W9-AEF-428

Conversations with Elizabeth Spencer

Literary Conversations Series
Peggy Whitman Prenshaw
General Editor

Conversations with Elizabeth Spencer

Edited by
Peggy Whitman Prenshaw

University Press of Mississippi
Jackson and London

Library of Congress Cataloging-in-Publication Data

Conversations with Elizabeth Spencer / edited by Peggy Whitman
    Prenshaw.
        p.   cm. — (Literary conversations series)
        Includes index.
        ISBN 0-87805-527-4 (cloth). — ISBN 0-87805-528-2 (paper)
        1. Spencer, Elizabeth—Interviews.   2. Novelists, American—20th
    century—Interviews.   I. Spencer, Elizabeth.   II. Prenshaw, Peggy
    Whitman.   III. Series.
    PS3537.P4454Z64   1991
    813'.54—dc20   91-19455
                                                                CIP

British Library Cataloging-in-Publication data available

Books by Elizabeth Spencer

Fire in the Morning. New York: Dodd, Mead, 1948.
This Crooked Way. New York: Dodd, Mead, 1952.
The Voice at the Back Door. New York: McGraw-Hill, 1956.
The Light in the Piazza. New York: McGraw-Hill, 1960.
Knights and Dragons. New York: McGraw-Hill, 1965.
No Place for an Angel. New York, McGraw-Hill, 1967.
Ship Island and Other Stories. New York: McGraw-Hill, 1968.
The Snare. New York: McGraw-Hill, 1972.
The Stories of Elizabeth Spencer. Garden City, NY: Doubleday, 1981.
Marilee. Jackson: Univ. Press of Mississippi, 1981.
The Salt Line. Garden City, NY: Doubleday, 1984.
Jack of Diamonds and Other Stories. New York: Viking, 1988.
On the Gulf. Univ. Press of Mississippi, 1991.
The Night Travellers. New York: Viking, 1991.

Contents

Introduction

In many respects the life and literary career of Elizabeth Spencer have mirrored much of the social history of the American South in the mid-twentieth century. A native of Carrollton, Mississippi, she grew up in a time in which an agrarian life was the typical experience of southerners, whether they lived as farmers in the country or as farmer-merchants in town. In her first three novels, beginning with *Fire in the Morning* in 1948, she wrote of rural and small town Mississippi, portraying a region with a troubled history and an intricate system of class and caste made more complex by strains of racism, poverty, religion and capitalist ambition. She wrote from deep knowledge of a pattern of family life in which individuals strained to reconcile private dreams with the demands of intense and often vexing relationships within the family clan.

As a young writer just setting out, she intended "always to be a southern writer and live in the South and explore southern society," she told Gordon Weaver in 1974. "I thought of myself as a country and small town person." But like the region itself in the latter half of the century, she came to be vitally and directly involved in a larger world, came to be for better and for worse, a "city person." She moved from Mississippi to Tennessee, and then to Italy, with occasional time in New York and visits to Mississippi; she married an Englishman and made her home in Montreal for many years; and in 1986 she returned to the South to live in Chapel Hill, North Carolina—a South vastly changed from that of Carroll County in 1921, the year of her birth.

In these interviews, which span twenty-six years, Spencer talks of her life's work as a writer—how she set about developing her craft, whom she credits for giving support and direction, why she writes. In the Weaver interview she speaks of the need she feels to respond to a world that is always changing. "We don't have a closed, stable society, as writers in the pre-World War II South had, or as writers of the eighteenth or nineteenth centuries had. This changeableness in the world, the kaleidoscopic nature of the world, is something that has got to be said in writing. This is my conviction."

In the early novels Spencer looked back at the more stable society of a Mississippi largely untouched by changeableness, but with her departure to Italy she began to write of a fluid, modernist world. With the publication of *The Light in the Piazza* came literary celebrity and a new direction in her fiction. From "about 1960 on," she tells Charles Bunting, she began "to try to come to terms with, not the southern world, but the world of modern experience." More recently, she has observed to Amanda Smith that "Italy had a lot to do with changing the focus" of her writing, particularly in bringing about a separation from the South. It is, in fact, "the South and Italy" that she refers to in her 1990 conversation with me as "the two concepts that are the strongest" in her life and work.

At some point in each of the eighteen interviews collected here Spencer is asked about the significance of her southern background for her work. She discusses her childhood in Mississippi, her immediate and extended family, her strict Presbyterian upbringing, and the beloved family plantation, Teoc, which she often visited as a girl. "The thing that I didn't like about Mississippi, though I love it in a sense," she tells Irv Broughton, is that "there wasn't anything I could do ever to escape." The first real watershed in her life, as she explains to Broughton, was leaving "the Mississippi environment, complete and total Mississippi saturation," and attending graduate school at Vanderbilt. In the most recent interview, Spencer recalls for Terry Roberts the associations with students and professors she had at Vanderbilt, remembering that "the Agrarian theories were very much discussed in our group, but for the most part they were taken with much reservation. We didn't understand the fanaticism. We understood the brilliant side of Donald Davidson and highly regarded it, but his fanatical approach to the South we resented in ways."

Spencer's reading of Faulkner and other southern writers began seriously, she says, at Vanderbilt. Her early love of books goes back, however, to a bookish childhood and a mother who read to her. She recalls, too, the talk of books around the table of her mother's family and a family library that held the European and American classics.

She often speaks of her parents' ambivalence about her ambition to be a writer, noting that to her father a career seemed not particularly desirable for a young southern lady and a career as a writer not even a good choice of career. In a very brief interview not included here, Spencer tells Laurie L. Brown that it would have been an unusual southern family who "would want a young girl to turn into a serious novelist. . . . My parents were somewhat divided, I think, about my writing: my mother wished me to continue, my father wanted the whole nonsense stopped. . . . If I had been born a boy I might have found more freedom in living as I chose, but as a young man wanting to write I would certainly have faced much stronger opposition, as a man's 'career' was thought to be much more important than a woman's and had to be on firm economic and social ground."[1]

She talks, too, of the reaction from family and from southerners generally to her forthright treatment of racial themes and local politics in the 1956 *The Voice at the Back Door.* "At the time," she recalls in the conversation with E. P. Broadwell and R. W. Hoag, "tempers were overheated about racial issues; and I guess people felt that I was mounting the platform to tell them what they were doing wrong. They didn't understand the spirit in which I wrote the book." Speaking to Dorothy Hannah Kitchings, she notes that she "wasn't trying to preach to anybody. I was trying to straighten out my own attitudes about blacks and whites in the South—that was the impulse of the book." Spencer recounts to Broadwell and Hoag the period in Italy during which she did most of the work on the novel, an experience of distancing, she says, that helped her to know what it meant to be "southern." As she worked on the book, she says she began to hear again "whole conversations that had passed over me and that I had never really analyzed. I began to listen to these inner voices, to people saying things that I had accepted all my life without question; and suddenly I found myself questioning." She calls the experience of writing *The Voice at the Back Door* a "healing" one, and she speaks of the novel as the work in which her "style came to maturity."

In several conversations Spencer takes up the question put to her

[1]*Women Writers of the Contemporary South,* ed. Peggy Whitman Prenshaw (Jackson: U. Press of Mississippi, 1985), 6-7.

by many interviewers regarding the relationship between southern experience and the boundless outpouring of books by writers of the South since the 1920s. She talks to Bunting of what she sees as a tendency of the southern mind toward the "mythical," the "imaginative," and the "primitive," attributing the sensibility in part to the "South's more fundamentalist approach to religion." To Broadwell and Hoag she talks of southerners' "Proustian sense of time," in which "the past is never gone." She also points out the coexistence, ironically, of a widespread belief that the old ways of life in the South were—and are—dying. "There used to be almost a tangible tension between the movement of what might be called American civilization and the more static aspect of things in the South." Following a line of cultural analysis reminiscent of that of Allen Tate, Spencer attributes the burst of literary creativity commonly referred to as a "renaissance" to that "tangible tension" and to the desire to depict a waning way of life, to "get it all down," before the modern world assimilated it.

Spencer is often asked "the same old tired question," as Charlotte Capers puts it, "Did Faulkner and Welty influence your work?" Spencer always speaks respectively and admiringly of Faulkner's fiction, but her personal acquaintance with him was very slight, as she tells John Griffin Jones on one occasion and repeats in slightly different versions in other conversations. When she was on the faculty at the University of Mississippi in Oxford, she was introduced to him—twice, as she recalls. "I said, 'How do you do, Mr. Faulkner?' and he nodded, and that was all." Later, their paths crossed slightly at a memorable party in Rome. Spencer takes good-naturedly the inevitable comparisons with Faulkner. "Listen," she tells Robert Phillips, "if you write a novel in Mississippi, North Mississippi at that, you are bound to be compared to Faulkner . . . [but] I couldn't escape the Mississippi subject matter—I was brought up in it."

The friendship with Eudora Welty is long standing, going back to a meeting that took place during Spencer's senior year at Belhaven College, which is located across the street from Welty's home in Jackson. She explained in the *Paris Review*, "Some of us in a little literary society wanted her to come over and be our guest soon after her first book appeared. She came and we chatted later and she did not forget the occasion; nor, certainly did I." Spencer speaks of her admiration of Welty's achievement, but adds that her own approach to fiction is quite different from Welty's. Still, she remarks to Robert Phillips that she "once threatened to give *The Golden Apples* to a new acquaintance, and if she didn't like it, I doubted we'd have much in common."

Asked about her response to reviews and other critical estimates of her own work, Spencer is usually accepting and generous, finding much pleasure, as she tells Gordon Weaver, in reading a commentary that shows she "got through to the critic"—whether the review was favorable or unfavorable. She confesses to continuing puzzlement, however, over the extraordinary popular and critical reception of *The Light in the Piazza*. All told, the novella took her about a month to write, and that it should be the work for which she is most widely known strikes Spencer as a caprice of literary fortune. In the *Paris Review* interview, she speaks of the book's "charm," and describes it as a work written "under great compulsion," but finally she tells Robert Phillips that it has been an "albatross." She still finds it disconcerting to hear from readers who know her only as the author of *The Light in the Piazza* or who suppose it to typify everything else she has written. She tags the observation, though, with a casual and self-deprecating comment of the sort one encounters throughout the interviews: "I suppose I should be grateful they've read that."

Spencer speaks of the disappointing reception of *Knights and Dragons* and of her continuing reservations about the separate publication of the work as a novella. She predicted that after *The Light in the Piazza* people would be looking for "another delicious little romance," and, "as a matter of fact, that's what happened." She answers in much detail interviewers' questions about all her work, but especially about the novels that followed *Knights and Dragons—No Place for and Angel* and *The Snare.* Shortly before the publication of *The Snare,* she talks to Charles Bunting about feeling "a purer imaginative force" in her work. "There was an intermediary period between the time I left Mississippi and I wrote *The Light in the Piazza,*" she says, "when I didn't see any center to my work at all. . . . I had to get all this energy in some kind of perspective I could understand and feel. I think I've done that in [The Snare]." She goes on to say in this 1972 interview that she hopes to continue her direction of "catching up large patterns of modern experience in

American terms," having largely left in the past "the American abroad experience."

The era of the 1960s and its aftermath, charged with social tensions and moral uncertainties, form the central action of Spencer's last four novels and many of her recent short stories, including *The Salt Line,* the story collection, *Jack of Diamonds,* and *The Night Travellers.* In the 1990 conversation that I had with Spencer, she spoke of the sixties as a major turning point in American life, noting particularly the psychic forces unleashed by the Civil Rights Movement and the Vietnam War protests.

She discusses the 1960s as a period of recent history that has especially engaged her imagination and her effort to find meaning and give shape to the world she knows. She also emphasizes that it is through her writing that she finds the necessary vehicle for understanding and ordering her world. She remarks to Weaver that every novel is "not a departure from the person I essentially am, but a new experience of discovery for me, a new experience of a segment of our cultural life or of our current scene that is necessary for me to put down in order to understand." Sixteen years later she reiterated the same point to me: "I'm not a remarker on the world," she says. "I try to get hold of characters that seem to me to be involved in some way." With characters who "move ahead in their sphere of interests," who "transect with all the business of the world," she explores the common experience of us all. She speaks of working from "the particular outward. I try to make as much fictional use of my sense of the times as I can, but just standing outside, without a character to guide me, I don't know what I could say about the present."

In her most recent novel, *The Night Travellers,* Spencer combines her interest in the sixties with her knowledge of the South and of Canada. In several recent interviews she talks of the action and characters of the novel, noting that the move to North Carolina gave her an opportunity to sharpen her knowledge of the locale she used as her fictional South in the novel. Of Canada and her long sojourn in Montreal, which stretched from 1958 to 1986, she speaks with a degree of ambivalence. In 1984 she told Mark Morrow in a short conversation connected with a photographic session, included in *Images of the Southern Writer* (Athens: U. of Georgia P., 1985), "I don't think that it's entirely good to have moved to Canada. I've been personally happy there, but as far as my work is concerned there may have been other places it might have flourished more" (72). More recently, she has said to Irv Broughton that living in Canada almost put her "in a backwater," for although she found Montreal "a big international city," she also found it far different from the warm regions of the South and of Italy that she so much cared about. "It seemed to me I stayed up there too long. . . . This latest move to Chapel Hill is definitely a step I was glad to take."

Among the Canadian experiences that she discusses with special enthusiasm are close friendships that she has maintained over the years, which she describes to Terry Roberts, and her teaching of young writers at Concordia University, which she recounts to me in the 1990 interview, as well as in a number of other conversations. She speaks of having learned much about the teaching of writing from Robert Penn Warren, and she describes her classroom method as a combination of reading-discussions and writing-seminars.

Throughout the interviews Spencer talks of writers she reads and admires, writers whom she has studied as models of style or masters of plot, writers whom she recommends to her students and friends. She reads the Greek classics, Boccaccio and Shakespeare, and she speaks of having drawn upon *The Tempest* in writing "Jack of Diamonds." As a beginning writer, she was an avid and close reader of Thomas Hardy, and she frequently names Hardy as a signal influence upon her early work—more central than Faulkner, for example. "I thought *Fire in the Morning* was more like a Thomas Hardy novel than it was like James or Faulkner," she comments to Broughton. She talks of reading Jane Austen and George Eliot, Dickens and Thackeray, Victor Hugo, Chekhov and Turgenev. She frequently mentions Conrad, Proust and Joyce as shaping forces in her literary life. She remembers as a girl, she tells Amanda Smith, her uncle's urging *Les Miserables* upon her, and she reveals to Dorothy Kitchings her great admiration of Stendhal, naming *Le Rouge et le Noir* as a favorite novel.

Spencer indicates in these interviews a wide reading among southern writers; she discusses not only Faulkner and Welty, but Warren and other Fugitive-Agrarians, Katherine Anne Porter, Thomas Nelson Page of an earlier era, a number of her literary contemporaries in North Carolina, Walker Percy, and her Mississippi colleague, Ellen Douglas. She reads Updike and she speaks frequently of John Cheever's fiction. She admires Willa Cather, and she remembers reading the earlier American classics of Hawthorne, Melville, and Mark Twain. She has her students read James, Fitzgerald, Hemingway and Borges, and she describes to Robert Phillips her pleasure in returning to Dreiser, whom earlier she "simply couldn't read. Now," she says, partly because of Robert Penn Warren's *Homage to Theodore Dreiser* and partly because of an affecting visit to a region of New York reminiscent of that in *An American Tragedy,* "I'm hooked."

Some of the most interesting comments Spencer makes about admired authors and her own reading of them concerns Virginia Woolf, Katherine Mansfield, and other women writers of both the nineteenth and twentieth centuries. "At the start," she says in the *Paris Review,* "I felt put off by sensitive women writers whom I'd read but did not want to be like, even though I'd started by admiring them . . . someone like Katherine Mansfield, then later Virginia Woolf." She was apprehensive that their "lyricism" would have a deleterious effect on her still maturing style. She was trying, she said, to exorcise her own "natural bent to lyricism" and develop "a plainly-stated, hearty style—hospitable to sensitivity but not dependent on it."

Spencer's account to Robert Phillips of the editorial advice that she followed in writing and revising her first novel and her comments about her attitudes toward Woolf and Mansfield, largely shaped, one assumes, by her education at Belhaven College and Vanderbilt, give an indication of the mainstream literary attitudes toward women writers that obtained in the 1940s when Spencer was getting started. She describes her initial drafts of *Fire in the Morning* as "long, lyrical, girlish passages about the young woman who came to that town from a past outside it and married the central character. I had looked on it," she continues, "as primarily her story, as it might indeed have been if I could have got my prose to measure up. I think I was too girlish then myself to write well about her various sensitivities, hesitations, et cetera. My first editor urged me to cut all that out, so little of it remains, enough I guess to see what the rest might be like; and the weight of the book fell on the men and some of the older women who were part of the town, and they held it up."

Occasionally, Spencer has been asked about the term "woman writer," and she bristles slightly in her response: "Would you mind the term 'man writer'? 'Woman writer' is just next door to 'lady writer.' " But she goes on to attribute her reservations mainly to her early resolve to be "tough-minded"—a "novelist only, as distinct from a woman novelist. That was my early reaction—it had nothing to do with women's lib, of course—but I think for me it was the right beginning."

Throughout her career Spencer has steadily explored a variety of fictional forms—novels, novellas, short stories—and recently has seen her first play, *For Lease or Sale,* produced. In answering many differently phrased questions about how she writes, she reiterates the power for her of a compelling image or a "strong impulse" as the starting point of many of her short stories. Too, she attributes her turn to short fiction after the novels of her early career to changing circumstances. "I started writing short stories very consciously because my experience after I left the South got more fragmented," she says to Weaver, "and I couldn't see life in novelistic terms in the sense of whole segments of society anymore." She emphasizes the demands of the short form—"it expects of you more perfection"— but she finds the complexity, planning and stamina required by the novel to be even more demanding. William Styron's quip—"writing a novel is like crawling from Vladivostok to Madrid on your knees"— is one she likes and repeats to several interviewers. Finally, the recent production of *For Lease or Sale* has led to a number of comments about playwriting in the conversations of the past few years, and she has declared her enthusiasm for working on other plays.

In all the interviews that are written up as feature articles, the authors comment upon Elizabeth Spencer's extraordinary physical presence. Her friend and colleague, Max Steele, describes her walk and voice as "young (she swims and does yoga)," adding that she "looks thin in her deerskin jacket and light wool skirt." He takes notes of her deep dimples ("Dimples, yet, and her a distinguished novelist!") But the sophistication of "the white streak in her hair" and the "deepest aristocratic eyes," as well as the long list of impressive literary awards and the wide shelf of distinguished fiction, say to him, "Here is a lady to be taken seriously."

These interviews bespeak an artist of serious and multiple gifts, a woman who has participated fully in the twentieth century, moving among many cultures and registering their rich stories in fiction. And the conversations encompass many moods, from the light-hearted to the solemn. They take, as well, many different directions—from autobiographical recollection to thoughtful commentary on a writer's professional life, to observations about the nature of literary art. In all, they give us a fascinating introduction to Elizabeth Spencer, the writer and the woman.

Of the eighteen conversations collected here, thirteen have been previously published. Nine of these, following the standard interview format, have appeared for the most part in scholarly journals or literary reviews. Four others were published as feature articles, based upon conversations with Spencer. Three interviews, conducted for television or radio, are transcribed for this collection and appear here for the first time in print. The two most recent interviews (Prenshaw and Roberts) were undertaken especially for this volume and have not been previously published. This collection comprises most of the extant interviews. In two instances I have omitted published texts because of their brevity and because the information they give appears elsewhere. References to these (Morrow and Brown) do, however, appear above.

In following the usual practice in the *Literary Conversations* series, I have not edited or altered the previously published interviews. The usefulness of this policy for literary scholars is obvious, and I hope the variations in contexts, locales, decades, and moods that so shape and characterize the interviews will bring fresh perspectives and revealing information even in those instances in which some repetition may occur.

I should like to express my gratitude to the interviewers whose work made this collection possible, and to the publishers and other administrative agencies who have also given permission necessary for this volume. The support, good counsel, and abiding friendship of Hunter Cole and Seetha Srinivasan of the University Press of Mississippi have sustained me not only in the work on this volume but in the ongoing work, always gratifying, associated with the *Literary Conversations* series. The administrative secretary of the Honors College at the University of Southern Mississippi, Sandra

Roper Brackman, has supported me in ways too numerous to detail, and I am grateful to her for her extraordinary professional competence and for her friendship. In addition, Amelia Ruth Oden has given excellent assistance with the proofreading of the text, for which I am grateful. Above all, I should like to acknowledge my admiration and appreciation of Elizabeth Spencer, whose literary artistry inspired both the initial interviews and this collection, and whose support is responsible not only for making the project possible, but for making the work of editing immensely enjoyable.

PWP
March 1991

Chronology

1921   19 July, Elizabeth Spencer born in Carrollton, Mississippi, second child of James Luther Spencer and Mary James McCain Spencer. The McCain and Spencer families had lived in Carroll County since the 1830s.

1921-38   Childhood in Carrollton and at the McCain family plantation, Teoc Tillala (Choctaw name for "tall pines"). Graduates as class valedictorian from J.Z. George High School in Carrollton, 1938.

1938-42   Belhaven College, Presbyterian College for women, Jackson, Mississippi, taking B.A. in English. Second place for short fiction, Southern Literary Festival. Invites Eudora Welty to speak to the literary society.

1942-43   M.A. in English at Vanderbilt University; study with Donald Davidson.

1943-44   Instructor at Northwest Junior College, Senatobia, Mississippi

1944-46   Instructor at Ward-Belmont, private school for girls, Nashville, Tennessee. Studies short story writing with Raymond Goldman, Watkins Institute, Nashville.

1945-46   Reporter for the *Nashville Tennessean;* resigns summer 1946 to work full time on novel.

1948   *Fire in the Morning;* manuscript recommended by Donald Davidson to David M. Clay of Dodd, Mead. Joins English faculty at University of Mississippi.

1949   Participates in Southern Literary Festival at University of
            Mississippi with H.H. Kroll, John Crowe Ransom and
            Stark Young, a distant relation of Spencer. Meets William
            Faulkner. Awarded the Women's Democratic Committee
            Award. Visits Italy in August.

1950   "Pilgrimage," *Virginia Quarterly Review,* receives honor-
            able mention in Martha Foley's *Best American Short
            Stories.*

1951-52   Takes leave from University of Mississippi; brief residence
            on Mississippi Gulf Coast, writing full time.

1952   *This Crooked Way;* Visited by Eudora Welty and Ka-
            therine Anne Porter on the Gulf Coast, on another
            occasion by Welty and Elizabeth Bowen. Receives Recog-
            nition Award from the National Institute of Arts and
            Letters.

1953   Guggenheim Fellowship; leaves for Italy, settling in Rome.

1954   February, attends a party in Rome for William Faulkner.
            Five months in Florence, returning to Rome in Sep-
            tember. In Rome, meets John Arthur Blackwood Rusher
            (b. 1920), an Englishman who taught in a language
            school.

1956   *The Voice at the Back Door;* sails from New York to
            England; marries John Rusher, 29 September, at St.
            Colomb Minor in Cornwall, England; returns to Italy.

1957   Rosenthal Award of the American Academy of Arts and
            Letters; Kenyon Review Fellowship.

1958   Moves with husband to Montreal, Canada

1960   *The Light in the Piazza,* published originally in the *New
            Yorker.* Movie rights sold to MGM. McGraw-Hill Fiction
            Award ($10,000); O. Henry Award for "First Dark."

1962-63   Donnelly Fellow, Bryn Mawr College

1964   Spencer papers deposited at the University of Kentucky

1965   *Knights and Dragons,* published in shortened version in
           Redbook. "The Visit" included in Martha Foley's *Best
           American Short Stories.*

1966   O. Henry Prize for "Ship Island"

1967   *No Place for an Angel;* visits Eudora Welty in September,
           en route from Key West to Montreal.

1968   *Ship Island and Other Stories;* Bellamann Award; Lit. D.,
           Southwestern University, Memphis, Tennessee.

1970   Moves from the suburban Lachine into Montreal. Visiting
           writer at Gulf Park College (Mississippi) in March.

1972   *The Snare*

1973   Visiting writer at Hollins College, Roanoke, Virginia

1974   Death of Mary James McCain Spencer

1976   Begins teaching at Concordia University, Montreal; later
           holds positions as writer-in-residence and adjunct pro-
           fessor. Death of James Luther Spencer.

1981   *The Stories of Elizabeth Spencer* and *Marilee* ("A
           Southern Landscape," "Sharon," "Indian Summer").
           Spends spring at Yaddo. Lectures at Faulkner conference,
           University of Mississippi. Gives reading in Jackson,
           introduced by Eudora Welty. Pushcart Prize for "The Girl
           Who Loved Horses."

1982   Spring at Yaddo, working on new novel

1983   Award of Merit Medal for the Short Story, American
        Academy of Institute of Arts and Letters. Visits France
        and Italy in late summer on grant from National
        Endowment of the Arts. O. Henry award for "Jean-
        Pierre."

1984   *The Salt Line.* Manuscripts and papers deposited at the
        National Library of Canada, Ottawa. Reads at celebration
        of Eudora Welty's 75th birthday, Jackson. Invitation from
        Rockefeller Foundation for a month's stay at the Villa
        Serbelloni, Bellagio, in May.

1985   Elected to the American Academy and Institute of Arts
        and Letters, Department of Literature.

1986   June, moves with husband John Rusher from Montreal to
        Chapel Hill, North Carolina; O. Henry award for "The
        Cousins."

1987   September, one of a delegation of Mississippi writers to
        the Moscow Book Fair; addresses students at the Moscow
        State University School of Journalism.

1988   *Jack of Diamonds and Other Stories.* Awarded an
        honorary doctorate by Concordia University, Montreal.
        Receives a Senior Arts Award Grant in Literature
        ($40,000) from the National Endowment of the Arts. *The
        Legacy* (Mud Puppy Press, Chapel Hill); Pushcart Prize
        for "Jack of Diamonds"; O. Henry award for "The
        Business Venture."

1989   25 January, premiere of play, *For Lease or Sale,*
        PlayMakers Repertory Theater, Chapel Hill.

1991   *The Night Travellers* and *On the Gulf* ("Ship Island," "Go
        South in Winter," "Mr. McMillan," "The Legacy," "A
        Fugitive's Wife," and "On the Gulf," with the art of Walter
        Anderson).

Conversations with Elizabeth Spencer

Elizabeth Spencer: Writer in Perspective

Kenneth R. Tolliver/1965

From the *Delta Review* [Greenville, MS], July-August 1965, 43, 70.

"If you want to write, my advice is to sit down and start."

That is what author Elizabeth Spencer told a creative writing seminar at the recent Mississippi Arts Festival in Jackson.

Seated at a small table and speaking in a quiet voice, she answered questions from a large group of would-be professional writers, teachers and persons generally interested in literature.

When one lady asked Miss Spencer how important grammar was to the beginning writer, Miss Spencer said, "If you need to worry about grammar and spelling, then you need to go back to high school and not to worry about writing."

She told the seminar that a writer must strive to "express a vision of reality, as he sees it."

"You can't copy someone's style," she said. "Of course you can be influenced by another writer, but you must develop your own way of expressing yourself."

Author of such works as *Fire in the Morning, This Crooked Way* and *The Light in the Piazza,* Miss Spencer said that she herself had been influenced by the works of William Faulkner. A native of Carrollton, Mississippi, Miss Spencer now lives in Canada with her English born husband, John Rusher.

"I have never been able to write about Canada," she said. "I just have not been able to reach it."

She told the group that she felt that she presently could write about two places with feeling. "Mississippi and Italy inspire me," she said.

Miss Spencer told the group she felt the first step toward becoming a writer was to become a good reader.

"I think you have to explore and read to see what other people are saying," she said. "Then, you can try and join the chorus."

She told the seminar that she often revised her work and "revision can be the moment of truth for a writer."

She said that a "creative reaction for a certain place or people" generally gave a writer the material for his plot.

"Of course the more you write, the better each piece becomes," she said.

On the subject of critics, she said that "some people can help a writer, but it must be someone the writer has a sympathy with."

She said she considered her best work *The Voice at the Back Door* and that when *The Light in the Piazza* was to be made into a film she was horrified at the thought.

"But, I think they did a delightful job," she said.

On the subject of style she said that she felt that this varied from subject to subject and from locale to locale. "Style is rather a living, growing thing."

She said she was most comfortable with the novel and that her best short stories were "really tiny novels in disguise."

"*The Light in the Piazza* started out as a short story," she revealed. "But it just got away from me and wrote itself."

She said she felt that character and plot could not be separated and that the creative mind should move from character to character and deal with different plots.

"The novel today is sort of a time of experimentation," she said.

Speaking informally at a small reception following the seminar, Miss Spencer said she had a great love for Mississippi and its people.

"In Canada I often long for Mississippi's green and the lush outdoors. I look forward to my annual trips home."

She said she missed the conversations of Negroes and that often she was "hungry to hear their voices."

But, she said she seemed to be best able to write about a place after she left it.

"I guess I see it in greater perspective when I am away," she said.

Her new book, *Knights and Dragons,* is set in Italy and is an outgrowth, she said, of her five years in that country.

Under contract with the *New Yorker,* Miss Spencer said she felt there were too few places for a writer to display short stories.

"Our magazines seemed to be avoiding fiction," she said. "Of course the *Delta Review* is a bright spot in the country."

Miss Spencer has been a contributor to the *Delta Review* and she said that the magazine's existence was a reflection of the creative personality of the South.

An Evening with Eudora Welty and Elizabeth Spencer

Charlotte Capers/1967

From the *Delta Review* [Greenville, MS], November 1967, 70-72. Reprinted by permission.

I had supper with Eudora Welty and Elizabeth Spencer at Eudora's house in late September. Elizabeth, en route from Key West to her home in Montreal, via Mississippi, where she was born and raised, had stopped over in Jackson especially to see Eudora. Before supper we sat on Eudora's comfortable screened side porch, where we could see a full harvest moon through the pine trees that encircle the house. We admired the beautiful time of the year with its foretaste of fall in the air. And we talked.

We talked about Elizabeth's book, *No Place for an Angel,* just off the press. About the book, Eudora said, "It's terribly good . . . the most moving thing." And now Elizabeth, "She's at the top of her form." Elizabeth says she worked on the book for five or six years, as it came to her, in "explosions." Between bursts of work on the novel she was writing stories, most of which appeared in the *New Yorker.* She says her book belongs to the characters in it. There are five principals, only one with a vague Mississippi connection, and they rule the book. "I tried to get at the nerve centers of the time we have just lived through," she said, "and I tried to do this through the people in the book. It all comes back to the characters, and the way they are swirled around by the world, and the inroads the world makes on character." The characters are indeed swirled around in *No Place for an Angel,* which moves from Texas to Washington to Key West to Italy, swiftly as the jet flies. Now that the book is done, Elizabeth says it has left her, departed, vanished. "These things just kind of come and knock me down, and then I write them, and then they depart."

At this point Eudora departed for the kitchen, spurning our offer of aid. She returned with drinks and olives, and this reminded us of Italy, and a picnic at John Robinson's farm near Florence, where the traditional Italian picnic fare of country bread and cheese and local wine and fruit was embellished by stuffed eggs and fried chicken, and olive trees grew on the high hills around us. Then Eudora and Elizabeth remembered another picnic in Jackson a few years ago, this time with the traditional Southern picnic menu of fried chicken and tomato sandwiches, which Eudora fixed. John Robinson, home from Italy, took them to a sandbar in the Pearl River where they ate their lunch, and for all of them it was a time out, a special time. Elizabeth says the day was brushed with gold.

Because I asked the same old tired question, "Did Faulkner and Welty influence your work?" Elizabeth answered, as she must have answered many times before, "I write my own way, I don't write according to anybody. But yes, anybody has to acknowledge Faulkner and Welty, because they're the top." And this is why the question has to be asked.

The friendship of Eudora Welty and Elizabeth Spencer began when Elizabeth was a student at Belhaven College in Jackson. For four years she went to school right across Pinehurst street from Eudora Welty, but never met her. When Elizabeth was a senior, and president of a creative writing group, she summoned up courage to call Eudora, already an established writer with the first of an unceasing series of prizes in hand, following the publication of *A Curtain of Green.* Elizabeth asked Eudora, one of her "great gods," if she would speak to the writing group. Eudora said she wouldn't speak to them formally, but she would meet with them, and she did. This has been the format of Eudora's sessions with young writers ever since.

Elizabeth went on to Vanderbilt and a master's degree in English; she wrote *Fire in the Morning* and when it was published Eudora gave it a blessing, or in Elizabeth's words, "a little puff" on the book jacket. In the puff Eudora wrote: "Elizabeth Spencer seems to be one of the natural novel writers, moving about freely and surely in the world of her story." She still thinks so.

That was about 20 years ago. Today both Eudora and Elizabeth have been swirled about the world a good deal themselves, and they arrived at the September evening on Eudora's porch garlanded with laurel. This was disregarded as we talked on the porch, but I had to ask Eudora one more thing about her work. Elizabeth had said that she wrote "in explosions," and that when a book was written, finished, it was almost as if it had never been. I asked Eudora how it was with her.

"I usually work on something that has been bothering me for a long time," she answered, "some private concern, or something that has been going on in the world that I have been thinking about for a long time, or that I am emotionally concerned about. It's always from deep feelings that I write—then something may *happen*—something that may suggest a form."

With the *happening,* or the form which it may provide for Eudora to pour her feelings into, she gets down to writing. "When the idea is with me, I like to work on it immediately and very intensely until it's through. Then it's gone!"

Supper time spared the literary ladies further interrogation, for I had the grace to cease and desist over cold boiled Mississippi Gulf Coast shrimp, lettuce and home-grown tomatoes, hot bread, and a dessert which Elizabeth said was trifle, which it may have been. In any case it was good, and Eudora made it.

With coffee in the pleasant living room, filled with books and paintings and with windows open to the night, the talk was general, and concerned a number of things—books, people, and places, to name a few.

As a matter of fact, the coffee table in Eudora's living room generated a good deal of conversation. Thereupon were copies of Lehman Engel's handsome new book, *The American Musical Theater, A Consideration,* and V. S. Pritchett's and Evelyn Hefer's beautiful book, *Dublin,* a present from Elizabeth Spencer to Eudora. This brought on talk about Eudora's and Lehman's Mississippi project, a ballet to be produced by the Jackson Opera Guild, based on Eudora's children's story, *The Shoe Bird,* with music by Lehman and choreography by Rex Cooper and Albia Kavan. *Dublin,* naturally, brought on Ireland, one of Eudora's favorite places in the world, and Elizabeth Bowen, who has also shared Eudora's hospitality in Jackson, and with Elizabeth Spencer, too. It was when Elizabeth Bowen was a guest of Eudora's in Jackson that she said, speaking of Mississippians to whom she had been exposed, "You are like us, you are like the Irish, warm and gay and friendly!" The three of us could agree that Elizabeth Bowen is indeed warm and gay and friendly, in addition to her great distinction. And we remembered

Elizabeth Bowen's visit, when we had "the heart people" with us, so designated because of Elizabeth Bowen's *Death of the Heart,* Hubert Creekmore's *Chain in the Heart,* and Eudora Welty's *The Ponder Heart.* All of them, upon noting this bond, took off for supper together at the late lamented Allison's Wells.

Eudora has a new book in Japanese, not on her coffee table, and could not determine what it was about until she found a picture of herself and of her house in it, and a sub-title in English where we Americans would least expect to find it, indicating that the book is *Delta Wedding,* backwards.

When I asked Elizabeth why she was in Key West, she explained that Expo 67 brought crowds to Montreal and friends to visit the Rushers, and with the culmination of summer and of the new book, she needed to unwind. Key West is real Hemingway country, and she read Hotchner's *Papa Hemingway* while she was there, which she says was written from love and which she liked a lot. She visited the places associated with Hemingway, accomplished her mission, to relax, and drove back to New Orleans in a rented car. After her Jackson stopover, she went to Carrollton, her home town, to see her parents, Mr. and Mrs. J. L. Spencer, before returning to Montreal and her good-looking husband, John Rusher. I know he is good-looking because she had several snapshots of him. An Englishman whom she met in Italy, John Rusher now has a language school in Montreal.

Elizabeth likes Montreal, is getting used to the cold and snow, loved Expo, and says that apartments in Habitat, the spectacular apartment complex at Expo, are renting right along for $1000 a month. She mentioned the Canadian painters and the general interest in Canadian art. According to Elizabeth, the Canadians paint something like the French impressionists, only "stronger—."

I left them talking. The months ahead seem filled with good things for both of them. Eudora has just sold a 110-page story to the *New Yorker,* which will be published in the spring. She looks forward to a Santa Fe visit to her long-time friend Mary Lou Aswell, former fiction editor of *Harper's Bazaar,* now living and writing in New Mexico. Jackson's New Stage Theater expects to produce an evening of Eudora Welty in May. And I believe that there are prizes yet unannounced just around the corner for her. Elizabeth has a book of stories coming out in the spring under the title *Ship Island.* The book is dedicated to Eudora Welty.

An Interview with Elizabeth Spencer

Josephine Haley/1968

From *Notes on Mississippi Writers*, 1 (Fall 1968), 42-53. Reprinted by permission.

The following interview took place on the afternoon of May 31, 1968. At that time Miss Spencer was preparing for trips to Jackson, Mississippi, to receive the Bellamann Award and to Memphis to accept an honorary degree from Southwestern University. Her taking time out from a busy schedule to grant this interview is indicative of her graciousness and devotion to the literary art.

Q. Why, do you suppose, are there so many Mississippi writers today?

A. Mississippi is sort of a counterpoint to American culture. This state is relatively backward, relatively isolated from the rest of the modern world or, more particularly, modern America; therefore, more tension exists between Mississippi and the modern culture. For a long time this tension existed but was just not articulated. When Faulkner came along, he brought it out. There are more Mississippi writers because no other part of the country has this particular tension.

Q. Do you think that a writer born in the South feels more or less constrained at some point in his career to write about the South and its problems?

A. It is just natural for a writer born in the South to write about the South. Before I went to Italy, I had never been out of the South, so I naturally wrote about that with which I was most familiar—the particular part of the country I had grown up in. Then I got a Guggenheim fellowship and went to Italy. I wrote *The Voice at the Back Door* in Italy, although I had already projected the book before I went to Italy. Living abroad, I just naturally changed my subject.

Q. That is to say, then, that you wrote about the people and the environment that were freshest on your mind?

10

A. Well, yes, but I don't copy my characters straight from real life.

Q. It has been said, however, that your characters, especially in *The Voice at the Back Door,* are modelled after actual people living in your hometown, Carrollton, Mississippi. Is this true?

A. Well, I wasn't aware of this so much. I think that the whole thing of being brought up in Carrollton—its geography, its peculiar environment, the particular atmosphere which I think it has—I don't deny that it was carried over in the book. But I didn't try to do it house for house. As for the people—there is a little game played by the people in every southern town which produces an author who publishes a book. They play the game of picking out the people, and the clues they use are so devious. They swear up and down that this is so-and-so and this is so-and-so. There was a woman in one of my books that people said was undoubtedly a certain "real live" person, but I had no idea of anyone when I wrote it. The clues they used to establish this identity—I forget them—but I certainly had no idea of doing this when I created the character. Characters come to me in devious ways, and the fact that they show up in this particular atmosphere makes people think that they are actual people living in Carrollton. One time I deliberately tried to copy a character from life, and the people who knew him said I failed miserably, so it seems if you try you don't succeed, and if you don't try you succeed too well. But it doesn't do any good to tell this to people because they go straight on believing what they want to, anyway.

Q. You say that your characters are based on types of people rather than on individual people?

A. Oh, no—there's just a certain point when they come clear to me—like a photograph being developed. They come into my mind as being absolute, individual people, and I wouldn't say they were like anybody I had known before; but there is a metamorphosis that is very interesting because you take from one person you've actually seen one particular quality, and the odd thing—a lot of writers have commented on this—is that often you will use a person whom you don't know, whom you've only just seen and never have been introduced to but who sticks in your mind. I don't know what it is, but it is a common thing. I think the mind is a kind of scrap bag or attic of impressions that causes you to remember something for no reason at all. Do you find this true? Or just something you see out of a car window—you'll remember that more than anything else. Some people you've just seen or know only slightly will capture your imagination. My feeling is that if you get two or three of these kinds of impressions in your mind, they converge. I don't know how this happens, but it seems like some kind of reflector system. The mother in *The Light in the Piazza*—I know I've seen her somewhere before. I can see her in my mind's eye in navy blue with that kind of short blond hair that women have when they get rinses, walking off down the street. I can't place that woman, but I can see every detail about her. It was out of that impression that the whole character developed. I'm a great believer in central impressions. You have to trust that— everything develops from that.

Q. Do you become emotionally involved with your characters?

A. Oh yes, when I'm writing something—to a marked degree. It varies, however. Sometimes you identify too closely with your characters. When I was working on *No Place for an Angel* over a period of years from 1961 to 1967, I felt these people very deeply. They would come in my mind and live with me. When a particular character would stick in my mind, I would write about him or her. That's why the book is written the way it is—in pieces. Some days it would be Irene—she was so real to me that sometimes I felt I had a luncheon date with her. Then Catherine would stay with me, with all of her problems that were caused by the kind of life that those around here were projecting on her. These different characters would recede like chords of music, with different characters taking the spotlight at different times. I would write 80 or 90 pages in a hurry about a particular character and would then put it down until another character came into my mind.

Q. Is this the way you write all your books?

A. No. Before this, I had consciously mapped out my books. *No Place for an Angel* is the only book I've written in this way.

Q. How extensively did you plan or map out your previous books?

A. Well, of course when the work begins to live, it takes on a living quality and will surprise you. The characters do things that you would never have suspected them to do, and all very naturally. The plot takes on certain features that you hadn't planned before. I feel the presence of the characters; I get to know a great deal about them and what is pertinent to their relationships. You can always feel when the forward motion happens to the story, and then you can start writing, or continue writing.

Q. What difficulties have you had in writing?

A. In *No Place for an Angel* the difficulty was involved in the pace of the story itself—the shifting around from place to place—actually trying to keep up with the way these people lived.

Q. What about your style? How much importance do you give style?

A. Of course one's style should not live by itself, but should be adapted to the subject of the work. A good writer will not stick to only one style—"his" style. It is discouraging sometimes to read a writer's first works because you can actually patch out what he's read. His writing is a combination of other writers' styles. This is natural, because beginning writers tend to get enthusiastic over particular styles of writing. Faulkner's *Soldiers' Pay,* for example, started a new trend in style. And Joyce was perhaps an influence on Faulkner. Sometimes writers are hampered by a particular style; for instance, Faulkner, in his later works, tended to become bogged down in his style, with the long involved sentence structures. Some writers develop more slowly than others in adapting their style of writing to the various stories that they write.

Q. Talking about other writers, whom do you consider to be the best writers of today?

A. I enjoy many writers, but I certainly wouldn't attempt to evaluate their work in terms of "better," "best." I find Updike, for instance, very interesting, but somehow I can't really understand what he's saying. John Cheever I like because he's original—not like anything I ever read before. This is something in itself. I feel that the best of Robert Penn Warren's work will live. He has good things in all areas of his work—poetry, short fiction, criticism, novels. I've heard a lot of good things about William Styron, and I'm willing to be convinced that he's good.

Q. When and how did you begin writing?

A. As soon as I learned how—when I was about six. I was sick a lot as a child, and I lived down at the end of the street where hardly anyone travelled; consequently, I was alone a lot. It was during the Depression, and there wasn't much to do for entertainment. In fact, there is never much to do in a small town for entertainment.

Someone said that the reason there are so many southern writers is because there is nothing else for them to do but write.

Q. What kind of things did you write when you were this young?

A. I began writing poetry—I did this after I tried drawing pictures. Then I started writing fairy stories. A teacher read one of these in class once. One time I wrote a long story about the North Pole, based on the kind of thing you see in children's magazines. I presented this to my parents for Christmas. But any excuse to write was a good one—I used to love those assignments in which we were to write our own thoughts about things. Again, I would stress the importance of a strong central impression. Sometimes you are very receptive to ideas. Someone has called this intuition.

Q. Would you give an example of this type of impression as the starting point for one of your works?

A. In 1961 I was on the way to the airport to take a plane back to Montreal from New York. The night before, some friends and I had been talking about the Kennedy election and the power that was behind it. As I was at the airport, I saw a sleek silver jet rise out of the horizon and level off. Somehow I imagined this jet as going to Dallas—this image of a jet departing for Dallas stuck in my mind as representative of the strength and power behind modern politics and behind our way of life. Of course, the later assassination of Kennedy in Dallas made the impact of the association of the plane with Dallas even stronger. This impression was the source of the scene in *No Place for an Angel* in which Jerry and Catherine Sasser are on a plane to Dallas. In fact, I wrote this first, although it comes on page 65 in the book.

Q. The jet, then, was a symbol of this power and strength. How much symbolism do you feel that writers are conscious of?

A. Creative intelligence is partly subconscious, partly conscious. Out of this atmosphere of creation something occurs which can be called symbolism. Melville knew that Moby Dick was a symbolic creature, but he didn't know himself what it stood for. The author pursues the meaning of symbols along with the reader. But I think that a lot of English professors make too much of symbolism. Most of the time symbolism is unconscious, a result of the mysterious type of spirit that enters into an artistic creation. Sometimes there is deliberate symbolism, as in Hawthorne's works. Perhaps it is better to call this allegory. Faulkner said *Sanctuary* is an allegory, because the people represent different life forces.

Q. What about the characters in *No Place for an Angel?* Did you mean for them to be symbolic or representative of different aspects or forces of life?

A. I didn't consciously intend this when I started the novel. To look back over the book as a whole, I suppose that they are symbolic or allegorical to a certain degree. Just as I said before, a story takes on a life of its own. What it turns out to be may be something different from what the author intended. There is a chemistry to certain characters—certain qualities and ideas seem to polarize in them that make them representatives of types of people. For instance, I suppose you could put the characters in *No Place for an Angel* on a scale or spectrum—Catherine at the one end representing the light and Jerry at the other end representing the dark. The other characters like Irene and Charles would fall somewhere in the middle, representing the worldly, materialistic type.

In *The Light in the Piazza,* the different qualities or shades of light serve a certain purpose, although not so much of symbolism. But I started with the idea of light and carried it through the whole novel. In *No Place for an Angel,* I began with a certain idea and carried it out by means of the characters. I suppose this is why the characters seem at times allegorical.

Q. What elements do you consider to be the most important in a story?

A. It differs with the particular story. The setting in *No Place for an Angel* changes so frequently that it can't be an important element. In this story all depends on the characters—and their relations with each other. In *The Light in the Piazza* there is the story itself—it is the most important element. *The Voice at the Back Door* is a deliberately plotted novel—the intricate plot is deliberate. Plot is the most important element in this story. But at the same time it is a novel of ideas—the plot carries out the idea, and so do the characters—everything bears on the question of race, on the race issue. Likewise, *No Place for an Angel* is a novel of an idea—an idea portrayed by the characters.

Q. Why do you write? Do you have a goal, an ideal to reach in your writing?

A. I tell a story to clarify the world for myself. I hope it communicates to other people. My books and short stories are simply stories that I want to tell—they involve people in different scenes, furniture, nature. In Proust's works of analysis, he tells stories. Likewise, in order to make things clearer to myself, I tell stories.

Q. Why do you think there are so many women writers today?

A. Women have never been second in fiction. There have been many novelists since Jane Austen who were women. Jane Austen, you know, wrote novels of manners and made them interesting. Before her, you had to struggle through things like *Pamela*. Even Sir Walter Scott—he was a contemporary of Jane Austen's, but look who's more interesting to read? In Victorian times, the Bronte girls were very good. *Wuthering Heights* is still a good book today. George Eliot's *Middlemarch* may be better than works of Dickens and Thackeray.

Q. What do you think of writing as a profession?

A. I never counted on it as a profession. What I hoped when I started writing in earnest was that my works would be published and find an appreciative audience. I never really expected to make any money from it. The financial results of *The Light in the Piazza* were surprising, because I wrote the story as a sort of an amusement in six weeks. It is basically a comic situation, and I couldn't wait myself to see what the characters were going to do. A friend of mine read it—it was still in very rough form at the time—and insisted on sending it to the *New Yorker.* He did, and the magazine turned it down. After this, he kept nagging me to redo it, so one day I sat down and polished it up—retyped it, smoothed out some rough passages, revised some scenes. My friend sent it back to the *New Yorker*—they really liked it this time and published it. Then came the movie contracts and the book clubs. So the book was really a financial success.

But most good writers, I think, don't write for money.

Q. Are you working on anything now?

A. Not at the present, but I do have a book of short stories coming out in August—*Ship Island and Other Stories.*

Q. By the way, why are you living in Canada?

A. I live there because my husband likes it. Sometimes, I feel out of touch with the American society, which is unfortunate because I write about American people, but living in Canada is interesting. Canada, like Mississippi, serves as a sort of counterpoint to American society as a whole.

"In That Time and at That Place":
The Literary World of Elizabeth Spencer
Charles T. Bunting/1972

From the *Mississippi Quarterly*, 28 (Fall 1975), 435-60. Reprinted by permission of the *Mississippi Quarterly*.

The following interview was conducted over a three-day period in August 1972 at Elizabeth Spencer's high-rise apartment overlooking downtown Montreal, where the author lives with her husband, John Rusher. Graciously responding to my battery of questions, the tall, attractive woman, who is acknowledged as one of America's distinguished fiction writers, spoke in a soft voice which still carries a trace of her Mississippi origins.

Miss Spencer was categorized as a writer in the southern tradition when her first novel, *Fire in the Morning,* appeared in 1948. Two subsequent novels, *This Crooked Way* (1952) and *The Voice at the Back Door* (1956), furthered this reputation. However, *The Light in the Piazza,* the first of three novels exhibiting an Italian setting, demonstrated the diverse and complex talents of this outstanding writer. It won for Elizabeth Spencer the McGraw-Hill Fiction Award for 1960 as well as an international recognition. A film version soon followed. *Knights and Dragons* (1965) and *No Place for an Angel* (1967) were succeeded by a collection of short stories, *Ship Island and Other Stories* (1968). Two of the stories, "First Dark" and "Ship Island," were awarded O. Henry prizes, and a third, "The Visit," was included in the Martha Foley Collection of *Best American Short Stories* in 1965. Three months after this interview, Miss Spencer's latest novel, *The Snare,* which the *New York Times Book Review* called "Miss Spencer's largest and most ambitious novel," was published.

Charles T. Bunting: You once remarked that one of the reasons you felt Mississippi had produced so many writers was the tension existing between Mississippi and the modern culture. How important is the sense of place to your fiction?

Elizabeth Spencer: Well, I think a sense of place in terms of the imaginative impact that certain places make on me becomes very important in many of the stories I've done. It's more important in some than in others, but this I would take to be a measure of how much the sense of—this atmosphere—how much it meant to the people involved in the story too, not just me, but how much it had to do with my characters.

CTB: Do you think that the South has created its own folklore and myths which have served you in your life and writing?

ES: Oh, I think the South has much more a native tendency to the mythical and to the imaginative and to the primitive. There just seems to be a quicker access to those things. If the same is felt by people elsewhere than in the South, it isn't typically felt; maybe they feel it and just dismiss it, or don't know what to do with it, something like that. But in the South it's accepted and encouraged even. I think this has something to do with the South's more fundamentalist approach to religion, that the things of religion are to be taken literally, not rationalized, but to be taken instinctively and in an immediate sense. This is part of it. The other part comes from being a land-based society that is more immediately in touch with natural things.

CTB: The religious experience which Amos Dudley has as a young boy in *This Crooked Way* leads him to envision a kind of Jacob's ladder to material success. Were you intentionally satirizing the South's Bible Belt brand of religious fundamentalism and its effect upon the psyche of the southerner?

ES: Oh, dear, I wasn't satirizing it. I was trying to come to terms with it as a valid human experience and seeing where that took me. That was really the theme of that book. I don't believe anybody could call it satiric, could they? I mean I took this character seriously. He had his funny elements, certainly. He's a very strange man, but his inner convictions of his own experience, not with any secondary mystical force or any church but with God Almighty Himself, were just tremendously real to him. And it seems to me that if you look closely at Protestant belief it means that there you are with God, just you two. That was the way he felt, without very much rationalizing about it. That was his conviction. I was trying to test that experience, and, of course, some of it is funny and outlandish. Because he was not what we would call the educated, the sophisticated mind. But I thought his story made a good basis for a novel because it was basic in Mississippi experience. Then I thought it was true to the character, those two things, and so this was how the novel happened. When I had both the character and the culture he existed in, I thought there was a possibility for the novel to formalize itself.

CTB: Do you recall what inspired your last scene in *This Crooked Way* in which Amos returns with the disenfranchised bus load of Dudleys to his plantation "and the waiting Ary"?

ES: Well, I just thought it would happen that way. The last section of that book came to me in a great wave of writing, and it was one of those times in writing when I just felt everything let go, and I was just following what would happen, what would happen. And this kept happening, this kept happening. And I felt that the book could not be resolved on a religious level except in a partial disillusion, but by this man going back to the formalities of his own experience on the deep social level of family continuity and all that—and being able to fulfill his religious experience on a ritualistic level—these actions concluded the book. Because he couldn't come to direct terms with the God that he thought he experienced, there's a partial disillusionment. But ritualistically he could fulfill that. When he went back and threw the money sack in the water, this was a ritualistic fulfillment. His whole return home was a ritualistic fulfillment. And then more than that, the continual social upheaval in his life, which had been brought about by marrying this woman that was above him, had to be in some way resolved, and so that's resolved in the novel on the practical level when his relatives are about to be flooded out by the same river that baptized him and that had ritualistically fulfilled him. The river's coming in on that family and so he has to bring them home, and his wife has to take it. So this is a social resolution, and it's also partially ritualistic. The book is a fulfillment, even though it presents a disillusionment: the major things he started with are really impossible. But we see it worked out. I look back on that book, and it seems somehow kind of central to a sort of experience that Mississippians could have.

CTB: Were you conscious of the similarities between William Faulkner's Snopes clan and your portrayal of the Gerrards and the Dudleys in your first two novels?

ES: No. Other people said that. I never drew that comparison. I

guess it must be in there. I think inevitably one is influenced,
especially in earlier works, by one's contemporaries. It was both a
very good and a very bad time to be writing when I started because
the giants in literature were people who were dealing with the same
people I wanted to deal with. So these were tremendously strong
influences for a young writer to shake off. The problem was both to
use the same environment and to search your own identity as a
writer. This was extremely difficult. When I look back on it now, it
seems to me I must have had the courage of utter ignorance because
if anybody would tell me now to do this as the thing was drawn up
then, I'd say, "Don't be an idiot." You just do things by going ahead.

CTB: How do you regard Faulkner's literary style, particularly the
later works?

ES: I thought Faulkner, like James Joyce, became a victim of his
style. I think, for me, Faulkner reached a final peak in *The Hamlet,*
and after that I find less interest in the work, though there are flashes
of past greatness and of great writing. I feel that the tension, that
some sort of drive vanished, and he was not able to replace it with
what might have been a new phase that would be as rewarding as
what he'd already done or advanced what he'd already done, or be a
new and fine thing; you know, in the way that Shakespeare, after the
period of tragedies, went on to write *The Tempest,* and *The Tempest*
is completely different, but still enormously rewarding. To me,
Faulkner never wrote *The Tempest,* or *a Tempest.* The style becomes
more and more involved. He just ought to have stopped it, it seems
to me. It wasn't doing what he meant for it to do, to my way of
thinking. But apparently he couldn't stop. It was compulsive. I think
that Joyce must have gotten compulsive in his word play. In
Finnegan's Wake I find this was overdone. It takes an over-educated
person to follow *Ulysses* without a guide or a key, and then you
aren't sure, you know. Still, it is a great and important book, while
Finnegan's Wake, to me, is nearly unreadable. Faulkner never went in
for word play, but he did get terribly involved in long sentences. By
the time you get through the end of the sentence, you've long ago
forgotten the first. To me it's a violation of that kind of wonderful
middle ground of writing, which communicates.

CTB: Of course, when *Fire in the Morning* was first published, the
Southern Literary Renaissance was dominant. Were you affected, do

you recall, by the fact that you were a Mississippian writing about Mississippi?

ES: Well, I had this brought to me as a matter of self-consciousness for the first time when I went to Vanderbilt because there I heard theories about southern literature for the first time in my experience. However, we had many books at home. Our library stopped about the time of Dickens and Thackeray in England. There was no James Joyce, no Virginia Woolf, none of the later ones, unless they got there by accident through somebody joining the Book-of-the-Month-Club, and then nobody knew, I expect, what to make of them. Then, in American literature we had Hawthorne and Mark Twain, and *Moby Dick.* In southern literature we had Thomas Nelson Page. Nobody wanted a book by William Faulkner. It was known that some odd character over there in Oxford was writing *terrible* books about the South in order to make money. And wasn't that terrible? So we didn't have any books by William Faulkner, and it wasn't known that any stir in literature was going on in the South, in my home town. Now, I think in the little college I went to, something of this was known, but it was generally evaluated as rather interesting, but not something to command full attention. It was only after I got to Vanderbilt, I realized that . . . Vanderbilt was a terribly important movement in American letters, and the hour of self-consciousness had already arrived for them before I came. All their brilliant works, the major part of them, had already been published, but the ferment was still there. I wrote my first novel after having been at Vanderbilt. I was over twenty then. So the major part of my early life was lived without any idea that the South either was or was not important in a literary sense. I just didn't think about it. I only began to read Faulkner after I got to graduate school. It was a great discovery. It really was. Writing about my terrain and things I'd seen and heard. Very few people can ever make that kind of discovery because very few people have a novelist of genius living right up the road. Oh, I'll never forget the experience. Here was life as I knew it rendered in the highest literary form. Everything I've heard all my life, people I've seen, types I've seen all my life, speech I've heard all my life. Here it comes, you know.

CTB: Four of the five parts of your second novel, *This Crooked Way,* are told from the first-person point of view. Did you have any model for the structure of this work? What sort of difficulties did you encounter in writing this particular book?

ES: It was a hard book to write. One reason, just from a practical standpoint, I was trying to teach and write at the same time. So I had to measure the writing of it against my teaching demands, and I would write in spurts on it. I think that's why it has sort of a feeling in reading it that it came not in one smooth flow, but in a kind of disjointed way: this angle here, another here, and so. But that wasn't an invention in the novel. Things are often written, you know, with different sections from different people's points of view. As a matter of fact, while I was working on that novel and had decided on that form, Shelby Foote published a book called *Follow Me Down* that was done with that same form, and I know that in *As I Lay Dying* Faulkner's method is a constant shifting of short passages from different people. I wasn't trying to imitate, but it just seemed to me that a person obsessed as this man was, possessed by an inner vision, if he told it all himself, one would lose perspective totally. But the whole book, the point of the book, was a process of bringing this vision into perspective; therefore, one needed the viewpoint of other people, the witness of other people, on this person who almost seemed to be at times demonic.

CTB: Was it your original intention to write a chronicle of a southern family? Elinor Gerrard of *Fire in the Morning,* of course, is the daughter of Amos and Ary Dudley, the main characters in *This Crooked Way.* In *The Voice at the Back Door,* however, familial traces seem to disappear.

ES: Well, no, I didn't start out to write a saga, but there was a story in *Fire in the Morning* that came along kind of by accident. This woman, who's an outsider to this community, is talking at dinner, and she recounts the story of her childhood and her parents to another outsider. And that story interested me. I didn't have time in the scope of *Fire in the Morning* to go into it, but she interested me as a character, and she wasn't related except by marriage to any of the people in *Fire in the Morning.* She was an outsider married into that family. But her family background, as she expressed it, seemed to me to have a good deal of kick in it as a story, and I began to wonder what kind of people, where did they live, what were they like, and that unsolved, unexplored part of the first novel led me to the second, but I didn't have any deliberate intent to keep on expanding those into a big saga of the South, or something of that sort. In fact, though the town is renamed Lacey in *The Voice at the Back Door,* this substantial outline, the physical outline in location, is the same as the town of Tarsus in *Fire in the Morning.* I just gave it a different name. This was a good bit like the town I was brought up in. Just the way it's placed on the map and the hills around it and the vegetation. Everything like that. So that's a point for continuity too, you see.

CTB: Part Two of *Fire in the Morning* opens and closes with the presence of Randall Gibson, the arid intellectual lawyer. Do you recall how you decided to use Randall as a character and a device?

ES: No. Again, it was a kind of close attention being paid to a small-town atmosphere, where there're always one or two semi-intellectual loners, who are commenting upon things, I guess. I didn't self-consciously say, "Now I need someone who will be a commen-tator and an observer, a know-it-all." But something needed to be in there. The two people already in it were so inarticulate. The man's young wife couldn't evaluate what experiences she was going through because she was an outsider, a stranger. She was sort of a catalyst for that reason. The young man, while very upstanding and, I'm sure, attractive and everything else, was not very much of a talker, you know. He was a strong, silent type. His father had too much to conceal in the situation to talk about it. So somebody had to get in there who could really talk. So this character came along as being a small-town type, and once I got him in there and got him going, he practically took the book because he was so articulate. But he moved in a good way in that book. I think that he loosened it up and opened it up much better than the people that I had put in motion could because they were involved in the action. I think that's how literary devices are born. Other people come along and name the device . . . But it's just that you've got to loosen your story and drive it forward. So what do you do? The Greeks had a chorus. It's something on the stage that needed to be there. And in a novel you have many devices . . . Henry James had all sorts of embroidery worked out on these points. But the necessities of the moment are really very pressing. You think of the reasons later.

CTB: Concerning your treatment of race relations in Mississippi in *The Voice at the Back Door,* did you have a compulsive feeling that as a southerner, particularly a Mississippian, you had to tackle the race issue?

ES: Yes, I did feel that; it was somewhat on my conscience. It was a time of great stress between the local viewpoint and, well, the outsider's viewpoint, and I wanted to examine a local situation just with the people who might be there—not with people coming in to say this ought to be done or has to be done—just set up in historical and moral terms within a single community in order not to generalize—to make it specific. And though the book was an almost impossible task to write, it was a lot of fun too to create a whole town, to see the unfolding of a problem of that nature. It was partially motivated by my desire to straighten my own thinking out. I'd been brought up in a very traditional southern atmosphere, though many people within that traditional pattern were at variance with each other privately among themselves and within their own most private conversations, but if an outsider came, they would probably never express these things in the sense they would privately. That's why I was trying to do it, a book that was personal to the South. However, it wasn't written with the desire really to *re*form anybody—I say *re*form rather than reform—except myself. I thought if I wrote down a story—which is my method. Some people paint a picture, some people build a house; I write a story. If I wrote down a story, that I would come out of it with my attitudes firmer and stronger, whatever they might turn out to be. A story is a process of discovery to the writer as well as to the reader, and you go along with your story and you wind up different yourself, I often feel, from what you started out, and I think the book did that for me personally. What it did for other people, I don't know. But it did make a considerable critical success and was also something of a popular success, and it's been in four editions in the United States alone, and it was published in England both in hardcover and paperback. So I feel that my personal effort didn't go without an audience in terms of the story. Apart from that serious central mortal issue, I just thought some of the characters were themselves in that book in a most delightful way. I enjoyed very much dealing with a lot of them.

CTB: Were any of your friends, relatives, or residents of your home town of Carrollton, Mississippi, disarmed over your treatment of the racial situation in *The Voice at the Back Door?*

ES: Disarmed? Let us say they were *armed!* Oh, some didn't like it emphatically. Friends of my mother wrote and said, "What on earth does your daughter mean?" And Mother very disingenuously said, "Well, I haven't read it!" Which, I guess, is a pretty good out. But some surprised me. Some of the most reactionary people thought, and told me they thought, that my treatment of a home town situation, especially the people and the whole atmosphere of that town, was so true to life, and they loved the book as a result though they couldn't agree with me on many of the implications racially. And I cherish their comments because it meant there was a kind of honesty operating and a lack of prejudice. Some people get so prejudiced against an idea they can't see the worth in a discussion—I mean in a presentation in context of an idea they don't agree with.

CTB: You wrote *The Voice at the Back Door* while you were safely entrenched in Italy, didn't you?

ES: Well, yes. It was revised in New York—a lot of revision was done there—and I went back to Mississippi both before it was completed and after it was published. The whole novel was projected as a novel while I was working in Oxford, Mississippi, at the University of Mississippi, and it was the projection of the novel that I submitted with recommendations from people at the University to the Guggenheim selections committee. So I mean I didn't have to hide anywhere and barricade myself. I don't think Mississippians take literature that seriously. They may have been outraged at Faulkner's *Sanctuary;* that's the only instance I've ever heard of them being actually outraged. But I wonder if that wasn't one of the earlier shockers, and that people everywhere may not have been shocked. He claims in an introduction he wrote it to shock, so maybe if he got a result of that sort in Oxford, it didn't show that Oxford was prejudiced against literature, but only that it was maybe morally outraged by this book in—When did it come out?—about 1930. Something like that.

CTB: *No Place for an Angel* was published in 1967. Can you point to a central theme in this work?

ES: I could at the time I wrote it. And right now . . . I think it was seen by me in terms of a search, that all the characters were in search of something, each within a particular private situation. They were all in a sense rootless—not entirely but people who for one reason or

another had left the locale they were born in. A large proportion of
Americans are in their situation for one reason or another. So I
wanted to deal with this kind of person in the particular generation
that we had just been through or we were just at the end of, when I
wrote it. And I wanted to trace their search and their failure. I think all
of them failed to a certain degree, and yet their search didn't go unrewarded. They each in a way found a measure of truth without finding
maybe the absolutes they were searching for. The idea of the angel—
the theme is more or less stated in the title—the idea of the angel was
the absolute. Nobody finds it. The sculptor sculpts an angel, but his
life is never transformed. So that was the theme, and it bore on each
of the characters in varying degrees. There was also in the book a
sort of spectrum of good and evil. The woman Catherine, who was
almost an innocent, was deeply injured by her husband, Jerry, who
was, I suppose, the most corrupt one of the group. And those two are
at either ends of a spectrum of good and evil. And then in between
there were the worldly people, like the Waddells, Irene and her
husband. Then there was the artist, who served as a go-between, a
point of liaison with all the group. He was a very busy character. He
was not talking, like Randall Gibson, but shuffling back and forth,
making love here and falling in love there, and being rejected yonder
and a social guest or a messenger . . . I thought that was clear, that
the spectrum of the book was clear, but no critic seemed to pick it up,
so apparently I didn't communicate too well in that plan of it.
Reviewers took it as an assemblage of people without much cohesive
theme, so maybe the time for that book hasn't yet come, or maybe I
didn't succeed as well as I thought I had at the time. With several
reviewers a strong element of its vision, however, was communicated,
and I had several excellent essays which showed me that a good
many people did care for it, but I'm not sure that it reached as wide a
public as *The Voice at the Back Door* and certainly not as wide a
public as *The Light in the Piazza*.

   CTB: Your most complex narrative structure occurs in *No Place for
an Angel*. Did you have a great deal of difficulty finding the right
narrative threads to tie together the stories of the Sassers and the
Waddells?

   ES: No, all that came very naturally. Somebody wrote and said
that I was trying to do a great performance in the book by

orchestrating time schemes, but I just let that happen naturally. I realized that the canvas was enormous and that the people were going to have to be terribly clearly defined in order to stand out against, not a compact background like a small town, but the world background; you know, they're all over the place. They go from Sicily, to Texas, to Paris, New York, Rome; wherever you look, there they are. And I planned this. To me, in my mind's eye, they loomed—except for the artist, Barry, who always seemed to me smaller than real life—they loomed larger than life. I could see their outlines like people on a flat plain as they often were in the Texas scene—you know, as human beings stood up on a flat plain look giant sized—and I saw them as giant sized. One reviewer pointed out they weren't important enough to fill up the scale I'd drawn them to, and I suppose that's a valid criticism. They weren't big enough people morally or spiritually to fill it up.

CTB: They weren't meant to be, however.

ES: That's right. That was the irony in it, but still there's a valid point there because it's not good to draw empty giants. But going back to the mood and the frame of mind I was in when I wrote that is quite impossible now, but I remember writing it with a sense that I was getting down a passing scene that ought to be brought to life. But whether I succeeded or not, I don't know.

CTB: On the first page of *No Place for an Angel* Irene remarks to Barry Day: "Angels don't belong in America." Has all the sense of innocence gone out of America, do you think? Are all the characters in the novel entrapped in what you call the last section of your novel: "The Grey World"?

ES: That's right! That there's no absolute. Angels, as I take it, are intermediaries between God and men, and I suppose in the kind of America we've always thought of, we have the Great Spirit, we have the Protestant God, but we don't have a belief in any of this order of things, this harmony, and of divine intermediaries, such as angels, that the Catholic tradition in Europe gave rise to in the great ages of the church. That's not part of our tradition; that's all I was getting at.

CTB: When questioned about her style, Katherine Anne Porter remarked, "I simply don't believe in style. The style is you." Is this a fair assessment, in your opinion, or do you believe in the cultivation of a style of writing?

ES: My feeling is I don't write in any one style. The style that I can express myself best in in any one story or one novel bends itself flexibly to the situation, characters, and moments of the story; however, I think in any work you must have a sort of feeling of unity and euphony. There's a musical texture that any work will set up, whether it's a work of three pages or three hundred pages, so that you have an inner sense when you're going against that. And this extends to style. It extends to the realm of the sentences themselves. This can be counterpointed in all kinds of different ways. For instance, one character may take over whose style of speaking and thinking is at variance with the general tone of the book, but always it's different in a counterpointing sense, so that you're varying from the prevailing style only in order to return to it. So the flow in a way is musical in a novel. To me a novel is like a symphony in many respects.

CTB: Ernest Hemingway once remarked that he learned "as much from painters about how to write as from writers." What influences, other than literary, have helped you in your writing?

ES: Well, I don't know much about music, but I enjoy music so much that often when talking about my books I use musical comparisons. But painting also has been a great help, and especially sculpture. I think particularly of *The Light in the Piazza.* One of the things that overwhelmed me when I first came to Florence—I had thought about pictures from art appreciation courses, also about the architecture of Florence—but one thing that struck me unawares was the experience of sculpture as being a quite different experience from architecture and painting because, you see, it's in the round, and you walk around it. It's always there; it's always just itself; it's a single thing. But just by circling, changing your angle, it becomes like many different things, you know, depending on the angle you view it from, and I think that entered particularly into *The Light in the Piazza* because Florentine sculpture to me is such a high point of the experience of Florence. You can walk around *The Light in the Piazza;* you can look at it from this angle, from that angle, and it never completely gives up its final answer; you know, "Was she right; was she wrong?" You get all this sort of effect without ever really getting an answer, but it gives off a certain solidity just the same.

CTB: Would you comment upon the duality of the word "light" in your title, *The Light in the Piazza?*

ES: A duality, yes. It was firmly and actually had the meaning of the light in Italy, which was beautiful and an outpouring of light so that the feeling is that you can see everything. The shadows are very definite, and all the colors are very distinct. Then there was the symbolic meaning that's sought at several times in the book. Well, Clara. The name itself has an association with light. But, further than that, there's the comic element of it. Whereas light seems to reveal everything—you think you can see everything—really the motives of these people and what they are actually doing and why are absolutely opaque, and the girl's mother stayed in a state of confusion there all the way through. I don't think there was ever a thorough catching-on for anybody.

CTB: What was the feminine reaction toward the pawning of Clara?

ES: You mean the letters I got? I got some very funny letters about that book. One woman wrote me in anguish and said, "Margaret Johnson has got to return to North Carolina and justify what she has done to people there! *This* is the real story!" Then I got a lot of very touching letters. People I expected to object most deeply and that I really had qualms about when I came to publishing the book were people who might have retarded or afflicted children. I thought, "Oh, my God, to have added to the anguish of people like these is really wicked in a way." I had a crisis of conscience over it. But I got my most understanding and tender letters from women who had daughters or sons who were under this kind of shadow because they said, "What we have to have as we live day to day is a sort of hope which you have represented, even though we know it'll never be realized." It made me feel better, but I still had lingering doubts as to whether afflictions should be central to a comic novel.

CTB: Does it bother you that this is the work for which you are best known?

ES: Yes, it does. It really does. I think it has great charm. As I say, you can't view your own things objectively. You can to a point. I think it has charm, and I think it has that compelling thing that was apparently building up unbeknownst to myself, of the Italian impression, which was evidently very powerful in my life. I'm conscious of that being true, but to have this slight thing that I worked on only all told, I would say, about a month, the thing that I'm best known for and have people come up to me and say, "Oh, you're the one who wrote *The Light in the Piazza*. Have you ever written anything else?" But I try to be generous about it. I'm glad they at least have read that.

CTB: Were you satisfied with the film version of *The Light in the Piazza?*

ES: I thought it was better than I expected it to be. I had seen so many books that I was fond of, stories I was fond of, cut up and changed into something else in movies, and I expected them to do the same to me, as I had nothing whatever to do with writing the script. Instead I found they had tried faithfully to stick to the story, and they certainly spared nothing in photographing it elegantly in color in Florentine locales. I thought they tried their best, and they were an attractive bunch of people. It was a gratifying experience. Nothing quite like it to go and see your own book on the screen. I'd had a movie sale before, *The Voice at the Back Door,* but they never got farther than writing the script. I think there was one of those mysterious strikes in Hollywood. They had to cancel the production, and they never got back to it, and it's still shelved. You want to make a movie? You can get that. There's a script and a contract.

CTB: At Long Beach, Mississippi, in March of 1970, you mentioned in an introduction to your reading of "First Dark" that you felt you were "still in the mid-stream of creating my work" and that "the major pattern, if such there is ever to be, has not so far emerged." Four years have passed since *Ship Island and Other Stories* was published. May I ask what you are writing now and if the "major pattern" of your work seems any more defined as yet?

ES: Yes, I think it is. Looking back . . . Like all writers, I think, I write instinctively; I write because I feel the urge to write and while I'm doing it, the hell with it, but the total pattern is something that recurs as a question: What am I really doing in a large sense? I think I never questioned this as long as I was writing southern novels because in writing I was simply part of the southern tradition. We were in the midst of a renaissance. It was a thing of resonance and a natural activity in that time and at that place, and no question occurred to me until the whole first phase of my work was, I see now, over with, the three southern novels and the group of southern stories about southern themes, which I did then. But then I began to see myself, because of having married an Englishman and living outside the South, as being no longer part of the southern locale in a strictly realistic way and having to find my place in a world that was geographically bigger than that and was different from that. So I began to work out both stories and situations that would illuminate that larger world and would help me find my place in it. That's why it was so difficult at first. Everything I began went concentric. It wobbled. I couldn't find the proper center. I think the personal result of all these later books and stories I've done has been that I feel much more secure in being able to move and live, actually find life, outside that mystic community. Maybe that's because I'm instinctively still a part of it. A strict southerner would say that. You carry the South with you. Like the Englishman who has his tea in the afternoon.

But maybe it's not. Maybe it's a little of both, but I felt after I completed the last book that I've reached the end of a long path and that I was ready, if I was to write any more—not that I want to quit, but it's just that one never knows what will happen—that I will be entering at this point a new kind of expression. I don't know what it will be. The exciting thing about the creative life to me is that you don't stand in your own shadow. You keep moving, and the imagination does catch on to new themes and wants to develop them. It sometimes seems a total departure from the way you were or intended to be to start with. But you just have to trust it. I guess that's it. And live it and work in it. That's all I know. But I distinctly feel a purer imaginative force as central to my work now, whereas before I felt there was an intermediary period between the time I left Mississippi and I wrote *The Light in the Piazza* when I didn't see any center to my work at all. Even *The Light in the Piazza*—I know I wrote it, but I wasn't so much in control of it; it seemed to control itself. So I had to get all this energy in some kind of perspective I could understand and feel. I think I've done that in my last book.

CTB: Your latest work is *The Snare,* and it's scheduled to be published in October.

ES: That's right. That was part of your question, wasn't it? *The*

Snare is a sizable novel which takes place in New Orleans, a city I've known by personal experience from the time I was a child and also by hearsay from the time I was a very small child. So I have all kind of firsthand knowledge of it without ever having seen, strictly speaking, a resident. I went down there any number of times to write large chunks of the novel. A good excuse for getting out of the snow and the ice. I don't know what I'll do now. (Laughing.) Somebody said, "Write another novel about New Orleans." No, it's not a novel about New Orleans; it's about people who are in New Orleans. But it had a fine flow for me. I can say that before anybody else has a chance to tell me just how I succeeded or failed because, having had this kind of inborn knowledge of the locale and the city, everything that I called to hand, like the setting of a house, the growth of a tree or a flower or all different things that all furnish part of a novelist's milieu to move in, came naturally, just flowed into place. It was instinctively right, I felt, and fit in where it belonged.

CTB: What is the central theme of your new work?

ES: The central theme is about a woman, at first a girl, then a young woman, her discovery of her own life style and life, and it involves a complete change of society, mores, upheavals in other people's lives because of her and her finding a new realization of things.

CTB: What are your principal literary preoccupations in *The Snare?*

ES: Well, *The Snare* continues a concern I've had for some time. As I've already said, my work from about 1960 on, I suppose, begins to try to come to terms with, not the southern world, but the world of modern experience. The most ambitious effort in this direction was *No Place for an Angel.* The present book continues this effort, though it returns to the South, not a regional or agrarian setting, but a southern city.

The aim of this fiction is not just to illuminate New Orleans; it's to illuminate an area of modern experience that has to do with the underground, the drug culture and things that may pertain to that. The principal character is a girl, a young woman, and the book spans about eight to ten years of her life with a good deal of movement back and forth in time into her early childhood, how she came to be at the point she reached. The people she gets mixed up with cover a wide range of social types. Some of them are even criminals. Yet she might at one time have married a very wealthy young man from a prominent Mississippi family. The very vitality in her always leads her toward a different life style from his. She finds that if she denies this vitality within herself and her own tendencies she becomes like an empty person. But if she follows them, she becomes a very dangerous person, and it's the inherent danger in the way she has to live that creates the dramatic tensions in the book. This has a wider application in the sense that I think many people today find themselves in precisely that situation, and therefore, we have the inescapable fact of a counter-culture arising and growing like a simultaneous growth along with the square culture. The book investigates the lines between these two things, how far one extends into the other and the tensions created and what becomes of the people who are touched, affected; how much danger is there and what can it cause, what can it give? This girl's not sad, nor mad either.

CTB: Is Julia in *The Snare* similar to Martha Ingram in *Knights and Dragons?* Does she come to terms with her life by accepting the chaos of the world?

ES: Well, Julia is quite a different kind of woman from Martha, and Julia is not, doesn't ever come close to insanity. She is governed by life forces that are stronger and stranger than anything in her immediate environment. Well, it's a complex novel, and you have to follow it along by reading it. I like Julia better than any of the women I've brought to life.

CTB: How do you assess the problem of time in your novels? You are constantly shifting back and forth in time. This happens in *Knights and Dragons.* It happens in *No Place for an Angel.* It happens frequently in your writing. What determines the . . . ?

ES: What determines the shift? I think it happens when the character can't move forward in time without being influenced by the past. When something interferes with the forward motion, it must be something from the past or something peripheral. So then you try to find out what it is. Is it an interference from the periphery? Well, let's see what it is. It's generally an interference from the past because many modern people are introspective. We don't live in an action world. (Pointing to her head.) We live a lot up here, so this mental action of our lives is like, in some cases, static from an interference and, in some cases, a recharging of the spirit from a source in the past. Still, time has not been a major element in my books, except, I think, in *No Place for an Angel,* but the real theme was not time; only the people existed in a style that isn't structured consecutively. It's structured backward and forward; it's kind of like a cat's cradle. You know, you pull this thread here and it may respond over there. It's really rather complex, all that, but I had to let it come as it would.

CTB: The Swedish film director, Ingmar Bergman, once said: "You know, somebody studying sleep discovered that if they prevent you from dreaming, you go crazy. It is completely the same with me. If I could not create my dreams—my films—that would make me completely crazy." In your fiction the opposite seems to be true. The dreams, the ghosts of the past, seem to throw your characters off the deep end. Catherine Sasser and Martha Ingram come immediately to mind. How do you assess your use of dreams and memories?

ES: I'd like to think that I've turned a corner about this dream and memory thing. I admit that as a person, without going very much into things that are really important just to me, certain dreams and memories and replays of things did haunt and upset me for a long time and were destructive to me personally. I think that just in the last couple of years that's changed, so that I suddenly find that dreams and memories have become life-giving again. Well, there are certain reasons I can give for why that's happened. There have been certain reconciliations in my life, whereas before there were estrangements, and I think that this is a health-giving thing, and maybe this is the source of the dreams that seem superficially to be composed of the same factors as before, but now they seem to me to be life-giving. I don't want to be too mysterious about this. There are certain kinds of animals that I used to dream of that it afflicted me with horror when I would wake up, and now these very creatures seem to me to be not in any way changed, but my attitude towards them has changed.

I think the dream world, the memory world, the fantasy world is a necessary part of the human operation. But look at Bergman's work. What are these dreams? They're often destructive. They aren't necessarily life-giving. So look a little deeper into the work, rather than into what he said, and you find this same ambivalence. Some dreams give life; some do not. This is getting rather deep into the human psyche. I haven't read a great deal of Jung, but I think he investigates these things very intelligently. He seems to have a feeling for these kinds of worlds.

CTB: In your fiction I was interested in memories as they affect Martha Ingram, for example, who seems about as close to the deep end as any of your characters. Memories seem to affect her and Catherine Sasser in such a way as to throw them into an abyss.

ES: Yes, they're the two mad women in my books. I think the story you mentioned, "First Dark"—the girl in there. There comes a point when she doesn't know what her mother did, whether her mother killed herself or not, that she wavers on the brink of substituting or wanting a myth rather than a reality because she simply doesn't know the answer, and this young lover watching her knows that she's at a moment where her sanity might collapse, and he makes her get the hell out of there. Well, that was the closest approach, I believe, in my former books, my former work, before *Knights and Dragons,* to women going mad. Margaret Johnson, in *The Light in the Piazza,* was confronted by "What is really going on?" but she was too practical a woman to have her reason ever overthrown. You know, she might scream, "Oh, I'm going crazy," but women who scream, "I'm going crazy" seldom do. But Martha Ingram was a demon-haunted person, and I wrote this story at the time of great personal inner tension, which may have come out in some of the characters. She was afflicted by love-hate for the man she had admired so much and married and then saw beneath the mask of the good, great philosophic hero of her student days. She found the lurking horror of a cruel person, and she couldn't accept this. It was the discovery of good and evil in one person, the person who is closest to her, and then she couldn't escape it. And he apparently didn't want her to escape it. He kept writing her, you know, sending people to her, apparently wanting to keep his image alive to her, and then, disastrously, she meets the one person she shouldn't have met, who perceives this and takes advantage of it, and this is when, I think, towards the last, she really is a little mad. But in a way, by accepting the madness of the situation, I think she cleansed it, because by coincidence the man who was haunting her literally died. In a symbolic way, she could believe that she had exorcised the demon. The act of exorcism was complete, even though she herself was left. It's a little bit, in physical terms, as if you had an enormous growth, a tumor of some kind, and if this is removed, a large part of you goes with it, you see. There you are. You're alive, but you've lost.

CTB: In "First Dark" Frances is reading Jane Austen aloud. Does this allusion parallel your own reading? What literary influences are you aware of?

ES: I came very late to Jane Austen and to women writers generally because I had sort of a snob attitude toward women writers when I was a bright college student. I thought that they were apt to be oversensitive and too given to fluttering over details. I think I had an early dislike—because I really didn't understand Virginia Woolf— of the kind of people who seemed to admire Virginia Woolf. Later reading of Virginia Woolf assured me that she had a very hard intelligence. It's a very rich work that she did. Another writer that I had this kind of dislike for was Katherine Mansfield; I still find her oversensitivity a bit hard to take. But it wasn't until later on that I read and came to deeply admire Jane Austen. Another writer I have deep admiration for is George Eliot. *Middlemarch.* I began to see that women writers were right in there when the novel was being formed, and now they rank very high in my estimation, and I'm proud to call myself a woman writer; I used to insist that I wanted to be considered as A WRITER, not as a woman writer. But now my later judgment has taken over, and I begin to see that there is a difference.

CTB: What contemporary women writers do you most admire? What particular virtues do you find in their writing?

ES: Well, I've always placed Eudora Welty just about as high as you can go. I think of her particular sensibility that she's always had the courage to stay with and develop to its fullest extent. There are several of her works I would place very high in the scale of American letters generally. Other modern women writers? I haven't read extensively in Joyce Carol Oates, but I think occasionally she writes a most excellent short story. I find the novels a little bit hard to get through, though I was interrupted in reading a book called *Them* that I intend to return to. I thought the people were very real in that. There's an English woman writer named Jean Rhys. I liked a book of hers called *Wide Sargasso Sea.*

CTB: Have you read Joan Didion?

ES: Oh, yes. (Referring to *Play It as It Lays.*) That's good. But the sort of thing in which the pages are practically bloody with pain and wounds. But, I think, she has great talent. I don't know who else I would mention. I was never really in step with Flannery O'Connor's work. I could never shape it to my own way of looking at things, though obviously she is justly admired.

CTB: Is there any particular philosophical concept that you try to work into your own writing?

ES: I have often worried about that: that I don't have any tremendous central controlling philosophy even in my own life or in my work. I was having a very amusing conversation once with a friend and said that I wrote the same way I cooked, by God and by guess. I'm more serious than that, but I can't state a philosophic theme that's central to my work. At least I have the honesty to admit it. I keep thinking that there must be a basic pattern, since I do think I have a strong imagination and that this, in a way, is enough. Henry James said, "The imagination is always living a life of its own." This imagination in itself may be working out a permanent pattern without my consciously participating in it. But there have been controlling ideas that I've had, and over a good space of years these have dominated my work. For instance, that whole idea of a central intuition, the thing that starts you off, the thing that explodes and really forms the work. I believe that's an aesthetic idea rather than a philosophic one; it relates to how rather than what. I believe it is what gives centrality to my most successful things, a centrality of impression, and really brings about the complete work. I always return to these things, no matter how irrational they may seem to be. If they've had the power to start the work in the first place, then in themselves they have some control; if I want a title, I go back to them.

CTB: What changes do you ordinarily make in your writing?

ES: Well, I seldom change the beginning or the characters, but I often write, especially shorter things, I write them down very rapidly while I've got the first impulse. Then, often they don't fall right, and I'll put them away for a time. Robert Penn Warren says that the moment of revision is the moment of true vision. At first you're just writing under the impulse and the urgency. Get this down. Get this down. But, then, later on, you go back, and in an unimpassioned way you see what this meant, what was being attempted here. Then you can begin almost in cold blood to recast what needs recasting and make a final . . . make a thing. Be a craftsman. Make it right, you see. But both things have to be there. But the truest moment, according to Warren—and I've often wondered if maybe he wasn't right—comes when you're actually doing the making after the raw material has sort of splurged out there. Sometimes I discard things completely. I just set them aside and never . . . I may look at them again, but nothing in there seems to stir, so I won't continue. Then, in many other things, a vitality will persist. The character that I set in motion will come back and back and back, like Pirandello's *Six Characters in Search of an Author.* This character is searching for me. This character wants a story told. Please note. So I go back and rework.

CTB: What patterns do you see emerging in your work? Where do you go from here?

ES: I don't know how to answer that briefly. I think that in my last two novels I've come more to the heart of what I would like to continue doing, that is, catching up large patterns of modern experience in American terms—the "American abroad" experience is a good bit in the past for me now. So I really feel my direction is more toward doing the large American experience, but I'd like to do this as broadly as possible, that is to say, a new novel that brings a good many elements into focus around one theme: a large range of characters caught up in one broad thing, embodying our experience in our time. Though many of my books take dips back into the historical past, I've always been more interested in the present. This is nothing to say against the historical novelist; it's just not my bent to do it. I'll take a swatch of this, you know, just to bring it in sort of collage effect with the present. But the creative impulse being what it is, now that I've told you I want to write modern novels about America, (laughing) my next thing may be a historical short story about Italy. You can't tell what turns and switches you may come to. But this is my main current of movement now, it seems to me, and I would like to do, oh, well, two or three more large novels continuing what I've started at present. I feel more in focus with modern experience as a whole than I used to. There have been a lot of formative stages, I think, which anyone can go through. I hope they're over.

CTB: How do you generally feel about experimentation in writing? Writers like Joyce, Nabokov, and Burgess? Is there a place in literature for linguistical manipulation for its own sake?

ES: Must be because they've all done it, and have been influential. There came a time in writing—I think the modern period brought this on because the Victorian novel had gotten flat—when the tendency, the drive, was to go back to the bones of writing. Words take on new strength—they are like "thrown rocks"—and the skeletal structure of a piece of writing appears without padding. This was a way of ridding oneself of the soft elements in Victorian writing. I don't think we are particularly at that moment now, so I don't see any use of doing it now unless it just amused one to do it. I think the reason Nabokov has gotten into his sort of experimental writing is because he is a Russian in origin, and he finds himself having to express himself in another language and culture he never thought of himself as being a part of. Nabokov had done some marvelous short fiction: *Pnin, Lolita, Pale Fire.* Then he did this long thing, *Ada.* There are so many double images in that that it became confusing to me. And he has to make not only double images of words, at *least* double, but a double image of the *world.* The characters aren't even living on this planet. But maybe there are those readers who delight in working out these patterns.

CTB: Would you select one of your novels and one of your short stories which give you the most satisfaction?

ES: Well, I like that story "Ship Island" very much. I had to get a full private satisfaction out of that story because a lot of people didn't seem to understand it, but it didn't upset me in the sense that having many people misunderstand *Knights and Dragons* upset me. I felt "Ship Island" didn't mind being on its own. For some reason, that story stays with me, I don't know why. Maybe I just always liked the Gulf Coast.

CTB: Why is Nancy's story in "Ship Island" subtitled "The Story of a Mermaid"?

ES: Oh, that was worked out, at least to my own satisfaction. Again, maybe I'm a little like people who indulge in word play, but the symbolism of it was that she existed in the story on two levels: as a creature of myth and as an ordinary pretty little girl playing around one summer on the coast. She, in the first place, is visited by an unusual phenomenon, you know: the fall of scalding rain. She can sleep in the water; you remember once she went to sleep among the seaweed. Whenever she gets on land, in land situations, people seem to be insulting her and treating her as an inferior, which, of course, on a literal level they see her to be and she sees herself to be. She feels that she can swim around these people and look in the windows of their houses without being a part of the world they inhabit. On land all kind of bad things happen to her; she's almost bitten to death by mosquitoes, you remember that? But when she's in a water situation, she comes into her own. And the two strange characters that pick her up are kind of creatures other than human. And then at the last the symbol becomes very strong because it's as if she dove away when she is departing from him—from her boyfriend—it's as if she dove away from him and her refuge is the sea, of her identity.

CTB: Yeats once called the writer's existence "a solitary, sedentary trade." Have you felt any isolation as an artist?

ES: Yes, I often wish I were out going to a job where I'd be more with people because I'm very gregarious by nature, and I don't like to be alone as much as I have to when I'm writing. But I try to mix that with periods when I'm not actually at the typewriter but maybe just thinking about my work and getting out more and seeing more people. It's a lonely work and it's hard for a person who likes to be with people. You're stuck with it, but then you can't have it every way, and if you're a writer born, you can't not write or you would be less a person. It's one of the occupational hazards.

Elizabeth Spencer at Sycamore Fair

Hunter McKelva Cole/1973

From *Notes on Mississippi Writers*, 6 (Winter 1974), 81-86. Reprinted by permission.

This is the transcription of a short videotaped interview made at the studios of WNJC-FM at Northwest Junior College in Senatobia. It was recorded during Miss Spencer's second day of appearance at Sycamore Fair in April, 1973.

Q: In addition to short stories printed in *Ship Island and Other Stories,* several by you have not yet been printed in a collection. Miss Spencer, many hope that you do plan another collection.

A: I enjoy writing stories so much I wish I had enough stories of some weight, a choice selection, to bring out another volume. Unfortunately, publishers now do not like to bring out story collections. There's a feeling that they do not sell as well as longer single pieces of work. Therefore, it might be a better idea to do a long short story such as *The Light in the Piazza,* published separately. This is something I'm turning over in my mind.

Q: Are there forms other than fiction which you write?

A: I occasionally do a short non-fiction piece on request. I remember the *Delta Review* once wrote me as a struggling publication—and I thought it was a very attractive publication—and asked me to do a little recollection of my childhood in Carrollton and in Mississippi, and I did that. And occasionally someone asks me informally to do a book review. But I don't do book reviewing professionally or reminiscence pieces.

Q: What is your writing schedule?

A: When I'm working, I try to work three or four hours; at the most, five hours is about the greatest amount of time I can put into prime creative time. I try to get started as soon as my husband gets off to work, about 9:30 or 10:00. I work on through until about two and stop for lunch and other chores.

Q: What writers are you most enthusiastic about?

A: Well, there's our Mississippi's novelist Walker Percy. I admire his work very much, particularly the first two books—*The Moviegoer* and *The Last Gentleman.* And there's of course Miss Welty, Eudora Welty, a perennial favorite still going strong, I'm glad to see. John Cheever—I admire his work very much. And I'm always on the look-out for new younger writers to admire. There was a new book out by Ellen Douglas of Greenville—I admire that very much—called *Apostles of Light.* The subject is a difficult one. She was very courageous to tackle it, the plight of old people in our society. If you say *that,* as you have to say it on a book blurb, it might put readers off, but I think if readers get started reading this book, they will find it an absorbing, dramatic story.

Q: Do comments by critics help you?

A: Some critics overpraise, and some blame for no reasons or for the wrong reasons, which are bound to make a writer feel resentful, because the writer is in a bad position of not being able to answer or to defend the work. You cannot buy space in a paper to explain what you meant that the critic misunderstood. But, in the mainstream of criticism I've felt myself very much helped by fair comment, whether it was favorable or not, because I feel I can get better from sound comment.

Q: What are you working on now?

A: I'm not working on anything at present. I have a good deal of material in manuscript, fragments and things I started on and put aside for the time being. And I have a sort of chest I put these things away in. I never throw work away, because I feel that whatever inspired me, started me on this, if given a chance, might live again, and, therefore, sometimes subconsciously the work of a writer is going on and the writing will come to life again. I've often done things this way.

Q: What is your opinion of the term "woman writer?"

A: This is very dangerous ground at the moment. If you say you don't like the term "woman writer," then—I think it's a handy distinction. Of course women writers have many differences which they should defend. We should not feel that it's a pejorative term, a term of being second-rate, but simply a term of distinction of the work from the work of men. But, on the other hand, people never say "men writers." So maybe it's not really worthwhile to distinguish in this way.

Q: The sense of place is vivid and accurate in your new novel *The Snare.* In *The Voice At The Back Door* there are also a few vivid passages about New Orleans. How did you come to know New Orleans so well?

A: Well, from favorable and excited reports of it in my family when I was a child, [and from] people who used to go there to have a good time. Nobody enjoys New Orleans as much as a small-town southerner. It's our cosmopolitan, European city. The excellent food, the atmosphere, [and] something of the French past remaining there excite people. Then as soon as I went myself, I felt this same excitement; and so it's been a city of life-long fascination for me. One year I lived near there when I was working once on the Gulf Coast and visited it as often as I could. I hope to keep on with a life-long enthusiasm for this place.

Q: There are other recognizable settings in your writing, like the Gulf Coast, the ruins of Windsor, and the old Presbyterian church with the gold hand on top. What were some of your experiences at these places in Port Gibson?

A: There are no real experiences of mine in the stories. I remember it from childhood, too, as my brother went to the Port Gibson military academy, Chamberlain-Hunt. When I was a small child, we went down there for different school exercises and for graduation. My family was Presbyterian, and something about that church having that hand and then riding out in the country and seeing the ruins of Windsor—this is a childhood recollection that stimulated my imagination. So when I began to think of a setting for such a story as I did, the story you are referring to, "A Southern Landscape," imaginatively the two, the story and the scene, seemed to flow together. But as far as personal experience, it was an invented story.

Q: In your story "A Southern Landscape" these old Port Gibson landmarks were important to Marilee Summerall. Were they her gauges of permanence, along with Foster's continuous drinking and helling?

A: Yes, she refers to this as a permanent landscape of the heart and in a kind of bitter-sweet irony says that he's a part of it too. So we must take the good with the bad. But the performance of the thing is what she's really talking about in her own little way at the end of the story.

Q: When you were at Ole Miss a number of years ago, did you ever encounter William Faulkner, who by most reports was quite unapproachable?

A: I was teaching creative writing, and it would have seemed the normal thing to do with a very prominent writer in the town to give him a call or write him a letter and invite him to speak to the class, even though he would of course have been quite within his rights to refuse, but I never did because I knew his reputation as something of a recluse. John Faulkner, his brother, came out to the class. However, at the home of a mutual friend at a large party given for Stark Young, I did meet Mr. Faulkner, the first year I was in Oxford. He stood in the corner, during this cheerful and talkative party, without saying anything. Later on I would pass him on the street. Sometimes he would nod, and sometimes not. But I knew Faulkner best in Rome. When I was in Rome, in Italy on a Guggenheim Fellowship, he came there as a guest of the American Cultural Service. A large party was given for him, and I was invited. To my surprise, he remembered me, all about me; and we had a nice little conversation. I was later invited in a small group to dine with him, and he was more talkative that night. He said few words, but he did say those words. It was a pleasure to be with him, so I began to wonder about the nature of the recluse personality—if it isn't somehow fostered by the closeness of relationship in small towns, whereas the person in an anonymous and easy environment becomes quite different. But I'm not sure in Faulkner's case, ever, whether one can generalize.

Q: The National Book Awards will be presented next week. Have you any predictions—or favorites—in the fiction category?

A: Well, if Miss Welty is nominated, I certainly think it's time [for her to win]. She's never been ambitious for prizes. I just think it should be the conscience of the judges to feel that the time has come to give her all the prizes there are in this country, and I hope that she wins.

Q: Are there any young writers, other than Ellen Douglas, whom you especially admire and encourage?

A: I should like to find more young writers I could be enthusiastic about. Living in Canada seems to cut me off to some extent from the American literary scene, and I'm always looking to see if I can locate some writer that I'm really enthusiastic about. The books of Walker Percy, as I said, were a good discovery for me.

Q: Will you comment on the possible difficulties for the novel in the present technological age?

A: As far as reading time is concerned, people in a very complicated age, a very complex civilization, have very litle time left for fiction because a great deal of their reading time is taken up with reading non-fiction. A professional man or woman has a great deal of reading material to cover just to keep abreast of the field, for there's very little time to read as much fiction as people read in the past—I believe that's true. And then, as far as story-telling is concerned, the media more and more invade this field, and many of the great books of the past have been taken over and translated into media experiences so that this partly cancels out—to some people, at least—their appeal. So the only reason people keep writing fiction, keep on reading it, is just because of a special love for it. So we're in for a hard struggle is the way I look at it. I hope I'm wrong.

A Conversation with Elizabeth Spencer

Gordon Weaver/1974

This is an edited transcription of a Mississippi Educational Network program, taped in Jackson, Miss., on 17 June 1974. It was first broadcast on 19 August 1974, number 75 in the series *A Conversation With.* Jeanne Luckett produced and directed the program. Transcribed with the permission of the Mississippi Educational Network.

Weaver: Elizabeth Spencer, a Mississippi author of national renown, is a native of Carrollton, Mississippi. She received a bachelor's degree from Belhaven College in Jackson and a master's degree at Vanderbilt University, where she studied with, among others, Donald Davidson, a prominent member of the Fugitive poets. She has taught at Northwest Mississippi Junior College in Senatobia, the Ward-Belmont School in Nashville, the University of Mississippi, where she taught creative writing, and, for a short time, was a reporter for the *Nashville Tennessean.* She lives now in Montreal, Canada, where she is also Mrs. John Rusher. She is the author of seven novels and a volume of short stories. Her latest novel, *The Snare,* was published in 1972 by McGraw-Hill. Her short stories have won O. Henry prizes, and her novel, *The Light in the Piazza,* was a national best seller and also a very fine movie production. She has received a Rosenthal Award from the American Academy of Arts and Letters, a Guggenheim Fellowship, and the Henry Bellamann Award for Creative Writing. She has also published a number of uncollected stories in the *Virginia Quarterly Review,* the *New Yorker* and other magazines.

Let me begin by asking whether there are moments in your writing when you absolutely turn off your critical intelligence and don't think of terms like "point of view"?

Spencer: Oh yes, I don't ever remember the terms, but I know that there are certain rules a writer should be conscious of. I've been criticized for switching point of view too much, but if I feel I've made the thing clear, that I haven't lost the reader, then I let it go.

Weaver: I am wondering if you ever feel a kind of difficult or frustrating tension between your self-consciousness as a master of the craft, an academically trained person, and your imaginative involvement in something that you're working on? Does the self-consciousness always help the imagination for you as a writer, or does it sometimes inhibit or stifle it a bit?

Spencer: I think when both things get going at once you're apt to trip up, because one thing is interfering with the other and inhibiting the other. I work more from the imaginative point of view the first time and just let myself get carried away and go with the tide, just write instinctively. I don't know about emotionally, but certainly I draw upon whatever intensity the imaginative experience is having for me. I think revision is the time when all of your literary craft comes into play. Then you are almost removing yourself from the position of the writer to the position of the reader. You ask yourself, "Have I made this clear? How is this going?" You can see that you've used a lot of technique unconsciously, like you drive a car unconsciously. You don't think, "Now I'm going to shift gears." A good deal of that comes with practice and you begin to use your own techniques unconciously. Of course, there is always the necessity for strict re-reading and revision—and maybe an opinion from someone else, if you are lucky enough to get it.

Weaver: Do you take a greater or different kind of joy in the imaginative experience, as opposed to the less emotionally involved one when you go back and look at the writing from a critical point of view?

Spencer: Both are work—and I'm lazy. I remember something that William Faulkner was quoted as saying, "I love writing; I just don't like writing down." I think the greatest experience of writing is before you write, when you get this marvelous idea and see the great pre-vision of what the thing is going to be. Then I feel like it is just flowing through my head and on the paper. Of course, it is not— you've got to sit down and get it down. I get more kick, more personal joy from the first draft, when it is really flowing and going strong. Most days I get only three or four pages. Sometimes not one. Sometimes only a paragraph. But on really good days, I've been known to just ruffle out ten, twelve or fifteen pages. At the end I feel, "Boy, that was really going good." It's like going down a roller coaster."

Weaver: What about when your work appears in print? Is that in any way a letdown? How does the gratification of seeing the work in print, of having it popularly or critically accepted, compare to the experience of doing it?

Spencer: It is a different experience, and I think a good one on the whole, but there is something a little bit ego-centered about it. It is like being too mirror-conscious, yet no honest writer would deny going back and looking at the work after it is published, perhaps sneaking off and reading it again and feeling a satisfaction.

I know I can't go back, though. For instance, I have really nothing to do any longer with my first two novels. They seem to me something completely apart from me. I am gratified when people say they enjoy them, but they seem completely separate from me. When I have to do any kind of talk or program on those, I simply can't go back and read them because I feel my style was unformed. I get a curious feeling, "Oh, I shouldn't have written that." Some writers are tempted to re-write, go back and re-write their early work, but I think this is a bad mistake. The spontaneity would be the greatest thing about it, and that would be lost. I know Yeats rewrote some of his early poems, did he not?

Weaver: Yes. And Henry James went back and revised things. There was such a mass of it I don't know how he was able to do it.

You've mentioned the importance of the ego in this, and that can be meant in different ways. Can critical response, or even popular response to something you've done, ever trouble you? Or, does it give you a great lift to know that you've written a best seller?

Spencer: Sometimes I feel I have been overpraised. And sometimes I really get a joy when I feel the critic really got it, whether the review was favorable or unfavorable, just a joy from the idea that I got through to the critic. That's the greatest gratification, I think. I hate to say it, but I was actually astonished at the reception of *The Light in the Piazza,* that it was regarded as so much better than many other things I'd done that I'd labored over more. It was written very easily and quickly, and perhaps I felt—I hate to say this—less personal involvement with it on the conscious level than with some of my other work. Of course, one can't quibble too much if people say they really love a book. I was a little embarassed that so many people seemed to flip over that book.

Weaver: Let me ask you now about your concept of audience. Is this a self-conscious concept with you at some point, either in your revision or your working in the craft? Who or what is the audience that you are trying to write to?

Spencer: I don't know. I think I have very little concept of audience. I suppose I think in terms of people who are somewhat like me, who have a community of interest somewhat like mine, and I guess that means fans who have followed my books and who write me about them. Some of them are people whom I don't even know, whom I've never met. I know that through the years this kind of audience for me has built up. I was told at the publishing house recently, "No matter whether we do anything about your book or not, you're going to sell 10,000 copies anyway. But if we do the extra bit and you get a good critical response, it will go far beyond that." I guess what I am thinking about when I write, if I think of audience at all, is these people who dig me.

Weaver: There is a kind of trepidation that a beginning writer feels about venturing into writing, that it is a risky and difficult thing. Now that you have reached a point where there is very little question about your achievements and where you have built up a following, both critical and popular, are you past the fear and trembling stage? Do you feel secure now? Does that ever come to a writer?

Spencer: No indeed, I'm not past the fear and trembling stage. For one thing, I am a writer who has tried to do different things. As soon as I can do something well, write a certain kind of story that I can return to, I want to do something different.

It seems to me that the world is always changing. We don't have a closed, stable society, as writers in the pre-World War II South had, or as writers of the eighteenth or nineteenth centuries had. This changeableness in the world, the kaleidoscopic nature of the world, is something that has got to be said in writing. This is my conviction. Therefore a writer, though not changing fundamentally in character, has got to keep changing approaches, I think. Many people will differ with me, but it's the thing that keeps me stimulated and alive in writing. It is the thing that makes every novel of mine, not a departure from the person I essentially am, but a new experience of discovery for me, a new experience of a segment of our cultural life or of our current scene that is necessary for me to put down in order to understand. Therefore, the fear and trembling are always going to be there because there's always going to be something new that's being subjected to critical and public opinion.

Weaver: Your comment on culture and the world leads me to ask about your being a Mississippi native, a southern writer by birth and educated in the South. I know this is a subject you've been asked about many times, and I don't want to pursue it too far, but are you grateful, as a writer, that you came out of the South rather than New England or the Midwest? Has it been a great advantage?

Spencer: Yes. Well, it was at one time, when I first began to write. I shouldn't quarrel with this because it led me immediately to a wider recognition. The southern writers more or less dominated the United States literary scene at that time, wouldn't you agree?

Weaver: Oh, yes.

Spencer: Every new southern writer who gained any recognition at all was immediately puffed as being perhaps Ellen Glasgow or William Faulkner in embryo, with work that must be watched. Well, this situation does not exist any longer. The national literary scene is dominated by quite another set of values and talents and the southern writer now has to take his chances along with others.

I think the advantages of starting in the South were very great at that time. The permanent advantages remain—the southern literary person has a sense of continuity in literature, just as the southerner generally has a sense of continuity in life—though the South has changed a great deal.

Weaver: There is one more question in that area that I would like to ask. Do you think people might have come to expect things of you that you're not always intending? You have written not only about the rural South, small towns and so on, but you have also written about Italy and life there. Your most recent novel is about New Orleans. It mentions smaller towns, Mississippi, but it is really about a big city. Have you ever felt that because you were a southern writer, identified as such because you had written some southern fiction, that you had to satisfy some expectation of the critics or others?

Spencer: No, I can't ever satisfy people's expectations. I just have to do what comes to me naturally. I don't think my experience was what I intended it to be. I intended always to be a southern writer and live in the South and explore southern society. I thought of

myself as a country and small town person. After I went to Italy on
the Guggenheim and married an Englishman, most of my experience
has been in cities. I don't believe in writing from nostalgia, although
occasionally I do so because I feel nostalgic. But I wouldn't write
exclusively from nostalgia. Willa Cather was very successful in doing
that because the images of her girlhood were never lost. Other
images for me have overlaid the original. Now I guess I have changed
into being a city person. I don't say this with any sense of pride or
false sophistication, but it is just that my experience has been more
in cities.

When I returned in *The Snare* to write about the South, I
deliberately chose a southern city that I had great feeling for. Also,
there was an overlap there that my American and southern readers
may not have been conscious of. Montreal, where I now live, is a
French-speaking city, and as I read more and more history I find that
French-Canada had much to do with the opening up of New Orleans
and the surrounding country. There was a link there that was cultural.
In checking names in the New Orleans phone book so that I wouldn't
accidentially name a family after somebody who was actually there, I
found many, many of the same names that I found in the Montreal
phone book. So, you have a cultural overlap there. Though New
Orleans is not French-speaking anymore, the cultural influence
lingers.

Weaver: Has the fact that you have for some time lived in foreign
countries, not only of the South but out of the United States, given
you any sense of being a kind of exile as a writer?

Spencer: Well, one critic said that I was self-exiled. I thought that
was the most overly important, inflated word to use for having
married an Englishman that I'd ever heard in my life. No, I never
intended to leave the South at all.

I'm not exiled; I just happen to live outside of the South. Leaving
did force a crisis in my work, though. For a time I wondered if I could
continue, and then, out of desperation, I guess, I had to find ways to
continue. There was a book I wrote that many peope were fond of,
No Place for an Angel, but it didn't make a smashing success like *The
Light in the Piazza.* If you will look, you will see that those are people
moving in international scenes, but most of them are southerners.
The couple who were central to *No Place for an Angel* were from

east Texas. Now we all know east Texas was settled by Mississippi and Tennessee. And the small towns in Texas, though they have their particular flavor, are very southern. The artist in that book was from the Mississippi Gulf Coast, though he is discovered in New York and Rome and all over the place. Southerners may not be as popular as the British—the British show up everywhere in the world—but Americans show up everywhere in the world, too, and southerners show up everywhere. It is remarkable, I've noticed, how we have retained our characteristics. So Margaret Johnson from *The Light in the Piazza* was from Winston-Salem, North Carolina, and several people wrote me and said, "Why in the world did you say that woman was from North Carolina? She's really from Mississippi." Though, I had no person in mind.

Weaver: *The Snare* is your longest novel, but you have also written short stories. I understand that in recent years you have been more interested in short stories. What determines for you whether a work will be short fiction, a novella, or a great, full-blown novel like *The Snare?*

Spencer: A novel is a tremendous undertaking. I think of a short story as being related to poetry or short pieces of music. A novel is more symphonic in nature, and you've got to really take a long breath. Fitzgerald said about a novel, "You've got to dive down and not come up for air until the end." This is a great psychic weight. I started writing short stories very consciously because my experience after I left the South got more fragmented and I couldn't see life in novelistic terms in the sense of whole segments of society anymore. The nature of experience that was being forced on me was fragmented. You would know people for a short time. You would have experiences that didn't relate to a long historical past or express a continuity in society carrying it forward. This is the nature of modern experience for a great many people. To me, it lent itself more naturally to the short story and to a sort of myth-like form.

The Light in the Piazza I started as a short story. This was to be about thirty-five or forty pages long. It was like a horse that bolted; it suddenly ran away with me. The characters sprang to larger life than I intended. It turned out to be that lovely little form. I'm not praising the book, but I'm praising the form, the novella, that lies between the novel and short story. In *Knights and Dragons,* the book that followed next, I was again trying to write about a forty-page story. Instead of bolting and coming vividly to life, it seemed to grow more internally. It had a swelling effect. It went on for about one hundred twenty-five pages. In trying to write short fiction, I sometimes stumbled upon this longer form, but that was unintentional. The short stories were for me a more developed technique. I thought of myself as naturally a novelist.

Weaver: Do you find the short stories more difficult, craft-wise? A more difficult thing to do?

Spencer: They are hard to do. You can't say you're writing a short story because it is easier than writing a novel. It expects of you more perfection, because it is shorter. It comes in for closer scrutiny.

I have a tendency to rewrite a short story more often than I do a novel. I think a lot of the novel is in the forward sweep and the spontaneity. If you make little mistakes, somebody said you can kind of sweep them under the rug. Sometimes it adds to the richness of the novel if it's not too carefully wrought. But short stories have to be wrought carefully, and therefore I rewrite them a great deal more. I think about details and transitions, style, phrasing, almost as if I were weighing and judging the lines of a poem.

Weaver: We've touched on the matter of change. Is it a good time to be a writer?

Spencer: It's a hell of a time to be a writer. It gets harder all of the time, but there's the challenge.

Weaver: I was thinking of change in two senses. There is the fact of the market, economics. I've certainly heard it's a hard time. Secondly, I am thinking of the electronic age and attempts like Marshall McLuhan's to discuss this. It has had inimical effects on the possible audience for literature. I wonder whether you felt the past, perhaps prior to World War II in the South, might have been a better time than now to be a writer?

Spencer: You've said it already. All of the encroachments on the audience have been severe. People don't turn to writing as their first imaginative experience; they turn to the media. I guess there are still going to be devotees of good writing who look to writing as a source. And long may these people live.

Weaver: Although a number of writers in the American tradition have not been formally educated, you yourself are. What has it meant to you? How would you assess the role of a place like Vanderbilt, with teachers like Davidson and that marvelous literary tradition that had been established by the time you got there? Was that important?

Spencer: Oh, I think it was terribly important to me. In fact, to go on and get a master's degree after leaving Belhaven was important to me.

Weaver: You were not seeking out the Fugitives, then, when you went to Vanderbilt?

Spencer: No. I had a teacher who eventually went into the ministry in Jackson, Dr. McDill, who had graduated from Vanderbilt. He saw both my potential and what Vanderbilt might be able to do for me. There was a creative accent at Vanderbilt, an aura that still lingered, though Ransom, Tate and Warren had gone. Davidson, of course, was still there. The whole natural thing at Vanderbilt was to be creative—I am opposing "creative" and "academic." It is possible to be creative through the academic, though that is very hard to grasp. It is easier to turn your academic system into a mill, rather than being sure that the creative is paramount. With a number of people at Vanderbilt whom I studied under, it was paramount—it was highly considered. I think that it was the best place that I could possibly have gone.

Weaver: Later, at the University of Mississippi, you taught creative writing. How did you like that as a writer?

Spencer: I took my cue from reading what Robert Penn Warren said about teaching creative writing. He also taught creative writing. He said the class might not teach people to write because there is some question as to whether you can teach people to write. Certainly you can help stimulate and encourage. But it is a marvelous place to teach people to read. Here is one course you don't have to organize according to historical background and influences; you can simply confront the work and study it. It became, in Warren's hands, a reading course. Frankly, I copied him, but the students were writing, too, all of the time.

Weaver: You have also in recent years done stints in Virginia. Have you enjoyed these?

Spencer: I enjoy them for about a month. The idea of taking a writing residency for longer than that, I think, is a good idea if people have the free time, but it means a lot of manuscript reading and seeing students. I do enjoy it, yes. I get to know different parts of the country. I had never lived in North Carolina until I went to the University of North Carolina, and I loved getting to know the people there. They are somewhat different from Mississippians. They have their own distinct flavor, but I feel right at home there.

Weaver: You told me earlier that you are now going to write about Montreal. [The voices become distant and inaudible as the program fades out.]

A Conversation with Elizabeth Spencer

Elizabeth Pell Broadwell and Ronald Wesley Hoag/1980

From the *Southern Review,* 18 (Winter 1982), 111-30. Reprinted by permission.

The following conversation with Elizabeth Spencer took place in Chapel Hill, North Carolina, in July, 1980, during a brief period when the author was serving as a visiting lecturer at the University of North Carolina. Elizabeth Spencer's distinguished career as a novelist began in 1948 with the publication of *Fire in the Morning.* She has since published six more novels, including *The Light in the Piazza* (1960), one of her best known works, and *The Snare* (1972). Her most recent book is *The Stories of Elizabeth Spencer* (1981). A long-time *New Yorker* author, Elizabeth Spencer has also appeared in numerous other magazines, including the *Atlantic, Journal of Canadian Fiction,* and the *Southern Review.* A native of Mississippi, she makes her home in Montreal, Quebec, Canada, where she is presently engaged in completing a new novel.

Interviewer: Is there a common theme or other unifying principle in your latest book, *The Stories of Elizabeth Spencer?*

Spencer: That collection spans thirty-three years of story writing; but, yes, I believe there may be at least one recurrent theme. I think many of the stories are about liberation and the regret you have when you liberate yourself. You see, however much you might want to, you cannot both hold on and be free. And that's the crux in a lot of those stories.

Interviewer: In your story "Mr. McMillan," would Aline be an example of a character experiencing this sort of internal conflict?

Spencer: Yes, Aline is rebelling against her southern family and even, in a more general way, against her whole southern background. She wants to free herself, that's true; but at the same time she also wants to hold on. I think her intention of using her inherited land for a town park reveals this desire to hold on. She wants, in some way, to retain a part of the place in life that would have been hers had she not left home to become a girl studying science at the university. But she *has* made an emotional break with her family, a break that sort of parallels Mr. McMillan's wanting his ashes scattered on the bay.

Interviewer: Another of your stories, "A Southern Landscape," ends with Marilee Summerall's somewhat sarcastic comment that she hopes Foster Hamilton will go right on drinking because "there ought to be things you can count on." Does her comment also reflect this ambivalent desire to hang on to a past that she knows she's leaving behind?

Spencer: Well, that remark, of course, is ironic. On the one hand, she knows that she can't marry somebody like that, a drunkard. But on the other hand, she realizes that she's not going to get rid of him in her consciousness; after all, he was a person she loved. So I suppose her last comment suggests a kind of rueful acceptance of what's not going to change.

Interviewer: Marilee appears in other stories, too. Do you find her character particularly appealing?

Spencer: Oh, I am very fond of her. I guess I feel closer to her than to any other character I've created. There are three stories about her, "Sharon," "A Southern Landscape," and "Indian Summer"; and maybe someday I'll come back to write more about her. There's a whole fabric of lives surrounding Marilee still to be explored. Marilee is a person who takes consideration of everything around her. She has a continuously expanding consciousness of her family and her environment.

Interviewer: Is Marilee perhaps a fictional Elizabeth Spencer?

Spencer: She's definitely not myself. Her voice, her attitudes, the kind of things she was born into—none of these parallel anything in my life. I do feel close to her, though—not as a friend but as a kind of shadow that I didn't leave. She's a kind of alter ego. Marilee continues my other life. If I had stayed in Mississippi and not become a writer, I think I would have been like Marilee, content or discontent in a Mississippi way. I don't know why it's not enough just to be Marilee; maybe it would have been better. There's still something very attractive to me about staying home and seeing how things pattern themselves and fit into my life. It's an unanswered question that teases me. I think southerners have this impulse very deep inside of them. If you split away, you always to some extent feel that split.

Interviewer: An important theme both in your own short stories and in southern fiction in general is the presence of the past. Can you account for this southern fascination with time?

Spencer: I think all southerners have a Proustian sense about time, a sense that the past is never gone. Faulkner said that the past isn't even the past, that it is the present. People get old and die, times change; but along with the continual recurrence of loss, you have the recurrence of memory. The glory is that through memory you can know. Faulkner does a great deal with time and memory as forces that govern the present; I think this concept is especially true applied to the southern experience and that it has become a part of the southern consciousness. You see, there used to be almost a tangible tension between the movement of what might be called American civilization and the more static aspect of things in the South. The southern families of my parents' generation tried to remain static. They held on to their values without ever wanting to examine them. You know the attitude: "Mama said it so it must be true." Well, to me this represents a kind of withdrawal and, in the long run, maybe even cowardice. What you're actually saying is that you won't examine your values because they might not pass the test. Eventually, I guess, people realized the change was inevitable; and I think this realization—that the life they knew was dying—led to a desire to get it all down. Probably that attitude accounted initially for much of the writing in the South.

Interviewer: Certainly some of your characters do have this heightened consciousness of the past, for example the woman in "The Day Before." But others, such as Aline, seem to resent ties to the past, especially family ties.

Spencer: Well, I think that may have come out of my own experiences. My own family and I went through many struggles because they were ambivalent toward my work. They never wished to have a daughter who would become a writer; I think few southern families would. When my books started coming out, I think my parents were a little embarrassed. Their hope was that I would get married and give up writing, as if somehow marriage was going to change all that. This was my personal experience, but I think southern families in general try to over-dominate their children. They try to mold their lives according to family and community expectations rather than letting the children reach out for things that might be different. "Different" doesn't mean "bad," but somehow they interpret it this way.

Interviewer: Did being raised in the South in any way help make you a writer?

Spencer: *(Laughs.)* I believed that I thought of it myself. I thought I got the urge to write when I was a child, just naturally, the way one might develop the urge to draw. I guess there had to be something in the South at the time that stirred people toward writing; but how my mentality fitted into that, I don't know. Southerners are great talkers, you know. People used to sit around telling stories just as shocking as some of Faulkner's. I suppose that this southern interest in people and this inclination to talk things over make for the kind of analysis of character and situation that one finds in southern writing. Of course, this storytelling instinct is not just southern; it's basic to human need.

Interviewer: While you were growing up, were you particularly interested in the work of any southern novelists?

Spencer: For the longest while I didn't know there were any southern novelists. We were very conscious of books in my home and in my town, but these were mainly English novels and American novels written in New England. When news got around that William Faulkner and Erskine Caldwell had published these very earthy, realistic novels about the South, people looked upon this as a kind of betrayal. These writers were frowned upon and not read. In fact, I never read a single one of Faulkner's books until I was in college. Nowadays, though, no southern writer could afford to be unaware of Faulkner. You simply could not write as if Faulkner never existed; you've got to be careful not to write the story of the Compsons again. Much of Faulkner's material was drawn from observation; it's very much derived from the culture. But so much of it has been worked over now that you just can't use it. Of course, you can't really say that any book exists that isn't influenced by other writing; all writing springs partly from other writing. And I'm not saying that you necessarily have to find new material. However, you do have to find what is still emotionally active and can command feeling, what can still provide a sense of discovery for the writer and the reader alike.

When you use southern materials, it's not enough to be southern. You consciously have to develop a style. Becoming a writer, I think, means developing a style.

Interviewer: What did you consciously have to do in order to develop your style?

Spencer: When I was in college, I had a natural inclination to write a little like Katherine Mansfield. So it seemed to me that if I was ever going to firm things up and be the kind of writer I wanted to be, I needed to escape a feminine sort of hovering over things, an overly-sensitive poetic prose like Mansfield's or Virginia Woolf's. To get away from that, I read a lot of Hardy and Conrad—excellent writers with a very firm, controlled style. This was the way I wanted to write, and in my early novels I deliberately forced myself to avoid a more feminine style.

Interviewer: How would you describe the style you've developed?

Spencer: Well, most of the time I'm leaving the language alone. I used to say to myself that Hemingway, whom I loved to read, kept language back, hobbled it, restrained it, while Faulkner inflated it. But I thought there must be a midstream, a beautiful spine of language, that would work for you if you left it alone. I think the style I've developed can reach toward a lyricism or an eloquence on one end, and then can become very colloquial and racy at the other extreme. I've tried to make my style flexible so that it will both work for me and always be in control.

Interviewer: Does your style change when you're not writing about the South?

Spencer: Yes. You can't graft the idiomatic language of the South, which is very distinct in its rhythms, cadences, and expressions, onto a subject that has nothing whatever to do with the South. When I wrote a story like "Go South in the Winter" or "The Search," I wanted the "southernness" out of those. What I had to do there was to rely heavily on decor and manners, observation and sympathy, in order to get some introspective depth. And in, "I, Maureen," my most ambitious story with a Canadian setting, I also used a great deal of external observation to move into personality.

Interviewer: At what point did you achieve full control over your style?

Spencer: I think my style came to maturity in *The Voice at the Back Door.* In my first novel, *Fire in the Morning,* there are shadows of my having read Faulkner and others. In both that book and *This Crooked Way* I see a little too much fancy eloquence, too many wobbles and mistakes in style. And in some of my early stories, I think I allowed my characters and dialogue to carry the whole narrative. For example, "The Little Brown Girl" works primarily because the characters take over, but that story strikes me now as being too flat and direct. I came to realize that it's not enough to depend on characters and dialogue.

Interviewer: Was there any particular reason why your style came into its own with *The Voice at the Back Door?*

Spencer: You see, I wrote *The Voice at the Back Door* when I was in Italy. Before I made that move, I knew only the southern scene and wrote only about Mississippi locales. *The Voice at the Back Door* is also set in Mississippi, but I think that my personally leaving that locale behind affected me deeply. That distancing helped me to sharpen the southern dialect in the book. You can't really know what it is to be southern unless you know what it is not to be southern. Robert Penn Warren said that you have to leave your mother's womb before you can get to know your mother, and I found that to be true.

Interviewer: Did the critics recognize your stylistic achievement in this book?

Spencer: Reviewers, because of the particular moment of racial tension in the U.S. during which the book appeared, concentrated on its subject matter. Some welcomed me as a "liberal," as though I had been born again; and some said I wouldn't have written such a book if I had been living in the States—they were segregationists and thought I was lobbying for the Negroes. At the time, tempers were overheated about racial issues; and I guess people felt that I was mounting the platform to tell them what they were doing wrong. They didn't understand the spirit in which I wrote the book.

Interviewer: What was the spirit?

Spencer: Well, I wanted to write a novel about the confrontation of races on the local level. I was not trying to stand up and announce that I was above these characters and could therefore write a sermon in the guise of a novel. In fact, I felt that the reactions of many of the characters were mine in a way. I was struggling through the whole thing with them. While I was working on that book, I would hear again in my mind whole conversations that had passed over me and that I had never really analyzed. I began to listen to these inner voices, to people saying things that I had accepted all my life without question; and suddenly I found myself questioning. I realized for the first time how outrageous these things were. It was a healing experience for me to write that book.

Interviewer: The title of the book, then, refers to these inner voices, to these conversations that you recollected?

Spencer: That book is full of voices and conversations. But I didn't think of the title until I had finished writing the novel. Then I decided to go back to the original image that I had had in mind when I began. In my own hometown when I was growing up, we lived on a hill, and the whole Negro section of town was in back of us. When Negroes would come to see us, they would come to our back door and call. So my central impression—the thing that started me on the subject—was literally this voice at the back door.

Interviewer: In that book is it significant that Duncan Harper, the only character who desires change, is killed?

Spencer: If he had been more complex, he wouldn't have taken such a firm, simple stand. He pushes everything forward to the breaking point. I think that a man who sees things in such simplistic terms—who says, for example, "this is good and therefore I will do it"—a man like this has a flaw in character. It's a failure in his character that he could never perceive evil. Duncan Harper was necessary to the book, of course; but he's not as interesting to me as a mixed character like Jimmy Tallant or even Beck Dozer.

Interviewer: Is Tinker also flawed? She seems to love both Duncan and Jimmy without any regard for their diametrically opposed political beliefs.

Spencer: Well, if you remember, she was opposed to their getting into politics at all; she cautioned them both against it. I think Tinker is almost a saint figure, a person without worldly interests. Her main concern is to love.

Interviewer: Beck Dozer also, at least initially, seems reluctant to get involved in the racial politics of this small town. Does this hesitation relate to his mixed character that you mentioned?

Spencer: Beck was the kind of black I was beginning to observe before I left the South and went to Italy. He was ambivalent because he was entering a new era of his own culture, passing from one static set of values and behaviors into another. His reaction is a sort of culture shock, which is why he vacillates in the way he talks and acts. Beck has moments of regressing and talking like an Uncle Tom; he has moments of sounding beyond himself. He also likes to play ironically on the guilt of whites, and there's even the suggestion of a death wish associated with Beck. I see Beck's whole character emerging in this novel; in fact, his is the theme of emergence.

Interviewer: Is Beck approaching a resolution to his ambivalence at the end of the novel?

Spencer: Well, he does have a kind of triumph of character when he simply refused to do anything for Kerney Woolbright; he has found the courage to refuse. But this book was not meant to be the story of Beck. *The Voice at the Back Door* is about incident and about the interaction between difficult cultural levels. It's written almost like a melodrama, cut into short scenes and tightly plotted, with the emphasis on events. I was trying to write a local novel about the confrontation of the races; and in view of subsequent historical events, I think this was probably the last time that that confrontation could be treated as a local issue. It was not my intention in this book to explore the psychological depth of a character, as I did, for example, with Amos Dudley in *This Crooked Way.*

Interviewer: Amos Dudley is a very complex character; and part of his complexity, I think, results from his affinities with the biblical Jacob. One commentator has suggested that you used this biblical allusion ironically. Did you?

Spencer: No, I meant it quite literally. A great many things in that book were played off against biblical stories. For example, the sending away of one woman so as to take another: in the Bible, Jacob didn't do that but his granddaddy, Abraham, did. Like Jacob, Amos Dudley has, in a sense, run away from his home and gone to find his fortune elsewhere. Of course, instead of having his own dream of angels, Amos merely reads about Jacob having such a dream. I think the major biblical parallel involving Amos is his direct experience with God. In the Bible, Jacob operates like a businessman with God, making bargains and trading things off. Amos, too, tries to deal in this fashion. No, I did not intend the biblical allusion ironically; there's a literal parallel between these two men. At the same time, though, I do hope I left enough to chance and nature so that Amos isn't just a replica of Jacob. In my opinion, *This Crooked Way* is my most originial book. In fact, I think I might like it better than any of the other Mississippi books. And of all my characters, Amos is probably the largest in heroic stature.

Interviewer: Is Amos Dudley's first name significant? There is a book of Amos in the Old Testament.

Spencer: Well, I couldn't name him Jacob; that would have been a bit much.*(Laughs.)* I think what happened was that I was looking for an Old Testament name, but one that didn't have an obvious biblical association and that would also be appropriate in this backwoods setting. As I recall, "Amos" is a rather wild, prophetic book, a visionary book; so maybe I did draw that connection. There is a good deal of the poetic visionary in my backwoods Amos. But you must bear in mind that I was trying to write fiction rather than to draw too many parallels.

Interviewer: Did Amos' belief that he could communicate directly with God cause his problems?

Spencer: In a way, yes. He thought of himself as a privileged child of God, and the wreckage he brought about was the result of this attitude. You know, strict Protestantism maintains that you are alone with God; you confirm the deity just because the two of you. But Amos pushes Protestantism too far. Then he discovers that he has to fall back on ritual, the ritualistic belief in family and roots. Amos had to accept his roots instead of trying to sever them in his attempt to rise in the world. So he goes back to the river where it all began and undergoes a ritualistic redemption, triggered by a kind of repentance when he throws the money in the river.

Interviewer: Is Amos' "way" no longer "crooked" at the end of the novel?

Spencer: I think he had reached the end of "this crooked way." I think he saw that his obsession had led him, in a sense, even to kill. And he *had* caused both death and destruction. Amos was deadly to the people around him because he valued them less than his obsession with his own destiny. This kind of obsession almost always leads to destructiveness in society.

Interviewer: In your first book, *Fire in the Morning,* what is the symbolic significance of the title?

Spencer: Well, a fire in the morning loses its psychological impact but not its physical force. As a child, I once saw a house burn down in the morning, and the flames didn't seem to exist. It was an unreal occasion—this house turning to ashes in front of my eyes and the flames almost absorbed into the sunlight. You could hardly see the fire as an outrage at all, as the cause of this destruction. In the book, the Gerrards have done a grievous wrong to the Armstrongs and to other people, but society now accepts them as a leading family. Everybody knows shady dealings once took place; but time has covered up the original crimes, and the Gerrards are now thought to be perfectly respectable. That's what maddens the young man, Kinloch. In this new era in the little town of Tarsus, he's about the only one who perceives the continuing outrage of what the Gerrards have done. The fire in the morning is an image of this situation, but I'm not very fond of it anymore. As a symbol, it's a little overdrawn, I think; and I regard it now as rather immature. The writing in that book is perhaps generally a bit too self-conscious.

Interviewer: Randall Gibson, the lawyer, speaks in a very prolix, literary-sounding manner. Would this be an example of self-conscious writing in *Fire in the Morning?*

Spencer: No, it's an example of a part of southern culture. Maybe you've never known southerners who spoke like that—something like oratory, something like poetry. But there were many people in my parents' generation who were awfully good at that sort of speech, especially small-town drinking lawyers like a Randall Gibson. The more they drank, the more elevated their style became. My own uncles could converse in that fashion. The ornate speech, the long rolling sentences, seemed to flow out of their considerations of the times, especially over a glass of bourbon with a friend. They had read a great deal and often drew from literature in their conversations; they knew how to weigh events and heighten them with their speech. This is exactly what Randall Gibson does, and that's what I use him for in the book. He has the poetic vision necessary to lift that story up to the plane of consideration it needs. His presence makes of the whole retribution theme something higher and grander than it otherwise would be. His mannered speech is a deliberate contrast to the homey chitchat of the other characters. Without Randall to elevate it, that book would have been a flat account.

Interviewer: Is there a fate at work in *Fire in the Morning?* Did you intend the retribution that overtakes the Gerrards to appear inevitable?

Spencer: What I got from reading the Greek writers was that it's in the nature of things that balances have to come even and retribution must be carried out. Maybe I did believe that a little bit at the time. You see, I read a good deal of Thomas Hardy in school and for my own amusement, so I might have absorbed some of his philosophy; I guess I do have a lot of what seems like fate and sheer accident in my work. I'm sure, though, that Hardy comes out much more strongly on that theme than I do. As a novelist, I personally try to avoid sweeping explanations for events, whether philosophical or theological or whatever, because they get me into all sorts of difficulties. For me, fiction isn't the ground for that kind of generalization. Of course, there is accident in *Fire in the Morning.* If Kinloch had not married Ruth, who then happened to mix with that other family without knowing what she was doing, well, that whole issue of the past wrongdoing might have been dormant forever. But you have to understand that, once things got started, it was the determination and persistence of Kinloch that pushed them to their resolution. In this one instance, retribution did take place; but that's not to say it was inevitable.

Interviewer: How much planning did you do before beginning to write *Fire in the Morning?*

Spencer: Well, I was very much aware that I was writing a first novel, so I tried to outline the whole book in advance. Initially, I wanted it to be the story of Ruth, the young wife; that's how I had it planned. But so much of her life had been spent away from the local scene, in places that I knew nothing about and could not successfully imagine, that I was forced either to condense or to eliminate much of that material. Finally, the story came to be concentrated on the one small town of Tarsus and on Ruth's husband, Kinloch. This same thing happened again with *The Voice at the Back Door,* which I had thought was going to be Marcia Mae Hunt's story, about her running off with a stranger. Then the local scene became so powerful and intricate that I couldn't pull away from it. As a result, Marcia Mae's story was no longer central. I guess you could say that my original plans don't always work out all that well. *(Laughs.)* Sometimes books and stories just insist on being written another way. Not always, though. Some of my short stories are written straight out in a morning or an afternoon; they almost bounce out of the typewriter. But for a longer story, and especially for a novel, I do need to have a plan for the episodes and their arrangement. Still, that outline has to change as I write in order to accommodate the needs of the characters as they develop.

Interviewer: You say that *Fire in the Morning* was to be Ruth's story. Did her character occur to you before the theme of the feuding families?

Spencer: No, I originally wanted to draw an extended observation of small-town life, much of which is marked by grudges and long-standing dislikes such as the bad blood between the Armstrongs and the Gerrards. But I realized that this would be a static situation that might ravel on forever and never reach a climax. I needed something to precipitate action; and I started wondering, what might that be? Then I thought of Ruth, the outsider. At that point, I became very intrigued with Ruth's own story. When I started writing, though, the emphasis shifted back to the town. I faced that problem of a static situation again with *The Light in the Piazza*. I began with a mother and her mentally retarded daughter, but I wasn't quite sure what to do with them. Suddenly I thought, what if the daughter met a boy? This idea was very fruitful, especially in view of the story's Italian setting, because it offered dramatic possibilities involving the contact between the two families.

Interviewer: This theme of contact between Americans and Europeans recalls the novels of Henry James. Did you have James's work in mind when you wrote *The Light in the Piazza?*

Spencer: Well, everybody immediately made the comparison because of the theme you mention and also because of the use of romance. But, no, I wasn't particularly conscious of Henry James when I wrote my book. In fact, to me that story was more the sort of thing Boccaccio might have done in *The Decameron*, a little tall tale to satirize Florence. *The Light in the Piazza* is really a comedy.

Interviewer: What, specifically, about Florence were you satirizing?

Spencer: Florentines, and Italians in general for that matter, have a wonderfully devious mentality about some things, especially romance and family matters. They love to complicate these issues; and when they get involved in a family discussion, it becomes like a cat's cradle. I lived with a family in Florence and saw this happen time and again, with them and with their friends. Italians take pleasure in involving people in imbroglios, in these labyrinthine, unsolvable situations. In fact, they even have an expression that so-and-so is an *imbroglione,* which means someone who enjoys orchestrating problems and trivial matters, confusing everything. A large part of Margaret Johnson's trouble is that she runs head on into an *imbroglione* in Signor Naccarelli.

Interviewer: Why does Signor Naccarelli register his last-minute objection to the marriage of his son Fabrizio and Margaret Johnson's daughter Clara?

Spencer: Oh, that man is a walking irony! I doubt if he really knew why he did it. More than anything, he probably just wanted a little complication; things were working out too easily and simply to suit him. Also, I'm sure he resented the fact that Margaret Johnson, a woman, had taken charge of the situation. The macho side of his nature couldn't abide that, so he had to exert his own authority to demonstrate his ability to take control. That whole book is the story of Margaret Johnson's duel of wits with Signor Naccarelli. He was a rather complicated man, don't you think?

Interviewer: With all their love for complication, why do the Florentines in *The Light in the Piazza* respond so warmly to the naïve innocence of the childlike Clara?

Spencer: Well, there is a kind of innocence about them too, especially about Fabrizio. Also, Clara resembles the Madonna, and that resemblance brings out the innocence in all their natures. Italians are very Madonna-conscious.

Interviewer: What is the significance of the reference, at the end of the book, to the statue of Cellini's Perseus holding the Medusa's head?

Spencer: For one thing, it underscores Margaret Johnson's moment of triumph. She, too, conquered her Medusa and got those children married. And she doesn't underestimate her accomplishment. She had played a tricky game in a foreign country, and she'd won. The statue also recalls the first scene of the book, in that same piazza where Clara and Fabrizio met. I like to think that the book itself bears a certain relationship to sculpture because it exists in the round; you can look at that story from different vantage points and get many different views of it. In a way, it too is an imbroglio; you get into it and there's no exit. This could be true, that could be true.

Interviewer: Will the marriage of Clara and Fabrizio work, do you think?

Spencer: *(Laughs.)* It's funny you should ask, because I do have this idea that characters who come alive in my books go on living somewhere, that they are alive outside of that book as well as in it. But I really don't know whether Clara's marriage will last. You see, what happened is that I had to drop the story when I did because it had reached a point of absolute balance. It just ends like one of those fireworks explosions that hang there in the air for a moment like a huge flower. So how long Margaret Johnson's triumph lasted, I don't know. You can't tell. In any case, she liberated herself with her decision to push through that marriage. This gesture shows that Margaret Johnson will not be dominated, not by her husband, her doctor, her culture—or even by honesty.

Interviewer: In your other Italian novel, *Knights and Dragons,* a woman also struggles to free herself from oppressive forces.

Spencer: Yes, that book was sort of a companion piece to *The Light in the Piazza;* but it's a much darker book. *Knights and Dragons* is to some extent an allegory. The characters represent elements in a psychic struggle; oh, not all of them and not at every point, but in general that's true. The story becomes a study in evil influences over one woman. Martha Ingram is obsessed with the idea of her ex-husband, Gordon. He becomes a kind of psychic image to her, the dragon in her life. And when the knight comes along, the man who apparently has everything necessary to free her from this obsession, well, he too is a destructive person rather than a truly liberating one. The story turns on this ironic liberation. Martha ends up going crazy at the same time she's getting free.

Interviewer: Jim Wilbourne is the destructive liberator?

Spencer: Wilbourne is a perverse man. I think one of the worst things he does is to send Martha's nephew away. You see, rather than the friends, the obtuse lawyer, and all those little messengers that come over to see her, the nephew is the one positive element that Martha remembers from back home; and she wants to make contact with that element. Wilbourne recognizes that that young man has brought the spring to her, and yet he sends him away. Of course, although Jim Wilbourne is a destructive influence, there also must have been some weakness in Martha's own nature, a tendency to be obsessed with things back home. To me this is the theme of the American abroad—this intense preoccupation with what's been left behind.

Interviewer: Do you mean "theme" in a literary sense, or is this something that you observed when you were in Europe?

Spencer: In the five years that I lived in Italy, I saw many Americans who were concerned with things they'd left. Sometimes they became neurotic about these issues because they could not do anything about them. There was no theatre for action except in the mind, and in the mind things get distorted. I think now, though, that *Knights and Dragons* becomes too much involved with the psychological dimension and too little with the outer world. I tried, when I wrote the book, to create a lot of physical details, to overlay the psychic images onto the literal progress of the story; but the critics didn't seem to think I succeeded. Probably I should not have permitted publication of *Knights and Dragons* as a separate book. For a novel, it is rather overly poetic. I started that story, as I did *The Light in the Piazza,* to be a much shorter piece; but then both just suddenly took off and expanded.

Interviewer: How overt did you wish the theme of "knights and dragons" itself to be in this novel?

Spencer: Well, I didn't want to go to the extent of having the book tell the story of Saint George and the Dragon over again, if that's what you mean. I have used myths and folk tales and fairy tales in several of my books and stories, but I generally use them just as a sort of framing idea. In *The Light in the Piazza,* the story sprang out of the tale of the princess with the harelip and the prince who fell in love with her. Love being blind, he could not see her defect. But when I use myths or tales, I do so only in a loosely allusive manner. I'm not trying to update them and retell them point by point because, for one thing, I'm sure I don't even know the details of the originals.

My source is simply whatever familiarity I happen to have with the outlines of the tales.

Interviewer: You say you've used myths and tales in other of your works?

Spencer: Oh, yes, many times. For example, my story "The Visit" recalls for me the tale about the old man in the mountain; at least, I believe there was a tale like that. And I think the story "First Dark" relates in a way to "Rapunzel," or actually to any number of tales that explore the theme of an enchanted princess imprisoned in a tower or castle. Now, in "Ship Island" I used folklore and legends in a much more conscious manner than I have done in other stories. In fact, for "Ship Island" I did read all I could find about mermaids—about their affinity for sailors, their breathing under water, their unhappiness when on land, all of that. I worked those ideas into the fabric of my story quite deliberately. But that was an exception for me.

Interviewer: *No Place for an Angel,* your next novel after *Knights and Dragons,* has a much greater scope than either the two Italian books or the earlier Mississippi novels. Did you deliberately set out to write such a sweeping narrative?

Spencer: No, that was not a conscious decision. This book really began with a single central impression. I was driving to the airport one day when I saw a huge jet rising slowly into the sky. It was a striking image, and it stayed with me. In fact, I found myself wondering who was on that plane and where it was going. Soon after that I had a dream about some national politicians arriving in Texas. There was a man sitting in a car, quarreling with his wife, having his neck stung by a bee. As I wrote all of this material down, I thought of other characters and other story lines, all related. At that point I realized that I was working on a kind of panoramic novel that I had never tried before. I ended up with an episodic book based on the crossings of many people's paths.

Interviewer: Would it be fair to say that in *No Place for an Angel* Irene and Charles Waddell represent a kind of moral norm? Are their manipulations and their infidelities meant to appear typical of the society you're describing in this book?

Spencer: They're the norm in the book and I'm afraid they were the norm for the world at the time, especially for this country. The

Waddells are just awful people who live in constant compromise. The real tragedy is that nobody regards them as being particularly bad. You see, it takes a critical society to perceive evil; and the society that I was writing about in that book, America in the fifties and eary sixties, was not critical. There was a general decline in values then brought about by too much affluence, too many possibilities. It was the kind of spoiled times that often follow our wars. Melville wrote about this after the Civil War. In one poem I think he says that if you look hard, you see that even the foundations of society are "slimed"—that's his term for it. So, you finish a war like World War II with great idealism and then discover that the foundations are slimed because the country is such a wallow of affluence. In my book, the Waddells are more typical of this postwar moral lassitude than anyone else.

Interviewer: But all of the characters are more or less caught up in this same syndrome, are they not?

Spencer: Yes, and the irony is that—with the exception of Barry Day, the poor sculptor who is nearly always starving but always getting rescued—these are well-off people. They're talented, intelligent, good-looking; they're ahead in their careers. They are people who appear to "have it made" and who should "have it made"; but somehow that basic discovery of values and happiness seems always to elude them. In a sense, they're doomed; they operate in a spiritual vacuum. Their lives are futile because they are not able to find access to happiness or to make successful human relationships. I tried to underscore the emptiness of their lives by playing off all sorts of sudden and violent events against the major developments in the story. Do you remember that boy who seems to electrocute himelf deliberately in the Florida Keys? Well, violent and mysterious acts like that suggest the inability of these people to cope with life, to respond to it meaningfully.

Interviewer: Is there a parallel between the moral wasteland of *No Place for an Angel* and the dark and violent world of *The Snare?*

Spencer: Not a parallel exactly. In fact, I think contrast might be a better word. I've never thought of this before, but it strikes me now that the basic difference between these two books is their approach to the question of evil. In *No Place for an Angel,* evil is simply an absence of good, the result of a vacuum of despair. I'm not a student of philosophy; but a friend of mine, who is scholar enough to give me the right context, says that this is evil in Augustinian terms. But I happen to believe that evil is also an active force with an existence of its own, and it occurs to me now that it's this active force of evil that's loose in *The Snare.* That book rests, so the philosophers might say, on a Manichean understanding of evil as an independent power to be dealt with.

Interviewer: A commentator for the *Hudson Review* said he wasn't sure whether the culture depicted in *The Snare* was meant to seem "incurably evil or just excitingly unbalanced."

Spencer: Oh, that book is a study of evil and, I think, is deeply marked by it. In a philosophical sense, *The Snare* is my mostly intensely thought-out book. I do believe that evil is incurable; but I wanted to show that, even in such a climate, life can still persist and perhaps grow into a kind of sainthood. The lesson Julia learns is that she has to make a place for herself in the world of *The Snare.*

Interviewer: Does Julia herself become a saint figure at the end of the book?

Spencer: Well, I would not put it quite that way. Instead, I would say that she arrives at a concept of saintliness as a result of her involvement with evil; and I believe that even this concept is something rather precious to emerge from so much sordidness. Julia has both evil and good in her nature, but the true measure of her character is that she never gives herself wholly to the evil. In fact, both she and Jake retain a kind of curious innocence despite their sordid experiences.

Interviewer: At the end of *The Snare,* Julia finds herself inside a cistern with the corpse of Ted Marnie below her and a vision of Henri Devigny above. What is the significance of this tableau?

Spencer: As I wrote the end of *The Snare,* I was afflicted with a real horror. I can't say what effect the reader might get, but the imagined vision of the thing gave me something of the sense of horror of reading Dante, his approach to the depths of hell, Satan chained at the bottom of the pit. At the bottom of the cistern was where Julia found the body of Ted Marnie. Marnie is a kind of debased image of Henri Devigny, and I think that association explains her vision. All through the book, you recall, Devigny keeps resurfacing in her consciousness just as Marnie kept reappearing in

New Orleans after he's thought to be dead. Someone once made the comment that Marnie is a shadowy figure in *The Snare,* but that's what I intended him to be. That's what he is to Julia, a shadow of her former experience with Devigny, the seducer.

Interviewer: Is there any correlation between the cistern in this book and the sinkhole at the end of *Fire in the Morning?*

Spencer: I never made that connection before, but I guess they do have something in common. The ground has always sort of symbolized the rational and the firm, and I suppose I had this symbolic tradition in mind when I wrote those scenes. In both stories, the ground has been undermined, either dug out or rotted away. Of course, sinkholes come literally from my childhood experiences around Carrollton, Mississippi. There was a great deal of erosion on the bluffs there, and we always had to be careful to avoid sinkholes.

Interviewer: Ted Marnie is a religious fanatic and self-styled saint. What is the relationship between the saintly impulse and the demonic impulse in this strange man?

Spencer: Marnie's is a maddened mentality—not at all balanced and certainly not saintly. I had to cut the pamphlets he was writing from the final version of the book, but you would have found that they were just gibberish. Marnie is without intelligence, it seems to me; all he has is a kind of grandiose sense of his own powers. People like Marnie have appeared in my books since *This Crooked Way,* men who become their own god first and then try to become everyone else's.

Interviewer: What made you decide to write a novel about the seamy lowlife of a large southern city? Was there a particular central impression involved?

Spencer: *The Snare* is not really a localized story. Although it's set in New Orleans for the most part, to me it has the sense of an encircled locality within a larger context. In other words, the story is larger than the setting. I got the idea for the book from the New Orleans newspaper. In 1952, I think, they were running a story about the strange reappearance of a man who was supposed to be dead. In fact, somebody had been tried for his murder. I thought at the time that this would make a good subject for a novel, so I clipped all the stories and put them away. Five years later, my husband and I were visiting in the South, and we stopped in New Orleans. I went to the

Times-Picayune office and looked up the story as it first appeared, when it was just surfacing. What really triggered me was coming across a picture of a young man accused of this murder. His face was very intense, very intelligent, and I realized that he was somebody really fine mixed up in a sordid situation. Then I thought, well, if a young man like this were down here, he would certainly have a girlfriend. That was how I stumbled onto Julia, who caught hold of my imagination and became the main character. In a way, I backed into her. You see, I know that because she lived in a world I could understand and deal with, I could use her to break through into that darker world I needed to explore. Julia was my threshold. I think it's always possible to reshape your material like this once you get yourself swinging around a central impression.

Interviewer: You once said that Julia was perhaps your favorite character. Is that still true?

Spencer: I must have just finished *The Snare. (Laughs.)* In a way, though, that's probably still true. Over the years, as I wrote about woman characters—primarily from Margaret Johnson on—I searched for women who could sustain a weight of experience, both intellectual and emotional. I think that often the women characters I found did not do this. For example, Margaret Johnson's triumph was not necessarily a triumph. It was a fantasy that could explode five minutes after the book is over. Then, Martha Ingram, as I've said, had a weakness in her nature that kept her from throwing off her obsession. And Catherine in *No Place for an Angel* had to retreat almost out of life in order to sustain herself. But when I finally discovered Julia, I found in her a person who could take it and survive. I guess that's why I thought of her as a success. She was very alive to me when I wrote the book, and I suppose she still is.

Interviewer: Are you more comfortable working with female characters or with male characters?

Spencer: Well, I have found that if I choose a woman character who is too much like myself, I have to work to get myself out of her, to clear the way so that she can be herself. For example, I know there must have been some relationship between Catherine and me because I spent a lot of time removing my impressions from her views and attitudes. I think I sometimes need the objectivity toward my material that a male character will provide. On the other hand, the book I'm working on now has a male character who is central; and, frankly, that's causing me some trouble. I finally licked my problems writing about women, and now here I am in the middle of a book that depends on my doing a male character really well. So I've got to come to terms with a different approach from the one I've grown accustomed to.

Interviewer: Would you tell us something about this new male character?

Spencer: He is a person who in a small way has lived through the turmoil of the sixties, a popular professor who got caught up in liberal campus causes. But this involvement, in a sense, ends his teaching career. When the reaction against the liberalism of the sixties sets in, he finds himself misunderstood and ostracized. In a short time he falls from hero to someone without social approval. You see, I think this sort of thing happens repeatedly in American life; people who have an hour of glory in connection with larger events find themselves shunted aside when those events fade. There emerges from a situation like this the question of the survival of the spirit. I suppose that this is really the theme of the novel. I also try in this book to invoke that encircled locale idea of *The Snare,* relating the local scene to the larger pattern of life outside the story.

Interviewer: Have you given the book a title yet?

Spencer: I think it will be called *Shadow Play* [published as *The Salt Line*].

Elizabeth Spencer

John Griffin Jones/1981

From *Mississippi Writers Talking*, Vol. 1 (Jackson: University Press of Mississippi, 1982), 95–129. Copyright 1982 by the University Press of Mississippi. Reprinted by permission.

She'd come back to Mississippi from her home in Montreal to attend the Faulkner Conference at Ole Miss, and to give a reading at the Old Capitol in Jackson from her newest book, *Marilee*. Before a substantial crowd in the House of Representatives, Miss Welty introduced her and she read "A Southern Landscape" and "The Day Before" in a soft accent unchanged by her years in Italy and Canada. Afterwards, as I waited for my chance to talk to her while she signed books, I overheard an older resident of her native Carroll County describing just how closely she resembled her mother, and how the county Miss Spencer had left in the 1940s had changed. The next day she called me to say that a motel was no place for an interview, and we agreed to meet in the Archives Building later that afternoon (10 August 1981).

Jones: This is John Jones with the Mississippi Department of Archives and History, about to interview Miss Elizabeth Spencer. Mrs. John Rusher is how you're known in Montreal.

Spencer: Yes.

Jones: Today is August 10, 1981. We're at the Archives Building in Jackson. I've got a list of questions for you. Looking during my research on your writing life I wasn't able to find out a whole lot about your early background other than the fact that you were born in Carrollton, Mississippi, and the names of your parents. Can you tell me something about your early memories, your family, and that type of thing?

Spencer: I was born in Carrollton. My parents were both from Carrollton or from Carroll County. My mother, I suppose, was born at the McCain family plantation. My mother's family were the

McCains. There were some military heroes in the family. There were two military leaders from West Point and two from Annapolis. My great-uncle was General Pinckney McCain, who was a general during the First World War. He trained the Allied Expeditionary Force which came under the command, I believe, of General Pershing.

Jones: Sure.

Spencer: Camp McCain at Grenada was named for him. Then my mother's brother William Alexander McCain, who went to West Point, I believe he served in both the Mexican Rebellion and the First World War, and later became head of the quartermaster depot in Philadelphia. He retired to Bucks County, Pennsylvania. And his brother, Admiral J. S. McCain, commanded the task force under Admiral Halsey during the Second World War. His son was another admiral, John Sidney McCain, who was in command of the Pacific fleet during the sixties. He retired about five years ago, and only recently died, as you may know. My mother, however, lived a very quiet life. Of her two younger brothers, she was—there were two crops in that family for some reason. There were my two uncles who were in military life, and a girl, Miss Katie Lou, who taught Latin for years at McComb, Mississippi, and was a very highly educated lady. Then there was a long gap. I think maybe two children died. Then there was my mother and two other brothers. My mother, I think, was the next to the last. Then my father was the youngest one in his family, and I was the youngest one in our family, so it happens that I was only two generations from the Civil War. My grandfather remembered it though he was too young to go. My father's father, who was dead before I was born, had fought at Gettysburg. So when I say that, that my grandfather was in the Civil War, people look at me like I'm crazy, but it is really true.

Jones: Right.

Spencer: Let's see. You were asking me about my parents. Well, my mother was born at Teoc—that was what they called the plantation—in Carroll County. It was a plantation near Malmaison which was Greenwood Leflore's plantation in the Teoc country. Teoc Tillala was the Choctaw name for tall pines. You may have heard of that. Well, my mother was a very pretty girl and she became a music teacher. That was one thing open to young ladies. My grandfather was elected county sheriff and moved into Carrollton, and she moved up to McCarley, a little town near Carrollton, to get what music pupils she could. That was the thing one did: you lived with nice people who had a piano and you taught music. She saw my father up there, or rather he saw her. I think they went together for a little while. Then he moved into Carrollton to start business on his own, and they were married there and lived there ever since. They bought a house there. I was born in that house, and they both lived there the rest of their lives. It was a long lifetime for both of them in one place.

Jones: Yes. I'd read where your dad worked as a farmer.

Spencer: Well, I don't doubt that he worked as a farmer when he was growing up simply because they were very poor. It was right after Reconstruction in the 1880s that he was born. His father died soon after. They had farms and apparently had good houses and friends and everything, but it was just a hard life. His mother had to raise the four brothers. There were four brothers and a daughter that died. She had to do her best with those children. So he went one year to college and had to go back home to take care of his mother who was sick, and then they all got together, because she got tuberculosis, and they chipped in and sent her out to San Antonio to try to prolong her life. It went back a long way, but he remembered it just as fresh. Then he left McCarley. The Spencers at McCarley were C&G station agents, and Railway Express agents. They had a country store and the station, a whistle stop. They had a house and a farm. My father moved into Carrollton, and I believe he bought a store, but first he worked for the Railway Express in Carrollton. But sooner or later he started doing absolutely everything. He had stores for this and that. You know, anything that was going, he'd try it and make money at it. It cost a lot to raise us, I guess, and he knew he had to do more than one thing. He had the Chevrolet agency and the Standard Oil franchise, and he sent the Standard Oil delivery truck all over the county. I think my brother used to drive it in the summer time. And he had a cotton gin, and he had a little farm down in front of our house. In front of our house was a good many acres, about forty acres, on the outskirts of Carrollton.

Jones: Is the house still there?

Spencer: Oh, yes. We sold it to a family that descended from a family that had always lived in town, so I know it's going to be done right by.

Jones: And who in your family remains in Carrollton today?

Spencer: Nobody. Friends. In McCarley were my uncle and his son who moved to Greenwood, and for a while his daughter, until she married and moved into Memphis. They skipped Carrollton. They just jumped from McCarley to Greenwood. We went to Carrollton and never got to Greenwood. You know, a lot of Greenwood was settled by Carrollton. Carrollton is in the hills, but Greenwood is in the Delta and richer.

Jones: But you grew up with a strong sense of the difference between hill people and Delta people?

Spencer: I was brought up on the margin of the Delta, on what they call Valley Hill. Valley Hill can be any road going down that last hill. There were many Valley Hills. Just like that song about the Tallahatchie bridge. Well, what bridge did she mean? Nobody really knows. Any bridge over the Tallahatchie might have been it. Those plantations dated back a long way, and they were just on the margins of the Delta. Usually the houses that were built—I know my mother's family home that burned in the 1880s was built on the last hill overlooking the Delta. It must have been extraordinary. But their plantation was—you know, part of it would be in the hills. But you get central to the Delta, most of that was swamp, if you remember. It was just dead things and swamp. Really ugly. All that's gone. The trees are gone, all those big trees that used to stand in bayous and swamps along the road. Most of that's gone, as I understand it. I've just ridden over to Greenville this trip, but it looks to me like it's all been drained and controlled. Where're you from?

Jones: From here. Jackson.

Spencer: Are you a lifetime Mississippian?

Jones: All my life.

Spencer: Where's your family from originally?

Jones: Yazoo County and the Delta.

Spencer: Yes. But the central part of the Delta is what I'd think of as new country. Right along the river, Greenville and those places, they were all old. The central part of the Delta was dangerous. It was a very rich land if you could control the buckshot and the bayous and get the mules out of the mud. You had to get the cotton picked in the fall. Black labor was what it came to. But Mexicans used to come in to do that too. They were called wetbacks. It's just a whole different thing now from what it used to be. There was also yellow fever. Everything bad.

Jones: As Amos Dudley discovered in *This Crooked Way.*

Spencer: Well, that's the book I wrote about tales I'd heard about the people who opened up the Delta. People like that.

Jones: Fascinating book. Was there anybody in reality that you fashioned Amos Dudley after? Somebody in your family perhaps?

Spencer: No. He was an imaginary character. But I used to hear a whole lot of stories. I remember that what started that book off was my uncle sitting and talking one twilight down at Teoc. Somebody asked him about two brothers who'd gone over into the Delta and made what amounted to a lot of money at that time. Somebody said, "Where did they come from?" And he said, "Just like a lot of Delta folks, they came from out of the hills dragging a cotton sack, and in ten years they had a fortune." That sort of stuck in my mind. And I thought about, "Well, why did they leave home?" You know, there had to be some impetus. I had conceived of there being two brothers, just following what he said, but then as soon as I set up that scene, I realized it might be a man and his friend.

Jones: Arnie.

Spencer: Yes. And then Amos developed a strong personality of his own. His resentments were strong already, and he was caught up in the whole opportunistic thing of the Delta and its really primitive condition. See, he married a woman from near the river. I thought there would have been older families over there. The part he was opening up was very new.

Jones: A lot of people who talk about the phenomenon of there being so many writers from Mississippi, especially from the Delta, say that there was a compression of history, a great deal of drama and life packed into a very short period, that took place in the Delta, so that a family could go to riches to rags often over one generation.

Spencer: Yes.

Jones: They say that is great for a writer, for developing his sense of his time and place. Did that help you, that much being packed into one generation?

Spencer: Which generation do you mean?

Jones: Well, just in general over the two generations that cleared the Delta, the people who went from rags to riches like Amos Dudley, and the ones whose riches were lost.

Spencer: Who were ruined. No, that didn't affect my family. We were from Carrollton as I was telling you, and that's a hill town. I separate my father from a man like Amos Dudley. His ambition was to make a living for his family, to raise his children and furnish support. He was very conscientious, responsible about money, but money was just so hard to make. It was only in the last years of his life that he had any kind of affluence, modest though it was. He was always just struggling away trying to put my brother through college and then medical school, and then me through college. I went to graduate school one year, but that was all. That kind of syndrome of just fabulous gains from cotton land, and failure, largely depended on . . . I suppose unexpected crop failures might ruin people, or two or three bad years. But I don't think that in *This Crooked Way* Amos Dudley fell on evil times financially. Do you?

Jones: No, ma'am.

Spencer: I did hear stories about people going broke. "Becoming land poor," they said. They acquired more land than they could manage. Sometimes there would be accidents like that. I never personally knew anybody who went under that way. I know my mother's family plantation was always mortgaged, but I think it acquired the mortgage just after the Civil War. They probably had a large investment in slaves, and they couldn't sustain themselves after what happened. I just don't know how they managed the debt. But it wasn't until the 1940s that my father and my uncle got together and laid it out. They put it under single management rather than leave it divided property among the heirs.

Jones: Right. Tell me about your early life. You were born in Carrollton in 1921?

Spencer: Yes.

Jones: Can you tell me where the literary influence came when you were growing up?

Spencer: Well, I wasn't a very healthy child and Mother loved to read. She had extraordinarily good taste in children's literature, and also other literature. She came from a family that liked to read. I told you they had a plantation house that burned in the 1880s. They always said that they lost everything, but there were a great many books somebody had grabbed and got out with. Either that or maybe the library wasn't destroyed. There were Dickens and Scott, and then there were a vast accumulation of the things my uncles and my aunt had studied at college: Latin texts and histories and things like that. I don't think the McCains were literary or bookish people, but they made ready reference to books. They put great weight on education, like a lot of Scots Presbyterians do, and they were a strong Scots family—I think my grandmother was one generation from Scotland. I have heard that. I'm not quite sure that's true. She was from an old town that vanished, called Middleton. You might have heard of that. It was between Vaiden and Carrollton. It was a very thriving town before the Civil War. There was a shoe factory there during the Civil War to make shoes for the soldiers. They read an awful lot. I suppose my father's family had nothing against reading, but they probably had too rough a life to give themselves over to too much literature and music. I'm not certain of that. But among the McCains, you were supposed to read and talk about books. When I was sick a good deal as a child my mother used to read aloud to me all kinds of things: Greek and Roman myths. She was very strong on the Bible too, so she used to read Bible stories. Let's see, she read King Arthur's stories, Robin Hood and other children's books. Later on I became fascinated by all this, and as soon as I began to write in school I began to write down stories I imagined. I had a little black playmate. I knew far more blacks than I did whites when I went to school, because I used to spend a lot of time down at the plantation. Around the house the cook's children played with me. Our house was out from the center of town anyway. I used to make him listen to stories I'd made up. I think he was bored.

Jones: That's interesting, because certainly the kind of relationship a small white girl living on the fringes of town had with blacks in the '20s and '30s is something you have always investigated from "The Little Brown Girl" to "Sharon."

Spencer: Yes.

Jones: So listening to your mother read instilled in you an early love for the language?

Spencer: Oh, I think so. Some people probably have this naturally. I'm sure my brother was read to, too, but his bent wasn't literary. He was inclined to want to study medicine and scientific things. Since mine was literary, I had all that to catch on to. I kept on with it. I got encouraged when I went on through school by the teachers I had who were also interested in literary things.

Jones: You came to Belhaven after graduating from Carrollton High?

Spencer: It was J. Z. George High School then. They

consolidated some schools. J. Z. George was the senator from Carroll County who had brought Mississippi a new constitution after the Civil War.

Jones: Why did you choose Belhaven?

Spencer: I didn't! I liked Belhaven. I'm sure it is a good school. No, I wanted to go to the University. My family were all Presbyterians and they had ties with Belhaven, and they decided I should go there. So, I guess I counted my blessings that I could be given a college education. I think I got a scholarship there too. That was a little bit of a help. It was because I was first in my class.

Jones: Yes. At Belhaven did you have someone who took you by the hand and said, "You have talent. You could be a writer." Was it that early that you knew that's what you wanted to do with your life?

Spencer: I wanted to be a writer for a long time. I started writing stories when I was in grammar school. The teachers said they were really good, and they read them aloud to the class. I'm sure they weren't any good at all, but it was just the idea of having done this that was exciting to me. I used to sit up in trees and write. I would sit out by myself. It was a large property and there was a gully in back of the house and a steep fall of land. I used to sit back there and write in notebooks and hide the notebooks in some old machinery that had been dumped down there to prevent erosion. Then I wrote long stories and copied them in tablets and gave them to my mother and father. They were generally adventure stories about people getting isolated at the North Pole about which I knew absolutely nothing. Crazy things like that. I must have picked up fragments to put together in stories like that from books and from magazines my brother had.

Jones: So even that early you knew?

Spencer: Yes.

Jones: It's interesting to me to talk with writers about the first impulse to write.

Spencer: I can't explain it. I think there's something chemical about it. I remember when I first got this terrible urgency. I stayed awake all night with a kind of excitement about something or other. There was a fire in the room burning and casting shadows. The next day I tried to paint that, I tried to draw, but I had no talent for painting, so I wrote a poem. You know, it was some way to release this inner excitement. I don't think that's explainable. Mississippi doesn't explain it; nothing explains it. Being read to as a child doesn't explain it. It's a kind of chemical excitement you feel, and you're drawn toward one sort of expression or another. As I couldn't draw it, I wrote.

Jones: So you almost had to do it?

Spencer: I think so. I think some people have that kind of urgency. But where it comes from, I don't know.

Jones: Yes. You went on to Vanderbilt and studied under Donald Davidson, a man whose name I've heard many times. What about the academic training for a writer? Faulkner and Shelby Foote disparaged it. Do you think it's something every writer needs?

Spencer: I never took creative writing at Vanderbilt. I know that was a center for writers. It was assumed in the English department that it was more a center for literary studies. It might, as a by-product, stimulate writing. I really think that's what creative writing, which I've spent so much time from time to time teaching—it's something I hardly believe in myself, except that I think you can encourage and stimulate and direct students. Sometimes it's your Christian duty to discourage, de-stimulate and defuse students. You just know that they're never going to write anything. Not everybody has to be a writer. It seems to me you should relieve them of the idea that they have to be writers. To my mind for a certain type of person it's a waste of time. Be that as it may, Vanderbilt—I didn't study creative writing there. I took a little creative writing course at Belhaven. We had a little club—like they had the French Club for students interested in French, and a Music Club, and we had a writing club.

Jones: That's where you first met Miss Welty.

Spencer: Yes. We decided to ask her over to the college. She and I both have told that story many times.

Jones: But what about the idea that a college campus is probably the worst place for a working writer, being isolated and stuck off away from life in the unreal world of a college campus?

Spencer: Well, unfortunately writers have to make a living, and universities have been marvelously generous in giving a place to writers. Writers-in-residence are not required to teach full time, and yet they are given good enough money so that they can exist and write. If they want to live off-campus it's generally all right, if they report for their duties. Sometimes the choice is like that. I suppose a writer doesn't have to take it. Nobody is making you be a writer-in-residence, or associate yourself with a college campus unless you want to. Faulkner chose not to. I was just reading a biography of Faulkner. I've never read a biography of Faulkner before. There's an excellent one out by David Minter, who was at the Faulkner conference, a man from Georgia. Faulkner apparently was given books that stimulated him a great deal by Phil Stone, and was exposed that way to a kind of education that, it seems to me, was maybe even better than taking one course after another in college. But he was certainly bookish enough. He read a great deal. I've forgotten what our original question was. About colleges and writers?

Jones: Yes.

Spencer: And continuing your education? Well, you've got to get an education from somewhere if you're going to write. I don't believe in unlettered, untutored writers. It seems to me literature springs from literature. But whether you have the formal degree or not: that's empty as far as your writing goes. Your writing depends on the quality of the work—wherever it comes from. Have you ever heard of an unlettered, untutored writer who was a good writer? They might be good storytellers, and if what they say is taken down it might make what they call oral literature. There have been attempts made at that. I think at Mississippi Southern at one time they were drawing people in from a rather wild part of Mississippi called Sullivan's Hollow. You may have been associated with that?

Jones: No, ma'am.

Spencer: But you know about it. I don't know if this kind of thing transcribed makes for a true literary production. I'm just not sure. Certain untutored things have great interest. Louis Rubin, who was at the Faulkner conference, he was talking about a diary of a family— let's see, post-Civil War, I believe, and I believe either in Virginia or South Carolina—and he said, "It reads like a damn novel." You know? It was just unbelievably rich and full of, oh, I don't know, lost currents of emotion, violent relationships, this, that. I've forgotten the name of it. It's going to be published. I suppose literature just springs up sometimes. Something like that might be a great work. But I'm talking about the general pattern now. I think that literature springs from people who know about it, study it, read it, enjoy it.

Jones: You were saying before we turned the tape recorder on that you went to Ole Miss from '48 to '53?

Spencer: I taught at Ole Miss.

Jones: Right.

Spencer: I taught '48, '49, '50. In '51–'52 I took off to finish a novel I was working on. '52–'53 I taught there, but in '53 I got a Guggenheim Fellowship, and I left.

Jones: At that time you went to Rome?

Spencer: Yes.

Jones: I wanted to get your impressions of the influence Mr. Faulkner had on you, if you ever talked to him about your work or his. *Fire in the Morning* came out in 1948, so indeed you were a published novelist living in Oxford too.

Spencer: I was introduced to him twice and I said, "How do you do, Mr. Faulkner?" and he nodded, and that was all. This was passing chance social acquaintance. When I got to know Faulkner best—it shouldn't really even be called an acquaintance—was in Rome, of all places, even though I'd lived in Oxford. I don't think he was aware much of me or my work. I think he knew the title of a book I'd written because he mentioned it in Rome, but he said he hadn't read it. But at that time when I was in Rome in '53–'54, somewhere along in there, he came. You could look it up. Everything's documented about Faulkner now. I don't think he ever went uptown for a sack of groceries without them finding out about it now and putting it in a biography. He was there in Rome. There was a very nice guy who was head of the Cultural Service named Fox, and he and Mrs. Fox had a very beautiful apartment in the Renaissance part of Rome near the Tiber, and they gave an evening party for Mr. Faulkner. Of course, he was a small man. He was standing there in the corner of the room with a glass in his hand, which he never referred to, and they said, "Come on, you must speak to Mr. Faulkner." And I went and said hello, and he did remember me and asked me how I liked Rome and I said fine. Then someone else came up. But before the party Allen Tate, who was in Rome with his wife Caroline Gordon, asked me to go to dinner with them and Faulkner and another person. She was a rather wealthy woman who was a novelist and had a long car with a chauffeur. I suppose this was part of the deal. We went to a nice Roman restaurant. Tate talked to Faulkner most of the time. I was rather shy around Faulkner. I knew that he was shy. I felt shy, and I didn't want to talk to him. There's nothing worse than trying to talk to somebody who doesn't want to talk to you. Don't you think?

Jones: Yes, ma'am.

Spencer: So I was just in favor of leaving him alone. I remember we came back together. There was a girl with him named Jean Stein, I think. We came back together in the chauffeur-driven car. Something was said, because his hotel was near to where I was staying, something was said about his coming to lunch. I don't know who said it. He said, "If you will call me I'll come." I never did. I don't particularly like to know writers just to say I know writers. If they turn out to be warm and companionable people—I mean, Eudora Welty is a charming person to meet for dinner or to have as a friend and to chat with. I just can't imagine a more friendly person. But I would feel that about her whether she was a writer or not. That's what it comes to. Faulkner was strange and withdrawn from most people, so I didn't want to intrude on his thought processes, whatever they were. I met a good many people in Oxford that did have long friendships with Faulkner. I knew Phil Stone very well. Phil called up as soon as he knew I was in Oxford. He and Emily used to have me over for drinks and we'd chat a lot about writing. Phil talked a lot about "Bill" as he called him, and what he thought of his work. He was a very good talker, Phil, and an interesting man.

Jones: He loved Faulkner?

Spencer: Oh, I think they had one of those friendships you could call love or just lifelong devotion to each other. Maybe there were tensions. I don't really know. I think it was certainly a significant friendship.

Jones: But did his writing influence you as a young writer?

Spencer: Oh, I'm sure it did. I never did read Faulkner, in spite of the fact that my family read a lot and didn't exclude southern writers certainly. Stark Young was a distant cousin of mine.

Jones: I didn't know that.

Spencer: Well, my grandmother that married the McCain was a Young from Old Middleton. Then there was another branch of that same family that was at Como. They were Youngs. Some of these moved eventually to Oxford. He was brought up in Oxford but the family came from Como.

Jones: Did you know him?

Spencer: Oh, yes. Mr. Stark. Now, he came to make a speech to the Southern Literary Festival at Oxford that first spring I was there, '49, and I never had a lovelier time. My book had just come out and received good notices, *Fire in the Morning*, and both he and John Crowe Ransom had read it and welcomed me. Stark particularly seemed to take a liking to me. We wrote for years. He recommended me for a Guggenheim. When I was in New York he took me to lunch. That's what I mean. If Faulkner had been like that I would have been happy to try to be his friend. But there was just this enclosure—part, I think, of his art. But Stark was very receptive and really kind. Some of the correspondence he wrote me has since been published with his letters. So it was a nice relationship. But I never read Faulkner until I was in graduate school in Nashville. In a moden novel course I read him. The first semester was Modern British Novelists. It was excellent. Then I went on and took Modern American Novelists and inevitably hit on Faulkner. I immediately decided that since I was from Mississippi I would write a paper on one of Faulkner's books, and I wrote the paper and then discovered how woefully ignorant I was of what he was doing and the scope of it. Very little Faulkner criticism had been published at that time. It was a mystery of how the whole pattern of the county was fitted together. This was a great discovery, but I found it very late. Then I began to read everything he wrote. I know that some of his influence got into my work because I was from north Mississippi, so that was all I knew to write about. We were looking at the same things, like Italians painting madonnas—the same subject occurs over and over. I had to find some independence. But I don't think—do you think my books are too much like Faulkner's, the early ones? What do you think?

Jones: No, I don't. That's something I wanted to ask you about though, that charge. *This Crooked Way,* for instance, was likened to *Absalom, Absalom!* and also to his brother John's *Dollar Cotton*. It seems to me the similarity ends with *Dollar Cotton* after you state the basic plot of two poor hill country men coming to the Delta and striking it rich, Amos Dudley and Otis Town.

Spencer: But see, I never read *Dollar Cotton*. And I never thought about *Absalom, Absalom!* because the scale was so much more modest in that *Absalom* was pre-Civil War, and there were the magnificent mansion and millions of slaves and the dynasty thing. This made it an entirely different scope from what my novel purported to be, which was a novel of a man with a religious obsession. I don't think Sutpen had a grain of a religious obsession, do you? He was obsessed, but it was social. Okay. I never thought of *Absalom, Absalom!* because the scope was so different, and the time. *Dollar Cotton* I never read. So I guess the influence that I had to work myself out of was stylistic. I deliberately had to pull back if I found myself writing what sounded like Faulkner. My materials were coming first hand from what I knew from listening and from my own heritage. This is what I was trying to use. When Yankee critics compared me to Faulkner I thought they just didn't know. I suppose some comparison was inevitable.

Jones: Did any of that figure into the sharp stylistic break you came upon in *The Light in the Piazza?* Did you have a harsh reaction to being compared to Faulkner and Miss Welty and others in Mississippi?

Spencer: I think it's inevitable that critics compare. They live on comparison. If you're going to write a critical paper in college you're taught to do that, you know: compare and differentiate and so forth. They always do that. Women writers are compared to other women writers. Southern writers are compared to other southern writers. Mississippi writers are compared to other Mississippi writers. You know, you can't escape it. You were asking if that made me start to write differently?

Jones: Yes.

Spencer: I think that what made me start to write differently was that I spent five years in Italy before I came to Canada in '58. I'd never written anything about Italy. I'd written *The Voice at the Back Door* when I was in Italy. Then it looked like instead of being away a year I was going to be away five years, and then it looked like I wasn't going to be living in Mississippi, and I thought I could either give up since my subject matter had collapsed, or I could start writing of other atmospheres and sorts of people I'd been encountering for five years, even though that wasn't the South. So I started writing a

few stories like that and *The Light in the Piazza* was one of them. I
didn't plan it to be a short novel. I planned it to be about twenty
pages long, and suddenly it took off and became what it is: over 100
pages long. It was a new experience. But I loved Italy. I could see
things happening in Italy the same way I could see them happening
here. But then I thought it would be exciting to be a sort of roving
spirit in one's work instead of a fixed planet. You know? And then I
started trying other backgrounds. But the southern sensibility is
something that's sort of ingrained in me. If I get too far away from
that sensibility, I don't think I'll be able to write.

Jones: What about Miss Welty here in Mississippi, that influence.
Did it intimidate you?

Spencer: I often think that Eudora is even more an individual
writer than Faulkner. I think you have to be Eudora to write one of
her sentences. No, I don't think her work, except for giving me great
delight, has had any effect on my work. Do you?

Jones: No.

Spencer: I can't see it at all. No, I do think I am a distinctly
different writer. I think I read her later. She was publishing later. I
went through the big Faulkner kick of reading everything he wrote—
that ended about 1942 with *Go Down, Moses.* I don't think his work
since that date has had the enormous impact to me that the earlier
ones had. Eudora was just beginning publishing during those years,
and I think I read most of the things as they came out. But I read her
as a writer that was sort of concurrent with me. Faulkner was a great
idol. Her work seemed to me to be forming a little ahead of my own.
I think only in recent years she's finally gotten the recognition she
deserves, don't you?

Jones: Oh, yes.

Spencer: I used to say I liked her work extremely, and people
would say, "Now who is that?" It would be sort of like that. People
that knew anything didn't say that. No, I wouldn't say she was an
influence I had to fight off.

Jones: Who was? Who would you point to as your greatest
influence?

Spencer: Writers don't like to admit that they've been influenced
by anyone. But I think that when I started writing I'd been impressed
by Thomas Hardy, his novels, because I'd been brought up in a

farming background with a whole lot of family lore, with Anglo-Saxon people. The way he constructed his books seemed to me to be almost architectural. I think I tried in *Fire in the Morning* to pay attention to the way he constructed his books. I wanted to build something on my own that would be my own. But I guess structurally he would have been an influence. Certainly more than a writer like Virginia Woolf. She has a kind of magic in a way. But her novels are so fluid. A Hardy novel was laid like a structure, and I could see that.

Jones: Anyone else?

Spencer: I liked Conrad a lot; I think Faulkner was influenced a lot by Conrad if you want to talk about influences. That depended a lot on rhetoric. Conrad relied on the power—masculine power, mind you—evocation and descriptive forces and great rolling rhetoric. I didn't aspire to that. I thought it was wonderful stuff.

Jones: Let me ask you something about themes. With the Armstrongs in *Fire in the Morning* and the Morgans in *This Crooked Way* there exists something that literary historians these days are pointing to as inspiration for the outpouring of great fiction and fiction writers in the South from '25 to '55. It has been said that one of these great themes was coming to grips with the southern family romance.

Spencer: The family romance?

Jones: Yes.

Spencer: In connection with Ary Morgan in *This Crooked Way?*

Jones: Yes, that strong attachment to family.

Spencer: Yes, well, some southern families talk about themselves and each other as though they were the Plantagenets, even though they may be perfectly ordinary middle-class people. You know?

Jones: Yes.

Spencer: I likely satirized the Morgans, I think, but on the whole I thought they were a family of some dignity. They had their little family stories. But the main reason I made them what they were and the way they were was to show up the noncivilized origins of Amos Dudley. The contrast there helped me bring him in sharp focus. That's really a one-man book. It is so dominated by this man. In the end he's not a great person to be central to a civilization the way Sutpen wanted to be. I wasn't intentionally thinking of this at the time, mind you, but just looking back. He had to be shown as the dominant figure in the book, without having very many credentials to make him that way. It was kind of a religious strain, a primitive religious strain in the South that I was interested in showing. In bringing the Morgans into it I could show what he was and what he believed by showing what he wasn't and didn't believe. It's easy to pick up a family like the Morgans in Mississippi. There may be some literally named Morgan, though I did not have anyone in mind. I was thinking of a family over around Greenville or—oh, where else could a family like this exist? Meridian, Columbus, anywhere. I thought there was that family consciousness any number of places.

Jones: Let me ask you a question about *The Voice at the Back Door.* You are dealing with the tricky area of race relations in the South—I believe the book came out in 1956.

Spencer: Yes.

Jones: Knowing as you did the racial situation in the South at that time, was there something in your mind that you were trying to bring across to the reader, a sense of morality in terms of race relations with the example of Duncan Harper?

Spencer: Let's see. How all that came about was that up until the time I wrote that book I had taken the traditional attitudes more than I should, I suppose. I had actually believed what my forebears had told me about the inferiority of the black race. You know, I realized the time of personal examination had come. I wrote the book to explore any number of attitudes toward the changing social climate. I felt things were going to change. I didn't know they were going to change so violently and dramatically. I'd worked on a newspaper in Nashville, and it was a liberal newspaper, the *Nashville Tennessean,* and I had heard a lot of talk about more liberal policies toward the blacks. When I was at Ole Miss there were people who were somewhat tending that way.

Jones: Dr. Silver.

Spencer: Well, okay. Others too. I thought then that there could have been a student at Ole Miss who'd gotten somewhat exposed to this kind of thinking. You know, Duncan Harper was just a fair-minded man who'd been away in the army. Also, he'd known a kind of scope and perspective beyond just the local by having been an All-American football star. This could have given him more of a horizon, a perspective. Then there was that other man in there who was very attractive, but he was sort of a bad boy, and the other was the good boy. I thought they were both equally attractive.

Jones: Tallant.

Spencer: Jimmy Tallant. He also had been exposed to a wider scope of thinking, and at the end he came out on the liberal side of things. I was trying to explore it from a local standpoint really, even though they'd had outside experience to see how things even in small towns might be in flux. One certain thing was it was no longer static. There were forces working for change. I wanted to see one situation in action. But I deliberately planned the book like a melodrama with a sheriff's race, a possible murder, this and that. There were a lot of cross currents like that. I got into it and had a really good time writing it. It came out shortly after a really dreadful crime in Mississippi that had received national publicity: the Emmett Till murder, which you won't remember.

Jones: 1955.

Spencer: Yes. And it coincided with a lot of racial upheaval all over the country. This gave it a national popularity, reputation, huge critical notice. That was just purely and simply coincidence. I hadn't foreseen any of it. I thought it would be a fairly quiet novel, quietly received as the other books had been. But it did awfully well. It was translated into about a dozen languages. It was in several paperbacks. It was chosen for the Time Incorporated reading program. It was in print for twenty years, and it's now about to be reissued. So that's quite a distinguished history for a novel. There are still some people who like to read it. I hope it's not too dated. I really felt a certain moral pressure to do this. It was time for me to write a considerable work because I had two favorably-reviewed beginning novels, and I knew I was taking an enormous risk to write something timely that might seem to be a social tract or might seem to be polemical. You sacrifice more than you gain. But I still felt obliged to explore my own thinking about the racial issue. I couldn't avoid it. So even though I risked the whole thing being lost by just being timely . . . timely fiction is awful and you should never try to write it. It may succeed for a day, you know, and in ten years it's gone. I just had to take that chance. I think what's kept the book alive is that some of the characters in it are very real. I enjoyed writing about them and their speech and the way they met different situations, not just racial questions but romantic, family, political. I think that they were true characters.

Jones: Certainly. And when it came out one of the critics called it "an almost perfect novel," which is a nice review.

Spencer: Yes.

Jones: You left in 1953 to go to Rome? You were out of the state really during all the time of racial tension during which the state underwent so much change. My question is, is Mississippi today that different from the Mississippi that you grew up in and knew before you left in 1953? Is there a real discernible difference in the social tone here?

Spencer: Well, I remember the South of my childhood as being a great deal poorer. You see, the whole landscape has changed. You have all these soil conservation projects. Talking about the Delta, it's not recognizable from what I used to know. It's still flat. To me it's perfectly beautiful down here now, even though there're many parts that seem to have gone. Like North Street in Jackson. I had some cousins living on North Street, the corner of North and George Street, and I asked to be driven by there to see the old house. There's a Spanish-looking bank there now. All of North Street is gone. It's just that prosperity changes things more than almost anything else. I think it's a prosperous part of the world here now. These changes are just inevitable. No, I don't find much of the atmosphere that I grew up in. But, still, as long as I know people I knew back then—they seem pretty much the same with the accent and the friendliness and all that—so much has not changed. Don't you find that's true? Have you spent all your life here?

Jones: Yes.

Spencer: Never been away?

Jones: I've been away a lot. I really don't know. I grew up after the social change, really, so I really don't know much about Mississippi before integration personally. And I don't know first-hand anything about life in rural Mississippi.

Spencer: Yes.

Jones: What about your writing about Mississippi today as you do, completely out of memory? Do you come back down to fill your well springs?

Spencer: Well, one would hope to. It's not out of memory though. Let's see. I was in Rome for two years. I spent a year in the States finishing *The Voice at the Back Door,* and I was in Mississippi for about a month that year. Well, this is just personal.

Jones: Good.

Spencer: I had just been going with John, my husband, for a couple of years. We wanted to get back together. I didn't want to marry a foreigner, but the farther away I got from him the more I missed him. He kept writing me. Then I went back to see him and we decided this separation was ridiculous, so we got married. Let's see. That was two years away, but one summer after we were married we spent the summer in Mississippi. I've never been away for very long. Last year you had all that drought and chickens dying and people dying. I wasn't here that year because, again, for personal reasons it didn't seem like the time to come. All during the '70s when my mother and father were in their last years, they wouldn't leave Carrollton to stay with us or anybody else. I came back quite a bit and stayed sometimes for a month or two at the time. And I would take invitations down here for little readings and things that would just pay my air fare. I read on the Coast and at Natchez and in Jackson and at Mississippi Southern. Anybody who would offer me a plane ticket I would hop on the plane. So I haven't cut my ties here. If you mean that you have to write out of living day to day in a place, then I suppose that would finish me off, wouldn't it? I wrote a book laid in New Orleans called *The Snare,* and I was down there a good bit. So I'm not always in Montreal, or always away.

Jones: When you left the South, did you think that was the end of your career as a writer?

Spencer: I thought I'd keep on writing, but I didn't know how successful it would be. See, *The Light in the Piazza,* for better or worse, really did alter my vision of what I could do. It expanded me because it was so fantastically successful. The success was completely unexpected. For some reason everybody seemed to love that story. It was published in the *New Yorker,* then in book form. It was taken by a book club, it was made into a movie. You know, it went through one translation after another. Reviews poured in. I thought, "Well, maybe I should take a wider scope on things. Not confine myself to the Mississippi scene." So then I went on and wrote things that were laid in Rome. Maybe I made a mistake. Some people seem to think I did, and lectured me severely.

Jones: Really?

Spencer: Well, they didn't think I should have given up writing exclusively about the South. I thought I had proved that this other material was not only available to me but that I could handle it well. So I went on and did things that challenged me in a new way instead of just renewing the tie here. The outer world seemed to interest me more. I don't know why. It seemed to give me a bigger horizon.

Jones: Yes, ma'am. Yet you do return to Mississippi . . .

Spencer: Oh, yes. I never want to break the tie. But I don't know why I should just concern myself with that. But a lot of people who are attached to Southern literature and thought I was writing it well deplored the fact that I gave up writing it. Well, other things like *No Place for an Angel, Knights and Dragons,* didn't succeed as well as I thought they should. Maybe my critics were right. *The Snare* was laid in New Orleans.

Jones: And you personally don't think it hurt your fiction leaving the South?

Spencer: Well, it became my fiction, so I don't know if it hurt or not. You can't say—that's the road not taken, isn't it?

Jones: Right.

Spencer: You never know. You better watch out. Every turn you make you can't go back and say, "Well, I guess I can go back the other way." Then you've changed.

Jones: What about a story like "Ship Island?" That came out in, I think, '65. Tell me about that story. It was one of my favorites.

Spencer: "Ship Island." That was a very significant story for me. I think it's about my favorite of my stories. But it started a new theme in my work. I don't quite know how to put it, but it was the same thing in *The Snare,* it's the same thing in some of the stories in that book *(The Stories of Elizabeth Spencer).* It's that women feel themselves very often imprisoned by what people expect of them. You know? Some people mount rebellion: they are not going to put up with it. This has come to the surface in many aspects of my later work. That story was what started it. I just thought it had a compelling feeling. I felt it was very sensual and very right, and I liked it a lot. I think I wrote it in '63 and the *New Yorker* fooled around. It was long, and the *New Yorker* has a policy of bringing out seasonal publications. If you write a story that's laid in the summer, they'll publish it in the summer but they will not publish it in the fall. So they missed one summer with it, and they fooled around till the next summer, and I thought they weren't going to publish it then. It sat around for about eighteen months. I thought they should have come out with it sooner. It needed publishing when it was written. Let's see, then after that was *Knights and Dragons,* and then after that was *No Place for An Angel,* and the after that was the volume *Ship Island,* and then there was *The Snare.*

Jones: But you came across this girl that kind of rebels against this young insurance man just out of the fraternity house and runs off with those two sort of strange men, you came across her spontaneously and thought that that was right? What was her name?

Spencer: Nancy.

Jones: Nancy. You thought hers was a voice that suited you?

Spencer: Well, she didn't come on me as strongly as a voice as a character like Marilee. I think "Ship Island" is a third person story. But for some reason I began to feel an affinity to kind of waif-like women that were free. They have no particular ties, or no ties that are worth holding them, and so they become subject to all kinds of encounters, influences, choices out in the world. You know, they've got to find a foothold, they've got to find something to hold to. This affinity shows up in several stories like that. I think there swings in and out of Nancy's voice that kind of thinking all the way through, and it has the rhythm of the sea all the way through.

Jones: Was "Judith Kane" in that collection?

Spencer: Yes.

Jones: Another one of my favorites. Can you tell me something about that story?

Spencer: A lot of people feel that is a strange story. Some people don't like it. I thought it was very powerful. I thought it was a study of evil.

Jones: Yes. Evil with a beautiful face.

Spencer: Yes. This narcissistic obsession was what was victimizing the man and the girl that happened into the house. She perceived that too late to stop—I don't know if she could have stopped. The girl that tells the story. The full force of the situation strikes her later on.

Jones: Right. That house I kept picturing right off campus somewhere in Belhaven.

Spencer: I think I remember setting that in Nashville, that's where I pictured it taking place. Yes, it had a thread of fact. Most of all my stories, though they develop into something else, have a thread of something that suggests them. I remember staying in a rooming house with three or four of us who were in graduate school. There was one extraordinarily good-looking girl that was rather statuesque. I don't think she was in the least narcissistic, so this isn't trying to portray her as she was—she was a very nice person—but she had a room there. She told us one day that she used to walk around the room naked, and one morning she looked out the window and there was this boy in the house next door with his chin on his hand looking down. And it looked like he'd been doing that every morning since she'd been there. It gave her the creeps, she said. That was the end of that when she pulled down the shades. She was a nice person, and to put her in a neurotic situation seems unkind. She was very well adjusted. Years later when I thought of the story I thought of it in connection—I don't know; things scramble themselves—in connection with some man I'd known and his determination to get something back whatever the cost. You know, this kind of thing came together and made a totally different kind of character out of that incident. But the setting of that distinctly was Nashville. Don't I mention that? You thought it was Belhaven?

Jones: I kept picturing a house over near Miss Welty's. I just put you there because I knew you were at Belhaven when you were the age of the girl in the story.

Spencer: That's all right.

Jones: What about the story "Sharon?" It walks on shaky ground. Can you tell me something about that story?

Spencer: About the uncle next door that was living with the black maid?

Jones: And had children by her.

Spencer: See, I started this whole series about a girl growing up in Port Gibson, actually.

Jones: Marilee.

Spencer: Marilee. I don't know much about Port Gibson. The country just outside of Port Gibson was nice. It was a partly experienced and partly imagined image. I love south Mississippi, over toward Natchez and Vicksburg, Woodville. It's not the landscape I was brought up in, but for me it seems like a country I know imaginatively very well. I try to think of what's going on there. After I thought of her I put her in a rather plain house, and I thought, "Well, they've been there a long time." It started with a house. There are beautiful houses down that way, and I shouldn't have given her such an ordinary farm house to live in. I thought there must be a family connection. Then out of nowhere Uncle Hernan appeared in the house next door. And then his whole history came to mind. I wanted him to be alone to affect her life without a wife, and yet to be a masculine and virile personality. I realized he would have to have a woman, so the whole story emerged about the wife who died and the furnishings of the house reflecting her taste. Oh, I don't know. It just formed itself. If you put enough chemistry into a story it will make its own element. Do you write?

Jones: No, ma'am. Just interested. But I thought that was a fascinating story. Did you ever get any feedback on that?

Spencer: Yes, a lot of people seemed to like it. I read it once at a writer's workshop or conference in Indiana. One of the teachers was a rather militant black poet. I was a little nervous about reading it. I don't think she stayed to hear that. But some of the black people who were at the conference came up later and told me they liked it very much. I think that it would seem like a considered portrayal of all that to any black person who wasn't extremely militant. A militant black would have resented the fact that I represented Uncle Hernan in a favorable light at all, I think. Don't you?

Jones: Yes.

Spencer: He would have had to be some awful slob.

Jones: Yes, and maybe they would have resented that she submitted to it.

Spencer: Yes. And that he didn't honor his children, you know. They didn't go by his name, and he didn't send them to college and things like that. I guess that would have entered into their thinking, as of course it would have to.

Jones: Very interesting. Tell me about writing your short stories as compared to writing your novels. You said that *The Light in the Piazza* started off as a twenty-page short story and just grew. Do your novels grow out of your short stories?

Spencer: Well, no. That's about the only one, I think. *Knights and Dragons* did start as a short piece, but there were too many mysterious things in it and I thought I would clarify all that by just writing a little more and a little more, and finally it was what it is. No, generally the longer novels have all started as novels. It was just those short novels that were just sort of extensions of short stories. I do think *The Light in the Piazza* is like a novella, you know. It has the balance and proportion of a . . . mini-novel. I generally do undertake to write a novel. Sometimes I'll start those tiny little stories republished in the collection just on an impulse, just to see how far that will take me. I sometimes think that if you start something like that it may form itself very beautifully, like a little miniature. In six pages you can just see it, you know. It's like a little thing that has just sprung up. I do them in one afternoon. But a longer story that involved character and content—I have one coming out in the *New Yorker* this week. I started it as a story and it developed as a story. Usually those longer ones go through two or three writings. The first time I do them they are twenty-five or thirty pages long, and they almost invariably don't satisfy me. I'll mess around with them for a while, and then I'll put them back, and then two or three months later I'll get it out and see what it really needs. It may not need much rewriting, but it will need touching up. Most of the time they will come about. Aren't you tired of asking me questions?

Jones: Gosh, no. Are you tired?

Spencer: No, no.

Jones: Do you need to go?

Spencer: No.

Jones: I think this is fascinating. Certainly I'm not tired of asking you questions. I'll just ask you a couple more.

Spencer: All right.

Jones: I was reading a review of your book of short stories in the *New York Times Book Review* by Reynolds Price in which he says that you see the southern bourgeois female as a mirror of the world. Is that fair to you?

Spencer: No, I didn't like that. I was glad that he praised the book, that he came up with favorable things to say about my work. But as an appraisal I get sort of lost in that criticism, because I don't think I'm particularly middle class any more than any other writer from the South. The South had aristocratic pretensions, or cultivated aristocratic traits, but it seems to me that we're all predominantly middle class here. The other thing he seemed to ignore was that many of the longer stories like "Ship Island" or "I, Maureen" or several of the others are about women who are at odds with the middle-class view of life, you know. To them it *isn't* a sufficient view of the world. It's being tested through them and found wanting, and they are not going to let themselves be forced to submit to it. The other thing he missed is that some of the stories aren't even about a woman's view. A good many of them are about children. One or two of them have male protagonists. What can I say? To give that as a generalization on the stories seems to me to be a bit off-putting for a reader and not fair to the collection. But I felt he should be thanked for taking an overall favorable view of my work. I don't want to criticize Reynolds Price. But that did kind of rub me the wrong way.

Jones: Do you think you've gotten just criticism over the years? Do you think that the critics have gotten what you've put in your books?

Spencer: Well, no. Am I supposed to sit here and say that I am such a great writer and that they are missing it? You are putting me in a position of . . .

Jones: No, all I'm asking is if you feel as if you've gotten your just criticism, that your message has been received as you intended it to be.

Spencer: Well, I think that up through *The Light in the Piazza* I had a good many favorable—I had the favored regard of a great many people. I think *Knights and Dragons* was a story that was widely misunderstood, and possibly shouldn't have been published as a separate novel. I was very tentative about it. I wanted it in a collection and the publishers wanted to bring it out separately. I think it lost me a wider audience and I had to get that back. I don't think enough attention was called to the next novel or *The Snare.* How can I say? I may be wrong. Maybe they don't succeed as well as the others. But I thought in each case they didn't receive the notice they should have. How can I tell? Maybe there were other writers that were more interesting at the time they came out. Critics tend to take the whole spectrum of what's appearing, you know. They look horizontally, whereas a writer is always building out of the past into the present—not exactly a progress but a development. You know, you don't want to repeat yourself. Unless the critic takes the writer as a special focus of interest and shows how each book has advanced and developed him, then you're not being given the best judgment. But then very few critics have that much time to do that, or want to bring that much time to your work. Faulkner began to receive that kind of criticism only in the last years of his life only because of the accumulated body of the work hadn't been widely understood or favorably received before. He had to educate a whole new line of critics, you see, to come up to where he had already passed.

Jones: Yes, he was out of print until 1947.

Spencer: Not only out of print. Sometime look in the *New Yorker* magazine—maybe you already have—and read the review of *Absalom, Absalom!* that was written I think by Clifton Fadiman when it came out. Have you seen that?

Jones: No.

Spencer: The craziest thing you've ever read in your life. You know, silliest book he ever read, and he made fun of it for four or five pages of the *New Yorker.* And I think that's one of Faulkner's masterpieces.

Jones: You've said that you always think that your next work will be your definitive work, your best.

Spencer: Oh, you always feel that the next thing will be greater than the last one. You want me to talk about the next thing?

Jones: Yes.

Spencer: Well, I don't much want to because I have been fooling around with this novel for a long time. Occasionally it seems to come about as something that could be a very strong and wonderful work. I hope it will finally make it. Sometimes it seems elusive. It's laid on the Gulf Coast. That's one reason I came down here, because I needed to get down to where the scene actually takes place. I can always write much better in those circumstances. It may turn out to be a short, minor work instead of a longer thing. I'm just not quite sure at this point. You go through that in writing any novel. William

Styron said on the Dick Cavett show that writing a novel is like "trying to crawl from Vladivostok to Madrid on your knees." I thought that was good. Did you see that?

Jones: No.

Spencer: It was funny.

Jones: Well, I'll let you go. I appreciate your sitting and talking with me and being so very nice. It's been interesting. I'm glad I got to meet you.

Spencer: It's good to meet and talk to an interviewer who has actually gone and read your work. I've been interviewed by people who start off by saying, "I've heard about you and I'd like to read something you've written." I always want to say, "Well, what's stopping you?" You've been very good.

Jones: I've enjoyed reading your work. Thanks again.

Postscripts: Elizabeth Spencer

Dorothy Hannah Kitchings/1981

This is an edited version of a transcription of the entire interview, which was recorded on the Mississippi Gulf Coast on 24 August 1981. Final editing of the program was completed on 15 December 1983. A Mississippi Educational Network program, it was first broadcast on 16 October 1984 for an in-school audience and on 16 January 1985 as a prime time telecast. Ed Van Cleef produced and directed the program. Used with the permission of the Mississippi Educational Network.

Telecast begins with Spencer's reading an excerpt from "A Christian Education."

Kitchings: And that might have happened in Carrollton, Mississippi?

Spencer: It might have—in fact, it did, though I want to say very quickly that very few of my stories are autobiographical. That little reminiscence of childhood and one or two others are about the only ones you'll find in my work.

Kitchings: Carrollton is on that dividing line between the north Mississippi hills and the Mississippi Delta?

Spencer: Well, it's about ten miles from it. I'm not a Delta person at all. We thought of ourselves as an older part of the state really than the Delta. Actually, I think there were older plantations in the Delta— that were of the same period as Carrollton—but as far as towns went, most of the towns in the Delta are of a later date, I believe.

Kitchings: Today we're in a part of the state that seems to have attracted you on more than one occasion—and about which you have written *Ship Island and Other Stories.* You have an affection for the Gulf Coast?

Spencer: I love the Gulf Coast, just as I also love New Orleans. I think that these were our places to travel to when I was growing up. In high school and college, to get down here meant a sort of freedom from the restrictive background such as you find in the story I've just read.

105

Kitchings: Southern writers often say that close family ties have much to do with their writing. Would you say that's true in your case?

Spencer: Oh, I think so. Living in one place makes you remember things—but you also seem to have a family memory, things your mother remembered and told you, or your father, or your grandfather.

Kitchings: What sort of child were you? Would you be willing to describe yourself?

Spencer: I hate to look back on my childhood. It seems to me that I was a skinny, worrisome little girl. I was always tagging along behind people and asking them questions. I had an older brother. He and his friends seemed marvelous to me, though I seemed horrible to them, I'm sure. There were always occasions when I wanted to be with them and they wanted me to go away.

Kitchings: When you became a teenager, in high school, were you already writing?

Spencer: I began to write as soon as I learned how to write. It was an impulse. I don't know if it had to do with my mother's reading to me a great deal and my loving the things she read and my starting to make up stories on my own. I think it started that way. In high school, certainly, I did write a good bit because I had several teachers who thought I had talent and encouraged me.

Kitchings: Would you name a person whom you think of as most influential, other than your mother?

Spencer: Well, the town English teacher is always the rallying point of people who are talented in any way. I think Virginia Peacock, who came to teach there when I was a freshman in high school and stayed the whole four years, was probably as influential in high school as anyone I knew.

Kitchings: Do you remember feeling that you were somehow given special gifts of observation?

Spencer: I don't know about observation. I think I was especially aware from the time I can remember of having a strong imaginative tendency—of making up things that I thought were real and that became very real for me. And having fantastic stories in my head.

Kitchings: What do you remember as the books you enjoyed most when you were in high school?

Spencer: Oh, I loved the times when our teachers used to read stories aloud. There was a kind of a holiday feeling. You didn't have to do drills and diagramming, but could sit back and listen to a story. There were Poe stories and Hawthorne stories I remember enjoying. I came from a reading family. My mother's people read a lot, so school reading was just a continuation of what I was doing at home all the time.

Kitchings: Were there certain writers that you could point to, who have most influenced your writing?

Spencer: It's very hard to pin down, isn't it? I couldn't name any one person. Later, after I had finished graduate school, I read William Faulkner. I realized he was writing powerfully about the country that I had to draw on for my work—because I didn't know any other country. I had a hard time getting out from under his tremendous influence, though I think the way to escape the influence of any one person is to read a great deal from other writers.

Kitchings: Your first novels—*Fire in the Morning,* followed by *This Crooked Way* and *The Voice at the Back Door*—did you feel that they were influenced by Faulkner?

Spencer: I think Thomas Hardy probably had as much to do with *Fire in the Morning* as anyone. Hardy knows how to build a narrative—portioned out in segments, but quite different from the way that Faulkner works. People said *This Crooked Way* was influenced by Faulkner—and they said the same thing about *The Voice at the Back Door*—but I myself can't see that so plainly.

Kitchings: Do you take seriously what critics have to say about your work?

Spencer: Oh, I always read them, at least skim them if they come under my eye. And some of them seem to me to be helpful and instructive.

Kitchings: Would you talk about how you begin a story? How do you start?

Spencer: I start with a strong impulse. We're talking about short stories now, not novels. Novels are so much more deliberate, as you know. With short stories you may just get an impulse to write something and sit right down and do it. Some of the shorter ones in *The Stories of Elizabeth Spencer* were written in that way. With the longer ones, there might be an idea or a character hanging around in my mind for ages.

For instance, a story that people seem especially to like, "The Finder," was based upon a story I heard in college from a girl who lived in a town in Mississippi and knew somebody like that. Later, when I was casting around for something to work on one day, my husband said, "Why don't you write that story you told me about ages ago, about the man who could find things?" So after he left for work I sat right down and started—and I realized it had been simmering in my mind all those years. I wrote that story in one morning. When I looked up, it was three o'clock in the afternoon, and I was utterly exhausted, hungry and shaking all over. Later, I revised it, but I didn't change much.

Kitchings: In the case of a novel, which you said is more complex, do you make a complete outline of what you plan to do?

Spencer: Yes, I try to, though if it's got any life at all it will show that life by showing you that your plans are not absolutely correct. It will require a lot of consideration, and take false moves, though you try to plan it all ahead of time.

Kitchings: How much do you usually revise?

Spencer: Particular sections of a book I'll sometimes revise ten or fifteen times, but sometimes the original writing will stand just as it is. Some parts will kind of fight back at you.

Kitchings: Your experience is unlike that of some Mississippi writers. You're one of those who left home; you've lived in Nashville, in Italy, and now in Montreal. You're still writing stories set in Mississippi, however.

Spencer: Not exclusively. Some of my stories, like the recent one in the *New Yorker*, were set in Montreal. I've written several stories about Montreal; in fact, I have tried to write more about Canada since I've been there a good number of years.

Canada isn't all that different from us, you know. It's a whole lot colder, but many of the same blood streams are there. For instance, there were French-Canadians all over this country. And the English came here. We don't have as large a black element in Canada, but it's not all that different. Except this—whereas here we've got spreading oaks and gulf waters, there you would have a mountain with snow on it.

Kitchings: Is there anything you might say about how you developed your art?

Spencer: I happen to believe that imagined experience is real experience. I haven't had all the experiences that my characters have had, not their literal experiences. And no one can tell where your real experience—whatever that is—feeds into the imagined experience. But there must be a place where all that happens.

Kitchings: Let's talk about characters for a moment. Have you ever been accused of putting someone into your books?

Spencer: Oh yes. I have had certain people swear to me that they were that person in a story or a novel—and it just wouldn't be true. Well, sometimes there's a little bit of truth in it.

Kitchings: Do you have one character that you may be more fond of than another?

Spencer: I'm not sure. I think Amos Dudley in *This Crooked Way* was certainly a fully developed character. To me he was a very powerful and mysterious figure. There was a character in *The Voice at the Back Door* named Jimmy Tallant, typical of many Mississippi men I've known, who I feel was very vivid and alive. I like to think of my characters as living outside as well as within the book—that they've got lives that go on behind and around and outside those pages.

The character Catherine in *No Place for an Angel* also seemed very real to me. I felt that she was genuinely outside as well as within the book. And Julia Garrett in *The Snare*—I felt her live.

Kitchings: Do your characters ever get out of hand and do things that surprise you?

Spencer: Sure they do. They're always insisting on their way about things, rather than mine.

Kitchings: And do you usually give them their way?

Spencer: It isn't so much that. Eudora Welty says that the most mysterious, powerful moment in writing is when you have created something that isn't you, not when you've created the parts and parcels of yourself. To realize that something has come alive, a character that's not you, that's really a thrill in writing.

Kitchings: Would you talk about the times when you feel most successful?

Spencer: In writing? Ah, well, there's a wonderful moment in a novel or story when, instead of closing you off and resisting you, it suddenly opens up and you realize you can write it after all. There's a

moment of complete confidence then in your material, a rapport
between you and your material. There's another moment, too, when
you've actually finished something and you know damn well it's
good.

Kitchings: Do you have a particular audience in mind when you
write?

Spencer: I think of certain readers, people whom I've made
contact with in my life who have appreciated my work and whose
friendship, contact with them, goes on. I think of their understanding
and approving of or delighting in something that I'm doing.

John Cheever writes in an office in his house in Ossing, New York,
that's surrounded by trees and shrubbery. From this office he looks
out at some shrubbery and says he likes to think of all the nice
people he's known or will ever know as nestled in that shrubbery.
That's a nice thought.

Kitchings: Have you ever consciously addressed a certain group?

Spencer: People criticized *The Voice at the Back Door,* thinking I
had done that. Maybe to some extent I had, but I had some thinking
of my own to straighten out in that book. I wasn't trying to preach to
anybody. I was trying to straighten out my own attitudes about blacks
and whites in the South—that was the impulse of the book.

Kitchings: Do you feel a conscious moral obligation to your
reader?

Spencer: I feel an obligation to meaning, to what something
means. Certainly it would be a perverse writer who would make an
upside down world and try to pass it on. You couldn't believe in that.
Your beliefs are always being tested in writing, and some of your
beliefs may not coincide with your readers' beliefs, but there it is.

Kitchings: In the preface to *Marilee,* recently published by the
University Press of Mississippi, you talk about the moment in your life
when you heard Marilee speaking. Can you elaborate a bit?

Spencer: I had written a good deal at the time I started the first of
the *Marilee* stories, but hearing a character talking—telling a whole
story—I hadn't done that. And when she started talking, she wasn't
like a character *in* the story. She *was* the story.

Kitchings: In the first story, "The Southern Landscape," Marilee
says she has to have a permanent landscape of the heart. Do you
feel as a Mississippian that you have a chance for more permanent

landscapes of the heart than if you'd been born in California or
Montreal?

Spencer: I think so. That's been proved, I think, by the
abundance of southern writing and especially the writing that's come
out of Mississippi. There does seem to be a quality here either of our
experience or our long inheritance of experience that gives us these
images that reach to the heart.

Kitchings: I hope you'll forgive my asking you this perennial
question, but I'm interested in knowing your answer to why
Mississippi has produced so many fine writers.

Spencer: I don't know, though it does seem to me we are a little
bit different as a culture from, say, Alabama or Louisiana. West
Tennessee may be somewhat the same, but our small culture kept on
just as it was for many, many years.

There's a whole range of answers to your questions—I guess you
take your pick. By now we have a tradition of writing so that a young
writer coming along has that tradition in which to make a place for
himself. Is that an advantage or disadvantage? An advantage, I think,
not having to whack it all out like Faulkner did, or perhaps Miss Welty
did at first. Well—they may have had the great advantage of having it
all lying there, raw material. At the same time, they built up a
platform in a way.

Kitchings: I wonder whether you might be able to point to a
single book as your favorite of all time?

Spencer: Well, you have so many different moods in which you
respond to fiction, so many attitudes, that it would be impossible to
speak of one book. A friend of mine, Shelby Foote, always says that
Middlemarch by George Eliot is the greatest novel ever written. I
somewhat envy him in being able to keep his tenacity of vision
regarding that one book. I can't do it. But if I could, I think I would
name Stendahl's *Le Rouge et le Noir, The Red and the Black*. It's an
odd choice, maybe, but I find everything in fiction that I want to find
in that book.

Kitchings: In *Marilee*, I found this quotation, "You can't know
where you are if you don't know where you were." How important
do you think the study and knowledge of history in general is to the
writing of good fiction?

Spencer: Oh, I think it means everything to the kind of fiction I like. I was thinking about the modern tendency in fiction, which is to cut loose, so that you don't know where you are and you don't know who the people are. I suppose some works of power have been written that way—some spring to mind—I don't think it's fiction that will endure. By its very nature fiction is social. How can you escape that? It's based on observation, yes, but observation itself leads from some stream that's always flowing toward something. I can't see that you can separate the two.

Kitchings: Thanks so much. You've been kind to talk with us.

The Art of Fiction CX: Elizabeth Spencer

Robert Phillips/1986

Initially conducted in Montreal in 1975, the interview was updated through 1986. From *Paris Review,* 31 (Summer 1989), 184-213. Reprinted by permission.

Elizabeth Spencer has pubished a large body of work, yet she became famous for a novella she wrote in a month. The irony does not escape her. At the time of the interview, she lived in a modern high-rise apartment overlooking downtown Montreal. A southerner who still loves the rural South, this irony did not escape her, either.

Hers was an apartment full of light and books, many of the latter inscribed to Ms. Spencer by author-friends, for the most part American writers in the southern tradition. It is to this southern tradition that by most critical accounts Spencer is said to belong, despite her years spent living in Italy and Canada and the subsequent works of fiction she has set in both locales. The apartment had no separate den or study, her writing was done in the corner of the dining room, the typewriter being put away every evening. She lives with her husband, John Rusher, formerly of Cornwall, England. They have recently moved to Chapel Hill, North Carolina.

Spencer is the author of eight novels: *Fire in the Morning* (1948), *This Crooked Way* (1952), *The Voice at the Back Door* (1956), *The Light in the Piazza* (1960) (unquestionably her best-known work, having been made both a major book-club selection and a popular film), *Knights and Dragons* (1965), *No Place for an Angel* (1967), *The Snare* (1972), and *The Salt Line* (1984). Her subtle tales and novellas have appeared with frequency in the *New Yorker.* A short-story collection, *Ship Island and Other Stories,* appeared in 1968. In 1980 Doubleday published her collected stories under the title *The Stories of Elizabeth Spencer;* a new collection, *Jack of Diamonds,* appeared in 1988. Four of her stories have won O. Henry awards. Others have been included in *Best American Short Stories* and *The Pushcart Prize Anthology.*

She has led a life adorned by prizes: a citation from the

American Academy and the National Institute of Arts and
Letters for her first two novels in 1952; a Guggenheim
Fellowship in 1953; the Rosenthal Award from the Amer-
ican Academy of Arts and Letters and the Kenyon Review
Fellowship, both in 1957; the McGraw-Hill Fiction Award
in 1960; the Lucy Donnelly Memorial Fellowship in 1983;
and the Bellamann Award as well as an honorary doctor-
ate degree from Southwestern University in 1968 and
Concordia University in 1988. She received the Award of
Merit and Medal for the Short Story from the American
Academy in 1983, and was elected to membership in the
Department of Literature of the American Institute in
1985. In 1988, she received a Senior Arts Award Grant in
Literature from the National Endowment for the Arts. She
has been twice nominated for the National Book Award.

Ms. Spencer is a fashionable figure. She possesses a shy
smile and a soft voice which still carries traces of her
Mississippi roots. She was interviewed twice in Montreal
and then during a subsequent visit to her publisher in
Manhattan. Other questions were answered by correspondence, a practice of which she was wary. Both in person
and on paper, her replies were generous.

Interviewer: How do you work, and at what hours?

Elizabeth Spencer: I'm a morning worker. The minute my
husband is out the door to work, out comes the paper, the typewriter,
and manuscript I'm working on. I knock off at about two, eat and
take a nap if possible, then I'm out for groceries, socializing,
whatever.

Interviewer: You didn't teach until recently. Has that been a good
experience?

Spencer: Oh, but I did! I taught early on, at a girls' school, and
later I taught creative writing at the University of Mississippi. Then I
went abroad, met John, and I wasn't teaching after that. It's
something I got back into in 1976, on the request of a writer, Clark
Blaise, who was then at Concordia University here in Montreal. He
was due for a sabbatical. I did one course for him that year and liked
it, liked the students, was amazed at the variety of their backgrounds.
The next year the department invited me back as writer-in-residence.
And the *next* year they were stuck for someone to do two advanced

workshops, so I did those. This year I'm only doing one. I've found
the work stimulating. I always complain about anything that takes
time from writing, of course. But it is equally true that one can't write
all the time. On balance, so far, it's been worth it. A five-day-a-week
job saps up all the time. Teaching has many advantages this way, in
that time is more spaced out.

Interviewer: Can writing be taught?

Spencer: Was it Jean Stafford who had the best word on that?
Writing can't be taught but it can be learned? I think so.

Interviewer: You were a reporter on the *Nashville Tennessean* as
a young woman.

Spencer: The year I spent as a reporter was marvelous for me! It
took me out of a genteel world, gave me enlightening glimpses into
how things went on. I wouldn't have wanted it permanently; it got to
be drudgery like any job, only without much uplift. Some who got to
the more interesting top positions maybe felt differently, but I didn't
aspire to those.

Interviewer: Unlike your first two novels, *The Voice at the Back
Door* seems drawn from headlines rather than personal history. Was
this book influenced by your newspaper work?

Spencer: There's some truth in that, though I never thought of it.
It was, at least in part, "topical." I was under some sort of pressure
within myself to clarify my own thinking about racial matters; many
of my attitudes had been simply inherited, taken on good faith from
those of good faith whom I loved. It seemed like blasphemy to
question *them,* so I had to question myself. I could do that out of
materials—incidents, people—which I already knew about. It was
just in the melodramatic arrangement of the novel that I may have
stepped things up a bit.

Interviewer: I've wondered how that novel was received in the
South, particularly in your home region. Is that why you ran off to
Italy?

Spencer: Oh, I'm sure a lot of people in my hometown and
elsewhere objected. Some of the objections I heard about: I hadn't
been "fair to the South," and so forth. But, no, nobody wanted to
run me out of Mississippi. At least, nobody I know of wanted to. I
don't mean to make too light of this; it is doubtless still known that I
went against the white supremacy thing. The people who think like

that will use anything against you that comes their way. They've nothing against you except *that,* but it happens to be everything. It's the same thinking as that of the Inquisition.

Interviewer: There's a passage in that novel I marked—here it is: "In the South, it's nothing but family, family. We couldn't breathe, even, until we left." Was this your feeling, and is that perhaps why you no longer live in the South?

Spencer: Oh, Lord. Okay—while family is interesting for the range of character it offers a writer, and for the stability it may, at best, offer to the individual, it is in many, many cases stifling and destructive. There is always bound to be, at the least, *suppressed* conflict. The price is high. Someone much wiser than I once told me that southern families were cannibals. He was an enthusiastic southerner himself, so I felt even more the weight of that judgment. The family assigns unfair roles, and never forgives the one who does not fulfill them. Of course, a sense of freedom is a large part of my own nature. I can't be straightjacketed. Maybe they ask no more than all traditional societies do, one way or another.

Interviewer: When did you start writing?

Spencer: I started as a child, for me a time of total unconsciousness about the "South" in literary terms. I knew we had lost the war, that was about all. We had not so much a close-knit as a jumbled-up family, lots of them living right in the vicinity, Carroll County, Mississippi, and the moved-away ones kept coming back to visit. On my mother's side of the connection, writing was a natural thing. My rough, tough uncles had all written poetry and studied Latin, too. Imagine that today! They quoted poetry in great, memorized blocks, and what they wrote sounded like Kipling or Browning. Scraps of it were to be found around the house in old school notebooks. They all thought of literary things as meriting attention.

Interviewer: So your family was supportive?

Spencer: My mother's family was. Not my father's. My mother's family bought books, kept books, referred to books, read incessantly. I often heard my aunts and my mother talk of characters in a novel as though they were really living people—it was a shame Fantine in *Les Misérables* had to sell her hair and teeth; they wept over Dora in *David Copperfield,* but quoted Dickens that it was better for her to

die; my aunt fell for Darcy in *Pride and Prejudice* and so on. Others
in Carrollton, my little hometown, were equally strong on reading. I
did, I do believe, get the impression that here was a pursuit for good
families with their minds not exclusively on money, gossip, illness,
marriages and the crops. And unlike recipes, vegetable-canning, fruit-
preserving, sewing and going to church, it made for talk I was
interested in overhearing. I was also interested in political talk and in
that sort of reminiscence about people that led to long, partly
speculative stories. Dickens, Thackeray, and Victor Hugo were in no
way contradicted by the spirit of such talk, which in most cases was
done with kindness, compassion and even love, with regard to
human mystery. But I'm rattling about the older generation.

Interviewer: What about your own crowd? Anyone with a literary
bent?

Spencer: Well, there was a cousin, just up the street—a brilliant
boy slightly older than I, who talked a lot about books, music, poetry,
the best movies, and got the rest of us—tennis players, tree-climbers,
creek-swimmers, pony-riders, and stamp-collectors—more inclined
to these things as personal experience than we otherwise might have
been. He could come in while we were sitting barefoot on the piano
bench playing "Chopsticks," and, shooing us away, strike up the
"Anvil Chorus" from *Il Trovatore,* or a Chopin *étude.* His mother, like
mine, had given private lessons in piano, but he—unlike me—had
musical talent. He wrote some very good poetry later on, and
published one volume which I still admire.

Interviewer: What about you? Why do you write?

Spencer: Writing for me, I am trying to say, was *prepared for* in
various ways, but just the same, I always looked on it as a natural
impulse, one I would have had anyway. It had nothing to do with
William Faulkner, Eudora Welty, and the other writers of the South;
though I discovered them later with great joy. My true course was
already set by the culture that was happily mine from the day I was
born. When I started writing stories, my mother, my aunt, uncles and
others were immediately interested—I found quick audience and
some praise, a living kind of response. I take my experience as more
typical of the southern writers than not. I don't think southerners
were as culturally isolated as it is common to think. We had an "oral
tradition," true, but we also had an intellectual tradition. Translations

from Greek and Latin were on our shelves, and some originals, and if anybody mentioned Dante, he was there, too. In addition to the novelists I mentioned and their like, there were also Melville, Hawthorne, Poe, and the New England poets. A host of children's classics were read aloud to me, and one was expected to know the Bible backwards and forwards.

Interviewer: Why do you write the way you do?

Spencer: When I started writing I fell into a certain way of expression that was natural to me and that I liked to put down and read over. I used to sit up in a tree and write. Really. Just because you've nothing on your feet doesn't mean you've nothing in your head! I would also write stories in study hall to pass the time after I raced through my homework. Or sit up in bed on winter nights, scribbling into tablets held on my knees. Then I was getting the feeling I've always kept as the best part of it, that I was not so much writing as *letting something come through me.* This is a strange delight, but maybe many writers have it. I see it more strongly in some of my work than others, so it does not always prevail, but when it does I feel I am writing best. It comes from an inner way of seeing things in their plainest but truest way—not only seeing but hearing, smelling, feeling. The words go toward that. This can be refined, but its origin is obscure.

Interviewer: Could you say a little more about Faulkner? He's associated now with those same times in Mississippi. . . .

Spencer: That same cousin who played the piano and wrote poetry did tell me before I got to Vanderbilt that Faulkner was a great writer. I think I was in college, though, before I heard him say this. It was a marvelous discovery, but I don't recall reading Faulkner extensively until some years later. It was well-known that he was over there at Oxford writing books. But it was widely thought that he, along with Erskine Caldwell, was busy "giving the South a bad name" in order to "make money." This opinion did not spring from literary innocence so much as from a rather more complex reaction which I won't go into here, though I think I understand it. I remember when *Gone with the Wind* came out there were immediate readers in our town who came up with strong opinions. It was thought that the book left a good bit to be desired as fiction of the first rank, but that at least nationwide interest was drawn to the South by a popular novel sympathetic to our history. For this, they said, we could be grateful.

Interviewer: What other American writers impressed you?

Spencer: My cousin also talked about Willa Cather and I still admire Cather more than certain "complicated" southern women writers like, say, Ellen Glasgow. Cather seems at first simple, but the simplicity has its own difficulties—like some large natural phenomenon out west you can look at and contemplate for a long time. I knew Melville from my early days because *Moby Dick* was my brother's favorite book. He, unlike me, did not incline toward much reading that I know of, but he read that one over and over. He thought it was about whale-hunting. Of course people who say it isn't are wrong, too. Then I'd always read Mark Twain, and was too scared to sleep after Tom Sawyer got lost in the cave or something. I was surprised to find Mark Twain was taught in graduate school! Poe and Hawthorne were taught in the public schools—I still get a textbook feeling whenever I open them.

Interviewer: What about Henry James? Some have mentioned him as an influence for your later fiction, especially *The Light in the Piazza* and *Knights and Dragons*.

Spencer: Henry James I started reading at Vanderbilt, along with many of the "modern" English writers, like Virginia Woolf. It was an interesting labyrinth, enormous skill directed toward ends that did not seem then to be all that important.

Interviewer: James was not an influence, then?

Spencer: Listen, if you write a novel in Mississippi, North Mississippi at that, you are bound to be compared to Faulkner. If you write about Americans abroad in some sort of confrontation with Europeans, then you are bound to be compared to James. I couldn't escape the Mississippi subject matter—I was brought up in it. When I went to Europe, as anyone might, I couldn't help loving Italy . . . I just adored it, everything, and went back as soon as I could. That is, when I was awarded a Guggenheim. I wrote about it because I loved it, and had stayed there so long that I thought I knew it well enough. But I always wrote from an outsider's point of view. I think it must be clear that one has to do that, out of honesty. Well, right away, here came "Henry James" in every single review. The only odd thing was that I never once thought about it. It did occur to me and still seems obvious that the correct comparison for *The Light in the Piazza* might have been Boccaccio. Here was the kind of situation outlandish enough to have delighted him. Can't you hear one of his *Decameron* ladies beginning this tale: "Chancing to travel to Florence was a little countess from a town in France who had as a daughter, a beautiful young girl, a cause of great unhappiness. For, since an unfortunate accident had overtaken her at an early age, she had no little trouble with reasoning, reading being beyond her to learn and ciphering also, so that no doctor could tell her parents that she could never be cured, and no young nobleman, being exposed to her conversation, could dream of offering a serious proposal. Nonetheless, she was of so charming a nature, and so unaffected in her responses, which were all sweetness and delight, that anyone not knowing of her defect might take true pleasure in her company . . . ," and so on through to a satire on the empty-headedness of certain well-born youths around Florence. I don't think James should even be considered when it comes to that story, though the internal narrative of *Knights and Dragons* certainly seems, on rereading it, as I did the other day, to owe a good deal to his method.

Interviewer: There are other relations between those two novels.

Spencer: Oh, yes. *Knights and Dragons* was a kind of dark companion to *The Light in the Piazza;* someone with problems back home working free of them in Italy.

Interviewer: Both have mature women wrestling with heavy problems.

Spencer: Yes. Many of my women characters crack up under the strain of bad fortune or psychic miseries they cannot sustain. Margaret Johnson, the mother in *The Light in the Piazza,* had had a psychic break of sorts before the time of the story. Martha Ingram, in *Knights and Dragons,* thought herself tormented and pursued until she actually was mad for a time, I think, though she managed to surface. All that story is like an image seen wavering under water. I wish I could have let it all play itself out in Venice where it first occurred to me. When I got to Catherine Sasser in *No Place for an Angel,* I was able to see better what these over-strained psyches were suffering from. Catherine taught me a lot. But she got nothing except love in a pure state, which amounts to resignation. I didn't think that was enough, either, though to some lucky souls it may be. I've had

trouble finding fictional women—different from the search for real
people—who could take, or accept, what they had to be, and find
their way. Some of my stories seem to be testing out characters,
especially women, along those lines. When I finally got to Julia
Garrett, the central character in *The Snare,* I felt satisfied. Her path
led her right through the human jungle but she came out sane.
Maybe not safe and sound, but anyhow, at the story's end, coping,
and on a human level, too.

Interviewer: Did you intend the knights of that title to be the men
in Martha's life, and the dragons mental illness?

Spencer: Women often dramatize the men in their lives, they
assign them roles. Maybe I've done that too, once in a while. When
women friends confide in me, I often notice this theme. When I
wrote the story, I was going through a long phase of finding myth-
themes for stories centering on women. But I think the dragon for
Martha was clearly set out from the beginning as her ex-husband,
and Jim Wilbourne, the knight—remember all those old paintings?
—who perceived her plight and should have liberated her, turned out
to be rather dragon-like, too. So there's the irony.

Interviewer: Martha seems to feel so exiled that she suffers
paranoia. Was this a trait you saw among numerous Americans in
Italy? Did you share any such feelings?

Spencer: People abroad *do* experience the pangs of separation,
which is something like that graver word, exile. They want to be
thought of, not forgotten, but thought of with understanding at least,
not condemned. Any evidence that this is not possible . . . well, they
feel afflicted, and lacking other news, exaggerate it. People, Americans for example, who stay abroad too long do feel a sense of guilt.
I've heard this expressed many times.

Interviewer: We were talking about other American writers you
admired.

Spencer: I recently discovered Dreiser, whom I had tried several
times before but simply couldn't read. Now I'm hooked. Partly due
to Robert Penn Warren's fine study *Homage to Theodore Dreiser,*
but also because of something that happened. I was driving with my
husband through a desolate area of upper New York State. There
were lakes with dead trees standing in them, lonely twisting mountain
roads, ratty small towns with maybe one streetlight, a remote feeling.

I thought about the murder which happened near there in *An American Tragedy*—Clyde and Roberta—and the bird calls—was it a *weir-weir?*—it suddenly all grew unbearably real. So real it frightened me. It seemed all to have happened, just the way he said. This is the breakdown of that reality-line that fiction can make.

Interviewer: Your first collection of stories is dedicated to Eudora Welty. I take it you admire the work, or the lady, or both.

Spencer: Eudora Welty is a perennial favorite. My discovery of what she was doing with the old home landscape held as much delight as what Faulkner was doing, and I especially mean *The Golden Apples,* though many others are great. I once threatened to give *The Golden Apples* to a new acquaintance, and if she didn't like it, I doubted we'd have much in common. Eudora Welty I first met, personally, partly by the coincidence of having gone to a college, Belhaven, which was just across the street from her house in Jackson, Mississippi. Some of us in a little literary society wanted her to come over and be our guest soon after her first book appeared. She came and we chatted later and she did not forget the occasion; nor, certainly, did I. She wasn't so well or widely known back then as she deserved to be and later was. It was easier to see her occasionally both in New York and Mississippi. I certainly admired her work and do still, but we have such a difference of approach, don't you think? I can't compare things like this when I am involved. The same for Faulkner. If my material seems like his, as I say, it must be that we are both looking at the same society. For instance, there is a Yocona River in North Mississippi; the family in *This Crooked Way* comes from Yocona, which I knew about all my life. People used to say "Yocny." Only long after that book was published did I realize that Faulkner's Yoknapatawpha probably had the same origin.

Interviewer: What is the story of the publication of your first novel? Did you have help from anyone in placing it?

Spencer: I had written and sent off a number of short stories, and had had encouragement but no results. I started a novel based on some of these stories. I had been fortunate before that, though, in landing a graduate fellowship to Vanderbilt, ideal then, perhaps still, for anyone interested in creative study. The ghosts of the great— Ransom, Warren, and Tate—were still around, not that they were anything but alive then, but simply elsewhere. And one of the original members of the Agrarian group was still there, Donald Davidson, a superb teacher, one of the great minds I've known. I wandered away from Nashville, taught, returned to a job there, then worked on a newspaper as I said, then quit to work on my novel. Davidson knew I was working on it, and when David Clay, a New York editor with Dodd, Mead who had gone to Vanderbilt, came through, he brought us together. So within a short time of showing Clay the unfinished manuscript, I had my first contract.

Interviewer: Did you, or do you, keep a journal?

Spencer: I wish I had time to keep one. Sometimes I do; lots of good material comes along, just factual stuff, what I like to think about and make use of; but I forget it if I don't write it down. There will never be a shortage, however, of one inexhaustible thing—plain old life.

Interviewer: Were you conscious of writing autobiographically in your first two novels? Those families seem so well-realized, it is difficult to think of them as fictional . . .

Spencer: There is no autobiography in my early novels, or in any of the novels. Some of the stories, yes, but I can't find myself at all in the novels. I got in trouble, though, because people in our town all know each other, and have known about each other for generations, and because I had to draw on the locale, I found myself writing about people like them, though they weren't meant at all to be those people. But I've learned you can never tell anybody that what they want to believe isn't true. So no matter what I said, they still knew better, and I finally just gave up and didn't say anything. In *Fire in the Morning,* the portrait of my grandfather—a man I much admired—was deliberate, but all the events were fictional. Of course, there is a terrifying thing which may occur: *one sometimes invents what has actually happened.* This won't bear too much looking into.

Interviewer: Your family was upset with you over the Mississippi novels?

Spencer: My family was upset with me-as-novelist, especially my mother, because she couldn't make the jump to modern writing or to any published writing at all being done by anyone she *knew.* It was supposed to be done somewhere else by unknown hands. However, I could always "go home again," if that's what you mean. I live in

Canada to be with my husband. Nobody is keeping me away. Mercy, they've got more to think about than just me.

Interviewer: Whether you could "go home again" or not, you left the South for Italy, and then you left Italy for Canada. Why?

Spencer: I got married in Italy to an Englishman and lived there for a couple of years more, but my husband thought he could make a better go of things in Canada. His sister was in Montreal and wrote some good things about it and about Canada generally. His mother's family had been Canadian in origin.

Interviewer: You didn't consider moving to the South?

Spencer: No, John found the South impossibly hot and over-crowded with my relatives, so we set out to try our luck in a place I never dreamed of even visiting, let alone settling down in! It was really the best compromise I could make, so I accepted it. I've grown to admire Canadians and to love Quebec, especially Montreal.

Interviewer: Would you say that you are well-adjusted to Canada?

Spencer: Oh, no, I can never "adjust" to losing anything I really love. I still miss the South; to a lesser degree, I still miss Italy. There's some argument for being able to stay in one region all your life, especially if your roots are there. Whether you write or not, there's a powerful element of feeling involved, and once uprooted, those feelings weaken. I don't think I've ever really cut the root; I never wanted to. But there's a loss of immediacy in one's experience. You have to count on memory more and daily rhythms less. But memory is a Muse, after all, a girl with a vital life of her own.

Interviewer: What is the function of locale in your work?

Spencer: Some of my suburban or city-apartment stories could occur just anywhere, but these go only for a few pages. Generally I think of fiction through people in a place. They are particular people in a particular place. "Who" and "where" is then quickly followed by "when" and "what" and "how." "Why" relates to ideas. I think southerners are strong on ideas, but in a different way from writers elsewhere. I must be careful not to make a silly generalization, but my feeling is that southern writers (southerners generally) do not perceive any idea as abstract. We move toward an idea gingerly. Once formed, it is powerful and may eat you up. It's better to keep it young and playful as long as possible. But the way the southern mind seems to work is through particulars, through felt character, experienced atmosphere. Isn't life like that? We live it, only half-knowing what it is, aware of possibilities all along but often mistaken as to their full meaning. Then time may change it all, throw it in a new perspective. A strongly-felt locale and a strongly-felt character in it—these are usually the starting places of my work. I can see both—character and place—in my head. A person, or persons, in a place, something on their minds, a confrontation, an event, a fragment of memory, an action, something to start you watching it, your mind following it. . . .

Interviewer: Once you have your locale, and your characters, how rigidly do you plan your novels? They seem extremely well-made.

Spencer: I plan most novels ahead, they don't just happen. I think all the characters in them live in them as though the form were a house and they were the people, and none other, who resided there. Some characters have come to the novels out of stories, and some have migrated from one novel to another. I do not plan so far ahead for stories; it does seem that a story is a more spontaneous creative act. I sometimes just drop down and write a story. I could never do a novel like that. Both *The Light in the Piazza* and *Knights and Dragons* started as stories, but there came a moment when I had to see them as longer works, to stop and consider.

Interviewer: Many of your characters seem to be "loners." Why would you choose this type of character above all others?

Spencer: I guess I'm a mixture of sometimes wanting to be off alone somewhere strange, and sometimes liking people, desiring company. But "loner" characters are good to have in a work of fiction. They have a perspective, are less easily involved in an action; they can comment, are apt to be ironic, compassionate, witty, perceptive.

Interviewer: Is all your travel helpful to your work?

Spencer: I don't feel that I travel all that much. The trip to Greece in 1977 was my first in a long time, and my first ever to Greece. I was thrilled with Greece—a place I'd always wanted to go. I visited a Canadian writer, Audrey Thomas, for a time. She had part of a house in a fishing village on the south coast of Crete, Aghia Gallini. I loved the life. We swam twice a day. I used to go down early and see them bring the catch off the fishing boats, and the farmers coming

into the square with loads of fresh melons used to whack them open
and give me sample slices to eat. The whole town knew everybody.
The woman who owned the house had a loom in the parlor. I
watched her weave. Every morning about a hundred donkeys began
to go *heehaw . . . heehaw . . . heeeeeehaw. . . .* Just like Mississippi.
Greece inspired the South somewhere along the line. I love the
whole Mediterranean world. I think most people do. Maybe it's a
buried racial memory and we all came from there.

Interviewer: What differences have you perceived between
American and Canadian literature?

Spencer: That's an interesting question. Canadian literature has
made a worthy, self-conscious effort to be itself just in the last ten
years or so. Which is to say there is some needed walling-out of
American influences. Still, many have noticed comparisons. Alice
Munro's studies of small-town western life owe much to her reading
of the southern writers; I think she told me that herself. Think of
Margaret Laurence and Willa Cather. Parallels abound between
French Canada and the South—a conquered society with different
customs having to exist in terms of a larger, controlling nation, for
instance. The French here have their own language, to give them
unity, centrality. But it, of course, restricts their audience. Still, Marie-
Claire Blais is widely translated, as is Anne Hébert. Less well-known
are such good novelists as André Langevin and Hubert Aquin. There
are similarities between Blais and Carson McCullers; and Hébert has
a historical sense of French Canada—one looks to the southern
writers like Andrew Jackson Lytle for comparison. Novels that, to my
mind, are *just* Canadian, without any possible reference to another
society, are Margaret Atwood's *Surfacing* and Timothy Findlay's *The
Wars.* I admire Robertson Davies, his *Fifth Business* especially. But it
is rather a special case.

Interviewer: Are you at all conscious of being a woman writer?
That is, a woman who writes fiction?

Spencer: At the start, I felt put off by sensitive women writers
whom I'd read but did not want to be like, even though I'd started by
admiring them. I mean someone like Katherine Mansfield, then later
Virginia Woolf. I thought both were over-lyrical, not nearly tough
enough. So I tried to get a natural bent to lyricism (I had started out

in college writing poetry) out of my style, to develop a plainly-stated, hearty style—hospitable to sensitivity but not dependent on it.

Interviewer: Do you mind the term "woman writer"?

Spencer: Would you mind the term "man writer"? "Woman writer" is just next door to "lady writer." I wanted to be firm and even tough-minded—if not "tough" in the Hemingway sense—a novelist only, as distinct from a woman novelist. That was my early reaction—it had nothing to do with women's lib, of course—but I think for me it was the right beginning. Even in *Fire in the Morning,* my first book, I originally wrote long, lyrical, girlish passages about the young woman who came to that town from a past outside it and married the central character. I had looked on it at first as primarily her story, as it might indeed have been if I could have got my prose to measure up. I think I was too girlish then myself to write well about her various sensitivities, hesitations, et cetera. My first editor urged me to cut all that out, so little of it remains, enough I guess to see what the rest might be like; and the weight of the book fell on the men and some of the older women who were part of the town, and they held it up.

Interviewer: How do you determine from what point of view to tell a story? *This Crooked Way,* for instance, has four parts in the first person, only one part in the third person. Why not all five in the first person?

Spencer: Point of view usually comes with the story in my mind and can't be changed very fundamentally afterwards. I know that "trying from a different point of view" is a recommendation in creative writing workshops, but I could never do it; the whole integrates at once in one way, and there's just no disintegrating it. In the novel you ask about, I had the problem with point of view toward a central character, who was primarily obsessed—a God-driven person. I had some straining to do, but I felt I had to arrange significant points of view around this figure. How could he be able to assess his own story and have the reader believe that his assessment could be reliable? So, I balanced around him certain voices—a former best friend, a niece, then with deeper significance, his wife, then back to him again for the finale. This was experiment, if you like, but I think it had to be done that way to get the total picture.

Interviewer: And why was one part, the beginning, in the third person?

Spencer: It was my way of coming in from the outside, to lead both myself and the reader into the story. The third person is admirable for its power to move inward, then enclose.

Interviewer: What are your feelings about "experimental prose"?

Spencer: Writing is always an experiment. But, on the whole, I guess I am anxious to be understood, to be clear. That leaves out "experimental," to put it in its usual meaning. Flannery O'Connor once said, "If it looks funny on the page, I don't read it."

Interviewer: Do you consider yourself a religious person? *This Crooked Way* is really about religion.

Spencer: I was brought up to be very religious and sent to a Presbyterian school, so at various periods of my life I felt close to that sort of thing. I think I have a feeling for the Protestant southern experience just from seeing so much of it, as well as from some personal participation when I was growing up. There's a lot of variety in it, but it's mainly Bible-based. In 1975 when my father was in his late eighties, I was home to see about him and saw he had brought in some large pieces of petrified wood from a small cattle place he had near town. He said, "I reckon those things have been there since the Flood." I said, "What flood?" He said, "*The* Flood!" Well, the Mississippi River had been known to break out in notable floods, but I never knew the high water to get up to our town, which is in the hill section. I pursued: "You mean 1927?" He got angry: "I mean the Flood in the Bible!" That one, of course, covered the whole earth, involved Noah's Ark, and presumably left petrified wood outside of Carrollton, Mississippi!

Interviewer: Your mother was just as religious?

Spencer: She saw the Hand of the Lord everywhere. I remember when the British army retreated from the continent at Dunkirk, she remarked that the Lord had sent a fog to cover them. Being a Presbyterian, she got upset when people made fun of "predestination," but hoped to retreat with dignity by saying it was clearly set forth in the Bible. She took it for granted that everybody believed in the Bible or that if they didn't, they knew they ought to.

Interviewer: Is there such a thing as an ideal reader you write for?

Spencer: I never think of any one reader. But I do hope to be a

source of interest and delight to those who want to follow me,
which excludes, I guess, certain kinds of readership. It would mainly
exclude, I hope, people who want to see life only from one
aspect—sex, religion, politics, even "southernness." I doubt if those
who have special interests find my work offers a great satisfaction.
I'm a questioner, a searcher . . . I'd like to interest people who are
that, too.

Interviewer: Your books all have beautiful titles. How do you find
them?

Spencer: I like to choose around till I find the right one. There's
always an original impulse toward writing a work which has not yet
been formed. When I look for a title I go back to that. *The Voice at
the Back Door* . . . when I thought of the South and race, the blacks,
I first remember how black servants of ours or blacks we knew would
come to our back door when they were in trouble, they would stand
and call out of the night. It was further considered a breach of custom
for a black—or Negro, as we called them then—to come to the front
door. In our whole town, I think, only our old nurse, Aunt Lucy
Breckinridge, was permitted that. She was born a slave. In a recent
program on William Faulkner, photographed at Oxford, a black man
told about the old family nurse doing the same thing, going in
through the Faulkner's front door. I doubt anyone not born down
there would know the significance. So I went back to that germinal
thing, that small but significant custom, for that title.

Interviewer: What about the title, *The Light in the Piazza?*

Spencer: You like that title?

Interviewer: Yes.

Spencer: At the publisher's, they jokingly referred to it as *The
Light in the Pizza!* Oh, well. As a title, I hope it functions several
ways. There is the duality of the word "light"—the real light in Italy,
so beautiful and strong that one feels one can see everything. Then
there's the symbolic meaning, that's pointed up a number of times in
the book, light and enlightenment, I suppose. And of course, Clara's
name itself—her name means light. I was also playing up comic
aspects of the novel in the title, but most people missed that. I once
said, in an interview in *Mississippi Quarterly* where the same thing
came up, that just when you think you can see everything, the
motives of these characters and what they are actually doing and why

they are doing them are totally opaque. The poor girl's mother stayed in a state of confusion all the way through.

Interviewer: I'm glad you mentioned the significance of Clara's name. Many of your characters' names seem tip-offs to their function or meaning, such as Jimmy *Tallant*, Jerry *Sasser*, Beckwith *Dozer*. . . .

Spencer: I generally name my characters the way I do because that is their name. Sasser I see no significance in; Sasser is a fairly common name in the South. Clara did, of course, have the tie-in to light.

Interviewer: What about symbols, then? Are there any that you consciously utilize? There seem to be a lot of horses in your novels and stories, horses used in a Lawrentian sense of sensual power. . . .

Spencer: There are certain recurrent figures in my work, I know. I guess I am drawn to write over and over about horses because of a fascination I feel for them. One of my stories is called "The Girl Who Loved Horses." I was brought up around animals, and for riding I had first a donkey, then ponies, then horses. We lived on the outskirts of a little town, had a big property with a barn, kept mules and cows. It was no trouble to feed ponies and later a couple of riding horses, nothing fine though. I was lonely in the winters when none of my cousins were around and outdoor sports were practically impossible. So I used to ride a lot, alone. Then, on my uncle's plantation, I would ride with him some summers almost every day. In those days, you had to ride a horse around a plantation to see what was going on. I rode at school, too, and wherever I happened to be. At Oxford, at the University of Mississippi, when I was teaching there I kept a horse the whole time. So horses crop up in my stories—pun not intended. I think I love them aesthetically; actually I'm a little afraid of them, of the spirited ones; part of riding excitement is in the tension. I've been run away with, thrown, bitten and kicked, though not in the head, I'll have you know!

Interviewer: Are you conscious of any other symbols?

Spencer: Storms show up in my work a lot too, for much the same reason; they were fierce, dangerous, sometimes awesome around where I lived. Listen, if you want to find a symbol, there's nothing stopping you. Symbols should be like that in stories; not hauled in, but rising out of the possible, in feeling, and event.

Interviewer: Some of the events in your later fiction seem improbable, like Arnie mouting the large sea turtle he meets while swimming and proclaiming, "Take me to the deep," in *The Salt Line*. Such events give your work a dream-like quality. Any comment?

Spencer: It may be that most of these actually happened. The South is semi-tropical, near the coast especially, and many events partake of the strange natural phenomena in the area. South American fiction often sounds fantastic, but I bet a lot of it is to be thought of as actual. The sea turtle episode was related to me by my father. He used to go with a group on a chartered boat to fish in the Gulf. They once went ashore on a small island and there in the shallows one of them discovered a giant turtle which he rode out to sea for a distance. My usual theory is not to invent very much, only uncover what happens anyway, "strange as it seems."

Interviewer: I've been wanting to ask you: is *The Light in the Piazza* your glory, or your albatross? Its fame, I mean.

Spencer: It's my albatross. I think that it has great charm, and it probably is the real thing, a work written under great compulsion, while I was under the spell of Italy. But it only took me, all told, about a month to write, whereas some of my other novels—the longer ones—took years. So to have people come up to me, as they do, and gush about *The Light in the Piazza,* and be totally ignorant that I ever turned a hand at anything else, is . . . upsetting. I suppose I should be grateful they've read that. You know, I always thought it was so nice of President Kennedy to have said when he met Norman Mailer at the White House, "I've read *The Deer Park . . .* and the others." The fact that Kennedy didn't come out with *The Naked and the Dead* must have been gratifying to Mailer.

Interviewer: How do you feel about money, in relation to serious writing? Would you write better if you had more or less of it?

Spencer: It's nice to have it. It's ideal not to have money worries. However, writers have always proved their work can exist in extreme poverty or extreme wealth. . . . Personally, I just like to be well enough off. I've written under very poor circumstances and made do on a daily basis only by counting pennies and sometimes even dropping in on church suppers to cease from a diet of peanut butter sandwiches. I don't know if I wrote better then; it just seemed a nuisance.

Interviewer: Have there ever been long periods when you could not write?

Spencer: During the last decade, when my parents were in a long decline—they have since died—I was needed to help them out a good bit and I was disturbed by their aging, the whole implacable process of it. I did mainly short things during this time and found that any longer thing I attempted was broken up by recurrent problems. Otherwise, I am sometimes stopped in my work by a normal course of having finished up one crop and having to put in a whole new planting. This is gradual, almost a natural process of replenishment, and I get impatient while it's happening and think the whole thing's over, I'll never write again. Then I do.

Interviewer: Do you reread your own books?

Spencer: I often have to, to get together readings or comments. But not all of anything, I think. I feel I've heard it all already. I'm sometimes surprised that I let such awkward parts get by, and occasionally that I could have possibly written anything so good.

Interviewer: Have your sensibilities changed over the years?

Spencer: There were many things I couldn't see clearly when I was younger and I was inclined to make judgments about them out of ignorance. I don't know if there has been a change or a deepening of sensibility. If either, I hope my work reflects it!

Interviewer: One thing I had in mind was that your latest novels, especially *The Snare* and *The Salt Line,* seem built upon a fascination with the underworld—criminals and counter-cultures not found anywhere in your early work. Have you lived among such people in recent years?

Spencer: My husband would thank you for that! No, I don't know much about such people, except what I make up. Of course, I've read, inquired, and nosed around. I'm fascinated by these people, because they play by another set of rules, are in opposition to values we assume. Therefore, they can throw our values in relief, not so much by directly questioning them, as precocious children do, but simply by running counter to them. I don't know anything about criminal types except at second hand, i.e., reading, talking to people who know them, thinking of places where the boundaries are thin between the crooked and the straight. Everybody has something in his nature that's in the shadow world. I find a good deal of fun in imagining these parts, and just have to hope the underworld passages are convincing.

Interviewer: How much of writing has to be first-hand experience?

Spencer: That's an old question. My feeling about using such things is that anyone has got to be aware of the dark side of life; it gets into all human relationships, be they ever so joyful, balanced, and wise. No way around it. At a certain swivel of circumstances, the saint may turn into a devil; frightening but true. So when one brings on the scene the admitted crook or outcast or underworld figure, one is really just dramatizing what is latent in the nice little boy next door, or in one's old Sunday School teacher, the high school principal, or the U.S. President, and the next is—guess who?—one's self.

Interviewer: Given to thinking like that, does being a writer make relationships more difficult?

Spencer: I've found there are many different temperaments among writers. I am personally often distracted, absent-minded, fractious and anxious. I guess this makes me difficult at times. It's nice to be able to say, *Well, you see, I'm a writer,* especially if it saves you from losing a friendship or getting kicked in the behind.

Interviewer: Do you think you could have been as happy, or less happy, if you hadn't become a writer?

Spencer: I think I would be far less happy without a creative outlet. Everybody needs one in some form, to some extent. I'm just glad I found mine in writing, and early on.

Interviewer: Finally, do you have any advice to give young writers?

Spencer: Writing is hard work and guarantees no security, no rewards or pensions—it can't promise you anything. Bearing that in mind, you go ahead with it because you love it. Any art has the aspects of a love affair, life-long.

Landscape of the Heart

Beth Cooley/1987

From the *Spectator* [Raleigh, NC], 19 March 1987, 5. Reprinted by permission.

If you ask Elizabeth Spencer when she began writing, she'll break into a shy dimpled smile and answer, "When I began writing." In a soft voice that hasn't lost its melodious Gulf Coast lilt through five years in Italy and 28 more in Canada, she explains, "When I was a little girl I used to write down stories. First it was fairy stories, then adventure stories, then poetry." She began writing seriously in the '40s, sending stories to magazines and receiving rejection slips. In 1948 she published her first novel, *Fire in the Morning.* Two more novels followed, and then the *New Yorker* wrote to *her* asking for a story. "I sent them one they had rejected earlier. And then I sent them two others." Spencer's most recent book, *The Light in the Piazza,* is a collection of two previously published novels and a short story, "Cousins," which appears in the 1985 O. Henry anthology. A prolific writer, she also has stories in recent issues of the *Kenyon Review* and the *Southern Review,* and in *The Way We Live Now,* an anthology of contemporary short fiction.

For the past few months Spencer hasn't been writing anything new, but devoting all her energies to teaching creative writing at UNC Chapel Hill. Spencer is a veteran teacher who conducted writing classes at the University of Mississippi and in Montreal, among other places, and I was curious about what kind of advice she gives her students. Her answer was simple: "Mainly, I get them to write. They need to learn how to pull out the best and look for faults in their work." The only way they learn this, she feels, is through practice.

Although she enjoyed teaching last fall, like many other writers Spencer finds it nearly impossible to juggle her writing with other kinds of work. When she's teaching, she simply stops writing. She doesn't even keep a notebook. Instead, she prefers to immerse herself, to become intensely involved in whatever she's working on. And this requires free time. "Usually an idea will just hit," and she'll become absorbed in it. Sometimes the idea dries out, but Spencer just keeps writing. "If a novel goes dead or gets stuck in some way, I might write a story," she says. This way she gives herself and the novel a break.

Though she's lived half her life as an expatriate, most of Spencer's fiction concerns the South or southerners. She believes there is still something called Southern Literature, but that it has changed since she began writing. For one thing, we no longer have the Faulknerian Civil War character. "We're too far away for that, unless you want to write an historical novel." More importantly, though, society itself has changed. "During World War II the whole emphasis in culture shifted," she says. "The people of the South are less unique now, less remote from cultural currents. Everybody has a TV now. Even what we used to call tenant houses have great big TV antennas on the top."

Not to mention satellite dishes in the back yard. We can't deny that Americans are getting more alike, but it still seems valid to talk about southern culture—"We'll never really be all the same"—and southern literature. Spencer herself might be described as a direct literary descendant of Katherine Anne Porter and Eudora Welty.

But what characterizes the literature of the New South?

"It's hard to say what the characteristics are," Spencer admits after a moment's thought. "But there's a lot of southernness in the literature: manners, terrain, weather, food. A writer can't do without his landscape. It gets into his work." As she points out, John Cheever has New England in his, California writers have the West Coast in theirs.

Elizabeth Spencer has a lot of the Deep South in hers. Her most recent novel, *The Salt Line* (published in 1984), is about the Gulf Coast after Hurricane Camille hit.

"I was down around the Gulf after the big hurricane," she recalls, "I couldn't believe my eyes. It was a miserable thing to have happened." While the novel's setting is the storm-ravaged coast, the theme of the novel arose from the campus unrest in the '60s, "a political hurricane." So *The Salt Line* presents what Spencer describes as "the same theme in different aspects. It's an aftermath story—it involves the reestablishment of the self in a new context." It also involves the rebuilding of a once distinctly southern terrain into a less gracious environment.

Although she found the novel a challenge to write, *The Salt Line* is not her favorite. She considers *The Snare* (1972) her best work. The book is not well known, however, and she quickly points out, "Since it's not widely recognized as my best, I may be wrong. A writer is not always the best judge of his own work." *The Light in the Piazza,* which is set in Italy, is the novel she found easiest to write. The story grew from one of those ideas that just "hit her" when she wasn't "into anything else at the time." In 1962 MGM made a movie based on the book. But did Hollywood consult her about its production? "Not at all," she laughs, "but I'm still happy with it."

I asked her if she has noticed much change in fiction in the 40-odd years she has been writing professionally. "Mine's changed a lot—I hope for the better," she said with a smile that was somewhere between shy and wry, and then addressed the question more directly. She believes there is one perennial necessity for fiction; it ought to tell a good story.

"Some contemporary writers pull you along by other means, but they don't pull me along as well if they don't have a story to tell." Spencer sees the ability to tell a good story as something that sets current southern writers apart from most of their contemporaries. "Southern writers *always* have a story to tell." She finds most contemporary writing at least "interesting" and some of it very good, and she is especially enthusiastic about area writers.

"There's a lot of good work being done around here," she says, but judiciously refuses to name a favorite local writer. In fact, Spencer refuses to name a favorite author, period. She reads "different people at different times," and points to such broad categories as "the French writers" and "the Russian writers," as early favorites. Later, she read Hardy and Faulkner. "I came to Faulkner rather late," she says and admits that this is a little unusual, considering the fact that he was "something of a next door neighbor down there," in Mississippi.

Although Mississippi is her birthplace, Spencer hasn't lived in that neck of the woods for a long, long time. Last spring she and her British-born husband, John Rusher, decided to move to Chapel Hill from Montreal. North Carolina was a sort of compromise between the Deep South and Canada. She admits that she prefers the South to Canada, although she'll be the first to tell you that the heat wave last summer was no picnic—"The air conditioner saved our lives." While she wrote stories in Montreal, she says she never had "a feel for the climate," or any particular affinity with the place. "Order is a mysterious thing that writers need," she says. "I never felt it in Canada."

Spencer is uncertain whether a return to the South will be good for her writing. "It may make me lazy," she laughs. But anyone who knows her work must feel there's little chance of that. Her novels and stories are products of a careful writer with unusual gifts. The almost Jamesian subtlety of such works as *Knights and Dragons,* the gleeful humor in a story like "Moon Rocket," and the brilliant combination of both in *The Salt Line* and other works attest to her breadth and versatility. Even in her earliest stories Spencer's craftsmanship is superb, and a unique sensitivity to life and language lies at the core of her fiction.

PW Interviews: Elizabeth Spencer

Amanda Smith/1988

From *Publishers Weekly,* 9 September 1988, 111-112. Reprinted by permission of Cahners Publishing Company, a division of Reed Publishing USA. Copyright © 1988 by Reed Publishing USA.

Elizabeth Spencer is part of the grand tradition of southern writers. The distinguished novelist and short-story writer, author of such works as *The Light in the Piazza* and *The Voice at the Back Door,* Spencer has just published the latest work in her 40-year career, a masterly collection of short stories, *Jack of Diamonds* (Fiction Forecasts, June 5).

Spencer lives now in the South, after being away from the area physically if not spiritually for more than 30 years. She and her husband make their home in Chapel Hill, where two years ago Spencer came to teach creative writing at the University of North Carolina. They live in a pleasant suburban house graced by tall pines that drop cones on the front yard. Elegant and beguilingly gifted with a combination of strength and delicacy, Spencer talks to *PW* in a gentle, soft-voiced southern drawl.

Spencer's southern roots have been the central influence on her fiction. Her work has just been recognized by the awarding of a Senior Fellowship in Literature Grant from The National Endowment for the Arts—she is the only fiction writer so honored this year. Many of her subtle, luminous stories that explore the mysteries of the human heart are placed in the South, and even those set elsewhere have southern overtones.

Spencer was born the daughter of a businessman in 1921 in the town of Carrollton, Miss., population 500. "We were very family and land oriented," she says. "The outside world was almost a total mystery. Both sides of my family had been in that country since the Indians. My husband always said he'd never want to live in Mississippi 'cause I'm kin to the whole state, and that's pretty much true.

"I was fragile when I was a child, and my mother used to pass the

138

time reading to me, mostly fairy stories and myths. The summers
were interminable, long and hot." Though she wasn't allowed to join
her brothers in their sport of frog-gigging, Spencer accompanied her
father when he hunted deer, squirrels and doves on "a wonderful
island they bought in the middle of the Mississippi. It's a great saving
thing to the health of your spirit to get close to natural things. During
the Depression, I could never make anybody believe that we had quail
so often for breakfast—but everything we ate had birdshot in it."

Spencer's mother's family owned a large plantation. "They've
never been out of debt from the time of the Civil War, but it was still
carried on anyway by my uncle. I used to spend long summers down
there, but I was just too young or too gullible or too much a part of
the society to evaluate it as being a system of exploitation. Yet it was
also kindly and generous-hearted in many, many respects. One
didn't feel . . . any cruelty at all.

"It was not an ignorant society. My uncle was a great person for
demanding that his niece read certain books that he valued. One of
'em was *Les Miserables;* I read it much too young, because he was
standin' right over me practically the whole time. He felt I would
learn the whole scale of human misery and all the things that went
into making Jean Valjean a real man. My uncle thought the love story
of Marius and Valjean's adopted daughter was a very fine treatment
of love. It's odd, isn't it, a Mississippi plantation owner thinkin' this
French experience was so real and had to be understood? At home,
they were reading and discussing Dickens. The curious thing is that
the Southern Renaissance, so called, in literature was going on, but it
was judged that the books William Faulkner and Erskine Caldwell
were writing did not reflect the South in best light, and therefore were
to be ignored. To my family, William Faulkner was somebody up the
road who was writing to make money, and they didn't see the scope
of his work at all. I didn't read Faulkner 'til I was in graduate school."

After high school Spencer went to Belhaven College, a small girls'
finishing school in Jackson. "It was right across the street from where
Eudora Welty lived, and she had begun to publish when I was a
student there. Some of us in a writing group called up and asked if
she would come over for an evening, and she consented. She spent
a good deal of time on that first occasion talking to me and being

interested in some little thing I had written. We've been friends ever since."

Spencer got a scholarship to Vanderbilt and went off to Nashville, remaining there to teach after graduate school. Her publishing career began when an editor from Dodd, Mead came through Nashville, saw the manuscript for *Fire in the Morning,* her first novel, and sent her a contract before she'd finished the book. "Southern literature was in the ascendancy, and people were looking for new southern writers as a matter of course, so I seemed to fill that need," she says modestly.

Dodd, Mead also published her second book, *This Crooked Way.* Spencer later went to McGraw-Hill, then to Doubleday for a large collection of short stories, and subsequently to Viking for the current volume. On the basis of the first two works she won an award from the American Academy of Arts and Letters in 1952, and lived in New York on its proceeds. "I had a number of boyfriends who would take me out, and the $1000 lasted me all summer," Spencer laughs gently.

A Guggenheim sent Spencer to Italy, where she intended to stay for a year. She met her husband, Englishman John Rusher, there, and remained for the better part of five years. Italy has infused her imagination and her fiction ever since. There she wrote most of *The Voice at the Back Door,* about a racial situation that has its roots in the post–Civil War era. "That book depends so much on voice because it's totally about a small county in Mississippi. There are so many levels of speech that became very clear to me when I was in Italy because I was in a foreign atmosphere. If I'd been at home hearing them all the time, there would have been things that were merging and becoming vague." One reason for the book's "phenomenal success," Spencer thinks, was its coincidental timing with civil rights activism in the States.

"I began to get fascinated with Italy, and it began to seem like a possible second country. I still feel that way to a large extent. We would have stayed on, but it's hard for outsiders to make a living in Italy. It seemed too far from other bases where we might do better financially."

Eventually Spencer's husband took a job in Montreal, where they lived for 28 years, although Spencer says, "There hasn't been a year

in my life that I haven't come back to Mississippi or the South at least
two or three times. With experience first in Italy and then marrying
an Englishman, I began to see that my existence wasn't just one
straight line; it was being broken up into different packages, and I
began to try to adapt, write stories on that basis. Though many of
those stories I wrote in Canada must have been motivated a bit by
homesickness because a lot of 'em are about memories of the South.

"Italy had a lot to do with changing the focus of my work over the
years. Before I went to Italy I thought I would always be encased in
the southern social patterns and lineage and tradition, and if the
South changed, then I wanted to be part of that change. I didn't see
myself as separate from it. Then, especially after I married, I had to
come to terms with a life that was going to be quite separate from
that. I got to thinking that the southerner has a certain mentality,
especially southern women—you can no more change a southern
woman than you can a French woman; they're always going to be
French no matter what you do. So I thought that really nothing was
going to happen to me as far as my essential personality was
concerned, that it could broaden and include more scope and maybe
get richer. I looked at that from the standpoint of my characters, that
the southern approach was going to be valued no matter where they
found themselves. It seemed to me that there wasn't any need in
sitting at home in the cottonfield just to be southern, that you could
be southern elsewhere, in Florence, or Paris, or anywhere you found
yourself."

We go off to lunch at the local favorite, the Pyewacket, later pay a
visit to the small ranch house where Algonquin Books is located and
meet publisher Louis Rubin, to whom, along with his wife and Max
Steele, *Jack of Diamonds* is dedicated. We stop, too, for coffee, at the
delightful Hardback Cafe and Bookstore, whose owner, Grant
Kornberg, will shortly publish a single Spencer story in a limited
edition.

"The part of the States that is still *incredibly* attractive to me,"
Spencer continues, "is the coastal regions of the South. I've written a
lot of stories in the past about the Gulf Coast. Mobile isn't far from
the area I wrote about in *The Salt Line* [her novel about rivalries that
reemerge in the wake of a hurricane's devastation], and they have
bumper stickers that say, 'Thank God I live South of the Salt Line.' "

Indeed, Spencer has one in her writing room upstairs. "Somebody in Montreal said, 'Of course you took that from the common vernacular, but it made a good title.' I made it up!"

Spencer tells us that the stories in the current collection "simmered around with me since the last novel came out and before that." She was invited to the Villa Serbelloni in Bellagio, Italy, where she wrote "The Cousins," her exquisite story about five young southerners who go abroad together. "Writing that story was a sheer joy to me from beginning to end. I wrote to Walker Percy the other day and was going on about my new novel and said it took me a while to get to know the characters, and then I said, 'Writers are crazy. I made all these people up, and then I think I've got to spend time getting to *know* them. You ought to lock me up.' I get frustrated when I think of people like Eric and Ben [the two cousins that the protagonist, a woman, is enamored of], that I'll never meet them. I knew a lot of people similar to them, rather dashing and terribly well-read young men. When I was at the age to fall for somebody like that, they were all in the war. It was a long hiatus out of my life. I still admire that kind of guy very much, but I think they have their faults and weaknesses, too. The story brings out some of that."

Regarding the complex relationship at the heart of "The Cousins," Spencer says, "It seems to me that real relationships don't ever perish. My object is to bring people to a certain point—usually a spiritual point, an awareness of all the elements involved. It's like focussing a camera. In *The Salt Line* what I was trying to say was that the life force is hanging on and has to be reckoned with."

Spencer's stories are full of mystery about their characters. "If you got to the point where they cleared it all up, that story would vanish and another one would come on." Her friend, novelist Lee Smith, pointed out to her that in every story in her current collection people hide something from each other. Spencer's response: "There's a certain mystery at the heart of relationships that is difficult to penetrate.

"My idea of a story is that it's something that should go on living in your mind. I judge books and novels and stories like that, that there's something I can feel I'm living in, and after I finish that I can meditate on its various angles. I try to aim for that effect, because it's what I like to read. I have this optimism that the good things do have the tendency to last."

Soundings: Contemporary Fiction

Wayne J. Pond/1988

This interview, recorded fall 1988, was broadcast on 15 January 1989 on *Soundings,* the cultural-affairs radio series of the National Humanities Center. The interviewer is Public Programs Officer at the Center. Major funding for *Soundings* comes from the National Endowment for the Humanities. Copyright, 1989, National Humanities Center. Transcribed with permission.

Wayne J. Pond: Elizabeth Spencer teaches at the University of North Carolina at Chapel Hill. She's the author of eight novels, including *The Light in the Piazza.* Speaking of the title story from her new collection, *Jack of Diamonds,* here is Elizabeth Spencer.

Elizabeth Spencer: The impulse for the story came out of Central Park, where the story starts—an apartment above Central Park. I used to admire those settings when I came to New York. Once at a luncheon when I said I didn't have a plot in mind for a story or novel, an editor suggested to me, "You handle situations of young people so well. Have you ever thought about what a young person might feel who had parents involved in the theatrical, show-business world?" This germinated for years without my knowing about it.

Pond: The character Nat Jennings is involved in theatrical productions. He's the Jack of Diamonds, the man with the face we see, but don't see. Where did he come from?

Spencer: You turn the card, and there's the same face, you think. He just came walking in. I don't know where my characters come from sometimes.

Pond: Are these people real to you? Do you talk to them? Do they talk to you?

Spencer: They don't talk to me; they talk to each other. I'm the invader in their lives, though they don't know it. There have been a lot of amusing things done on this, you know. There's Pirandello's play of six characters in search of an author.

Pond: Do you have this chain of people behind you, following you around?

Spencer: I think I have been haunted at times by characters.

Pond: Another one of your stories in *Jack of Diamonds,* "The Business Venture," is a story with a female narrator who is talking about a friend of hers in the late sixties, or early seventies.

Spencer: It's 1976, though it could be the sixties, of course.

Pond: There are two people, a white woman and a black man, trying to get a dry cleaning business going. The story deals with the concentric circles that flow out from this business venture. Where did that story come from?

Spencer: That came from a lot of directions, too. I was driving through a small town in south Mississippi, and there was a Victorian house with a wing at the side and a sign up for some business that was going on in that wing. That stuck with me, the sight of that house just at the turn of the road in this little town, one of the biggest houses in the town—and of a Victorian rather than a classical sort. I thought, "Well, what kind of business would be run out of that house?" I don't know whether I imagined the business or not.

How it turned into a dry cleaning business is odd, too. There was a black man in my little hometown of Carrollton of whom my mother was always saying, "He's the best dry cleaner I've ever had." He used his G.I. mustering-out pay to study dry cleaning, and Mother would say, "Now isn't that a useful thing to do?" This was something I didn't forget.

Pond: You replicated that in this character in the story?

Spencer: Yes, but all the business of his working for a white woman who might have lived in that house, I imagined as happening in south Mississippi, not in Carrollton. It grew out of my wondering how women who are left coping in those big houses make a living when the money goes. How do they make a living? What is their financial alternative? One thing led to another.

Pond: It leads me to ask whether "The Business Venture" is a story about love and sex, or about business and race relations.

Spencer: The story is about the story. Oh, I think it really is about a business venture, though somebody teasing me in New York at a party we went to after a meeting turned to me out of nowhere and said, "Did they or didn't they?" We weren't talking about "The Business Venture" at all, but I knew at once what he meant. I said, "That's what keeps you reading. You don't think I'm going to tell you that?" I think it's really a religious story, to tell the truth.

Pond: The religion of what? Of money?

Spencer: No. I think this character Nelle was a nun-like character. And you can realize on the surface from reading the story that it is almost a medieval story. One way you could look at it is that he was a faithful knight.

Pond: Courtly love?

Spencer: Well, there is something courtly about his devotion to her. He is getting condemned by the black community at the same time she is getting condemned by the white community. The impact on this little sex-oriented, drinking crowd that she is always running around with is that she's just a complete puzzle. They don't know what to do with her. One falls in love with her and the other, the narrator, goes off for a weekend with one of her long time friends. Somebody else takes over the partying of the crowd. They just all fall apart.

Pond: One of the characters says about Nelle that she thinks she can live her own life, that she thinks she can make her own choices. Something like that?

Spencer: Yes. That's one of their means of trying to explain her.

Pond: Is this a feminist tract, a feminist expression?

Spencer: No, I'm not much into that. But if you have a real story, you can read things into it that weren't uppermost in my mind. It's about living people, and so it's like looking at life. What you find in it is up to you.

Pond: Another story in *Jack of Diamonds* is "Jean-Pierre," in which a young woman, Callie, marries a French-Canadian, rather unexpectedly. She meets him and, bingo, these two are married. You think, "O.K., let's see where it goes." Then he exits from her life. You made me think, as I read that story, of a Hawthorne tale called "Wakefield," about a man who just leaves his wife, moves a couple of blocks away, and stays there for twenty years. Jean-Pierre doesn't carry it quite to that extent.

Spencer: That story is set in the sixties, but what teased me about it, and made me want to write it, came to me later. The French-Canadian population politically became very powerful and assertive. There were a lot of submerged social envy and a sense of suppression among the French, which were beginning to surface in the sixties when we were living there.

Pond: Is that what happens with Jean-Pierre?

Spencer: It is an examination of the French-Canadian psyche reacting against the English snobbishness, or lack of knowledge of their community. Jean-Pierre himself was always afraid of the English put-down, that they would criticize him. Callie to me is rather heroic—one reviewer compared her to the faithful Griselda and another to Penelope, but whatever she is, she is just a kid. They had this powerful sexual attraction, and that's the core of the story. His act of marrying her was rather more of a protection than one might expect.

Pond: Protecting whom?

Spencer: Her. They were into this affair, this rather passionate affair, and he married her. That to me was creditable. But then he got frightened, and what frightened him, I don't know. It is suggested throughout the story that it was some kind of weakness in his own business arrangements and that he had to shore up support for himself elsewhere. He is afraid to tell her that because, for one thing, the French-Canadians are rather mysterious and inclined to be clannish and talk about their deeper problems of this sort among themselves. He was afraid of her betraying him to that community he was frightened of. The weight of the story falls on her—she's tried to the limit. His money doesn't hold out, and she doesn't get any word from him. She almost becomes attached to another man, but she doesn't.

Pond: Do you think of yourself still as a southern writer? You've lived in Europe. You write in *Jack of Diamonds* about characters who live in Canada. You still sound like a southerner—do you still think of yourself as a southerner?

Spencer: Oh yes. I'll always be a southerner, no matter where I live. I think it's a bit of a test of the culture, that you don't lose it. You could transport a French woman for many, many years to, say, California, but she would still be a French woman. So I think a southern woman, particularly, is always the same—as I suppose southern men are. By lineage, birth, everything, I was bred as a southerner, too much so ever to lose it now, any more than my accent. I never tried to lose it. Goodness, I don't think it's anything to want to lose; it's something to be proud to keep.

Pond: Elizabeth Spencer is the author of *Jack of Diamonds,* a collection of short stories published last fall by Viking Penguin. Elizabeth Spencer's new play, *For Lease or Sale,* premieres next week at the PlayMakers Repertory Theater in Chapel Hill, North Carolina.

Elizabeth Spencer
Irv Broughton/1988

From *The Writer's Mind: Interviews with American Authors*, Vol. 2 (Fayetteville: University of Arkansas Press, 1990), 97–125. Copyright 1990 by the University of Arkansas Press. Reprinted by permission.

Elizabeth Spencer was born in 1921 and grew up in Carrollton, Mississippi. She received her M.A. degree from Vanderbilt University and received a Guggenheim Fellowship in 1953. She won the $10,000 Fiction Award from McGraw-Hill for *The Light in the Piazza*, the Henry Bellamann Award, and the Award of Merit medal for the short story from the American Academy of Arts and Letters. She holds an honorary Litt.D. from Southwestern College in Memphis. Her books include *Fire in the Morning, This Crooked Way, The Voice at the Back Door, The Light in the Piazza, Knights and Dragons, No Place for an Angel, Ship Island and Other Stories, The Snare, The Stories of Elizabeth Spencer, Marilee,* and *The Salt Line.*

She is an American expatriate, although she might not call herself that, living in Italy and Canada before settling in North Carolina.

Her voice is mellifluously rich in its Mississippi accent, her manners acute, courteous, and pleasant. But within her finely crafted stories and novels beats the heart of a fierce and powerful writer, and one who is not recognized as fully as she might be.

Irv Broughton: What did people say when you were a kid and you said you wanted to be a writer?

Elizabeth Spencer: Oh, I don't know. They looked at me like I had a curious fantasy or something.

IB: What was your favorite myth when you were growing up?

ES: I think one of the Greek myths about Pegasus, the winged horse, I guess. There was a pretty picture in my book, *The Wonder Book of Myths and Legends*. It was all about the Greek myths. And next to that was the one about Jason and the Golden Fleece.

IB: What did you like about the book?

ES: It was the way it was written and illustrated. I counted a lot of illustrations in those stories. I also think it was hero worship. Jason was so brave and Orpheus was along on that voyage. I found a lot of heroes in the Greek myths, and they got assembled on that voyage to go and get the Golden Fleece. I remember it was kind of interesting that Orpheus played and the seas opened up; a lot of magical things happened when he played. I would drift away on dreams of this kind of thing. I didn't like so much the story of Daedalus and Icarus because it ended so badly—he fell in the sea.

IB: So you really believed in the heroic?

ES: I loved the heroic in these myths, and I guess the book I had played on my tendencies because it was very much shaped toward the heroes of great myths.

IB: Do you think you told more stories than most of the kids you knew?

ES: Well, I always liked listening to stories. I think I had a tendency to exaggerate and invent things. That was a very neat trick for covering up, because if you could exaggerate one way or another, you could get out of a little trouble. But my parents were very alert to that kind of thing and cautioned me against it. I do think I had a tendency to invent stories and they'd be things that wouldn't be acceptable around the little bunch of kids I knew—not acceptable in the sense that it would type me as a literary sort, which was something I tried early on to avoid.

IB: Were you really secretive about this?

ES: I don't know so much secretive as I just knew it wouldn't go down. I used to write things for my own amusement, but I'd show them to my mother. She was very encouraging about things like that and thought it was wonderful. I wrote a story once and gave it to my parents for Christmas. I remember sitting up late at night, and Mother said, "What are you doing?" You know, it would be cold up there; it gets cold in Mississippi in the winter. She said, "Come to bed. You'll catch your death of cold. What on earth are you doing?" I said I was just working on something, and I wrote all this in a notebook and gave it to them for Christmas. That was the secret of what I was doing.

IB: In what ways were you like your mother?

ES: Oh, I don't know. People always said we looked alike. They still say that, but I think she was very sympathetic to stories. She always liked stories and telling stories. She used to read fairy stories, and she always had a kind of child's delight in things. She was one of those people who never quite lost that. I think it was a wonderful trait to have—the enthusiasm and excitement. And in reading children's stories to me, I thought she was as excited about them as I was. My mother's family was not very literary, in a sense, but they were all great readers. One of my uncles said he found some children's books I would enjoy—they were George McDonald's children's books, things like *The Princess and the Goblin*. They were outside the canon of children's books like *Alice in Wonderland* that we had at home. So, when he got back, he sent them to me and we started reading them. And I remember she seemed thrilled about some of the phrases, and she'd say, "Isn't that a pretty comparison?" She got as excited about these children's things as I did, so we had a great rapport at that age.

IB: In what ways were you like your father?

ES: Oh, my father. That's another question. He had a bad temper and I have a bad temper. I don't know. People have told me that later on in life we clashed a lot because we were so much alike, but I don't think we really were. I never had a very good relationship with him. From the time I was twelve or thirteen, we were great pals, and I was running around with him everywhere. He was a businessman and a very active man. He never liked to read anything imaginative—he thought that was a waste of time. He was proud of accomplishment as long as it could be pointed to as something that people can admire in general, but he was very, very hard on anything about art or artistic effort or anything like that—it was a waste of time. I have to explain, though, that he was brought up when the South was quite poor and his family was rather impoverished and he had to work hard from the time he was a small boy. The work ethic was strong in his thinking.

IB: You seem to understand him.

ES: No, but I think he had many redeeming features, and probably he was nicer to people outside his family than he was to people inside his family.

IB: When you were a child, were there little exercises to try to make you into a lady?

ES: Oh, yeah. You see I was brought up in the summer on my uncle's place—I used to go down to the plantation. My mother's people were plantation owners and her younger brother was running the property. He and his wife didn't have any children so they were very receptive to my brother and me. We used to spend months in the summer. I always rode with my uncle—he was riding a horse all over the place in those years. (That was before the age of jeeps, before the Second World War.) I used to go fishing with Negroes way back in the swamp and climb trees. When it got to be time to go to church or visit with the ladies around home, they dressed me up with these little frilly dresses, white socks, and patent leather shoes. In the winter, I remember I had to wear little kid gloves. There was one lady who had a set of chairs that were covered with horsehair. It's a kind of satin, shiny, handsome fabric, but it prickled me in my little dress. And I was supposed to sit there with my hands folded, and not speak unless spoken to. And, "Don't scratch!" (Laughs.) And the damn stuff would be stickin' in my legs!

IB: But you wouldn't trade the milieu of the South, would you?

ES: I don't guess I thought it was remarkable at the time. I must have thought everyone was the same, but I know there were distinctions taught me by my mother. I was taught to be very democratic. A lot of the kids out in the country were riding horses and driving buggies in to school and they didn't have anything, and I was taught never to act as though I were better than they were. That was the mark of being the right kind of person. There were a good many people in that little town who prided themselves on their family background and therefore thought they could act superior to other people.

IB: You said once you see the world as a story.

ES: I think story has a lot to do with time and event that we're all involved in. We're involved in circumstance, event, and time, and so those things are indispensable to story. Then the things that are foremost in our minds, that we are living out in a way, are what we long for, and believe in. And those are the foremost things in a story. Then you find the forces that work against those things and you inevitably have a story at every turn of the road.

I was just reading an article in the *New York Review of Books* about certain writers whose characters seem static and characterless without qualities, because the writers are mainly interested in philosophic things—they are beyond events and actions. Well, I guess these may be the great writers of our times, but they don't please me at all. I find them difficult to read. But I guess I shouldn't say that. There's a philosophic point to be reached where you're not interested any longer in qualities, in characters, in events, in nothing but thought process or something. I just do not see that fiction can even exist without the other things.

IB: Some writers talk of the terrible need to communicate their point of view or ideas. Have you ever felt that way?

ES: No, I'm not sure that I have personally any one point of view. I learn so much from my characters. If I'm attracted to a character telling a story, I try to go along as much as possible with their point of view. Sometimes I can see around it—and the character's making a mistake, but I'm not inclined to sit in judgment on that.

The story *The Light in the Piazza* aroused a curiosity in my mind because I was following the main character in the story, the mother, and I thought a lot of times that she may have been deceiving herself. She wanted this marriage so badly for her daughter, she may have fooled herself into thinking—it was a wish fulfillment—"This is going to work out" when maybe it would collapse three days after the wedding. On the other hand, I didn't want to interfere with her in any way. I just let her have it. And a lot of people criticized me. They said, "It's such an ambivalent story. You can't tell where you stand." So I say to myself, "Well, they argued that about Shakespeare."

IB: What was the challenge in writing *The Light in the Piazza?*

ES: It wasn't hard enough—I wrote it very fast. I got the idea for the story when we'd left Italy and were living in Canada. The idea sort of came to me about missing the light in Italy very much. Someone said the wonderful thing about Italian painting is the quality of the light there. And I missed that, and it started out of that, but it also started out of an incident of a slightly retarded girl that my husband and I had known somewhere and the relationship she had with her mother. The story really came at me from a lot of directions. Another thing was the Italian attitude toward marriage and the arrangement of marriage. A woman was watching a wedding once and I was standing by her when the procession went by. She said to me, *"Le nozze! È una carta che si gioca."* "It's a card one plays."

IB: Did the Italians take umbrage at the idea of a retarded girl getting together with an Italian man?

ES: Well, some of them did. A friend of mine told me that she had a man friend who objected strenuously to that story. He said, "No father would do that to his son." I said, "I think part of the story might have been that he didn't realize what he was doing." I mean, that was one of the things in it. And several Italians that I knew thought it was perfectly wonderful, that the story had gotten hold of something in the Italian makeup that was just right. They told me that so often that I couldn't believe they were flattering me, but they just really felt that way and weren't offended at all. The preface of the Italian edition of *The Light in the Piazza* had this phrase: The father *"l'ha capito subito,"* that is he had understood at once the true state of the girl. And I don't know if he did or not. I couldn't tell that he had understood and I don't think he ever did.

IB: Was there anything that you never quite got used to in Italy?

ES: Well, I had a friend who was Italo-American, who complained about the same things I did after a long time. We both had lived there a long while, and it was like that marriage remark. She said that she had a dress promised for a party and it wasn't ready. She complained to the woman, and the dressmaker said, "Well, I haven't had time." My friend said, "You promised." The woman said, *"Che cosa è una promessa?"* "What's a promise?" This indicates a profound cynicism in the Italian character, and I just think it's bad. It was either there in every Italian I met, or it was recognized by people who didn't see that as being part of the Italian character, and I do think it is. But, of course, they've been there for years—the crossroads of nations. They've seen people come and go; they've been impoverished and seen all kinds of things happen to them, so I guess a certain cynicism has to develop out of that.

IB: Did you feel like an expatriate writing overseas?

ES: I haven't written much overseas except for *The Voice at the Back Door.* I wrote some short stories the rest of the time I was there, but mainly they were about the South. I started writing about Italy when I left Italy. The whole Italian experience meant a great deal to me, and when we left Italy and came to Canada, I had this kind of sense that I was going to lose a lot of that unless I started to write about it. I wanted to get it down. And, honest to gosh, I never did think *The Light in the Piazza* would be published. I just thought of it as a rather crazy story I was writing to get down a lot of impressions. I thought the central idea was exaggerated and that it wouldn't find an audience. It turned out to be the most popular thing I ever wrote, so I guess I'm not a good judge of that. (Laughs.)

IB: Bernard Berenson said Florence was a sunny place for shady people.

ES: Well, the Florentines do have that reputation. There was a lot of that irony, I think, in the story. That she has the experience of the light when she says, "It looks like you can see everything but you can't see anything."

IB: Were you naive when you got to Italy? Also, were there a lot of rude awakenings?

ES: I didn't actually think of moving there. I went there on a Guggenheim for one year. There were rude awakenings everywhere, but I don't think I was so starry-eyed and idealistic that I thought everything was going to be great in Italy. There were many minor things that were always happening, like people giving me the wrong change or promising me something or trying to rip me off in various ways. It got to be a way of life. You got ground down by it, and you just accepted that you had to be on guard all the time. I remember when we first came to Canada there was the tiniest accident— somebody bumped into us at an intersection. The insurance man immediately took the claim, and we called him about six times a week. He said, "Well, I know you people mean well and everything, but it takes awhile to process the claim." And we realized we were in a different country where we weren't going to be lied to, that the insurance was taking care of everything—and the check would arrive. I had this fixed idea when we were in Canada—good old, straight, honest Canada—that people would try things. I used to check things about fifteen times if I sent off a check or an order. It was a habit I had to lose.

IB: In what ways was Italy like the South?

ES: They didn't heat the houses well in the winter. (Laughs.) I think being very socially charming and correct was a point in common. I lived in Florence, but I lived mainly in Rome on that second trip, beginning in 1953, when I was on a Guggenheim. I lived mainly in Rome, but I went up to Florence and found a room in the household of an Italian countess and her family. They had a circle of friends, all of whom were related by old ties, family ties, or actual kinship, and the way their circle moved with each other and the way they talked about each other—they never dreamed of breaking these ties up—was like the South. Close-knit circles bound by long family connections.

IB: Are people sometimes surprised that a gentle lady from Mississippi writes with the kind of intensity and edge that you do?

ES: How do you know I'm a gentle lady? (Laughs.)

IB: Well, you just seem that way. Let me make that assumption.

ES: I think the people who know me well realize all that gentleness is probably a matter of being brought up well and having a certain Mississippi accent. I don't know. Eudora Welty said something like that in a preface she wrote to my stories. It's kind of like when I'm writing it's like being possessed by something else that's not so much me. I think most people who have some talent at times feel the talent possess them. I think those are probably the times when you're doing your most powerful work—when this force can get ahold of you and make itself felt. It's like being inhabited by a spirit that's not dictating to you, but coming out through the story.

I remember when I wrote "The Finder." That was an old story I heard at home. It's apparently a widespread folk belief, that certain people can find things, a psychic gift. So I went to write that one day in Montreal. I started about nine and I finished at two, and I thought I'd been working about an hour or an hour and one-half. It was all there—it just poured out. But that happens rarely. Usually, I have to hesitate and figure everything out.

IB: What was the hardest plot to develop?

ES: I think I had more trouble because I got involved with something in my own psyche in maybe an unpleasant way during *Knights and Dragons.* I had to back up and rewrite over and over and over. I thought, "I'll never get through with this." And I wanted to drop it. It may be, though I didn't think of the woman in it as being myself, that something of her psychic difficulty—it's very internalized experience—may have overlapped with certain psychic difficulties I was having at the time I wrote it. So the overlap was so intense I kept trying to pull back from it and be objective. I was trying to get a distance so that I could at least handle it, but it would pull me back in. It's like the story in Greek myth where somebody made a coat that's beautiful but it stuck to the skin. You couldn't get the coat off without pulling your skin off—it gave me that feeling.

IB: What things in your psyche?

ES: Oh, that's too personal. It just finally got absorbed in one way—I don't know. Some people think of writing as a pouring out of their own troubles. I don't. It was a coincidence that it was that way for me. Robert Penn Warren says somewhere that writing is a purgation of temperament. I think he said that in connection with Conrad. But I didn't do it to do therapy on myself. In fact, it turned out to be a laceration rather than a purgation. I just have to outlive it. I felt I had to go on and finish the story. I had a terrible time because I used to wake up at night and feel I was sinking in the sea. I was holding onto my story as a kind of life raft which was holding me up. But, anyway, this story is separate from me now and a lot of people think it's worthwhile. I'm not sure because it cost me a lot of pain.

IB: Did *Knights and Dragons* change a lot from your original conception?

ES: The original idea of *Knights and Dragons* was that I had already written about the light side of Italy in *The Light in the Piazza*—you know, the charm, the beauty, some dark things too like the runaway carriages, different things that happened. But on the whole it was suffused in light and romance in a way and *Knights and Dragons* was different. A lot of it takes place in the winter in Rome, when it's raining and people get colds. The apartments are not well heated—you know the landlords torment people. Things like that crept in. So I thought I was writing about first the light side of Italy and then the dark side—like the dark side of the moon. I thought the two were companion pieces.

IB: It seems you move in time very well in *Knights and Dragons*.

ES: People say that generally I do that well. But it seems to me that there are points in your life, or in stories—what you will— preoccupations, where the past does intrude. It becomes a living present. It's at that point that it's natural to relate it to the present because it is so necessary when living the present.

IB: What's the key to achieving that?

ES: To absorb yourself in the character so when the character has to have the past, through memory or feeling or continuation, that is when it occurs in the story, through dreams or recollections or conversation, or somebody coming. It's the actual pressure of the past on the present. Remember in *Knights and Dragons* when this man comes as a messenger from some property? Then in their conversation he explains what it's all about, and her feelings become very strong toward the past at that time—real misery on her part.

IB: Isn't *Knights and Dragons* kind of a liberation story of Martha?

ES: I think so. She had to destroy her psychic attachment in order to free herself, but in freeing herself she almost destroyed herself because the man she met caught on to this and was very destructive.

IB: What does short story writing owe your novel writing and vice versa?

ES: I look at them as different forms. I think the stories in *Jack of Diamonds* are almost novelistic because in the longer ones I was trying to awaken the resonance of a novel without spelling it out for three hundred pages. They could have been developed that way, but I thought I could do the whole thing in less space. I suppose that's a form in itself. I think of short stories too being sort of like tales that are told. You know, somebody might sit down at one sitting and tell this. I do think novels have to be thought out.

IB: Do you think the short story is the most difficult form as Capote and others have said?

ES: My stories all seem to develop pretty easily. No, I think novels are more difficult because they take so much longer to write. (Laughs.) William Styron said on a program once—it was so funny— writing a novel is like crawling from Vladivostok to Madrid—on your knees.

IB: Give me your three commandments when it comes to short story writing.

ES: Maybe I've got ten of them; what if I've got more than three? Let's see. Don't overwrite description in a story—you haven't got time. Don't bring in scenes that don't pertain to the central story. Don't bring in minor characters that might be nice in a novel to make a diversion, because again, you don't have time. But still try to keep the richness of the thing. Don't strip it down too far. I was never too partial to minimalist fiction for the reason it seems so stripped down that you hardly know where you are. So I think it's got to have some degree of fleshing out.

IB: Peter Taylor said the way to learn writing was to consciously copy the style of the greats. He said if you didn't you would do it unconsciously.

ES: I never have done that. I sometimes make my students do a paraphrase just so they'll be sensitive to prose rhythms—as the writers they admire are sensitive. They'll take a paragraph and do a paraphrase. For instance, in Welty's story, "A Worn Path," there's old Phoenix Jackson who's walking down the road. Well, turn that into a man coming to town for an entirely different purpose, in an entirely different season of the year, with entirely different things on his mind, but still follow the rhythm of the prose. And if Eudora has a simile, you put a simile. Instead of "on a winter afternoon," you say, "On a late summer morning." I thought that was a fun exercise. And, after they'd do a Welty, they'd do a Hemingway paragraph. After that, a James Joyce paragraph. There's one that I use a lot, a Joyce story called "A Little Cloud" where little Chandler is going from his office to meet his old friend. And the thoughts he has along the way are rendered ironically because Joyce is not in step with the characters; he's shoving them. So that's a little difficult for them. But, if they follow, they'll get more sensitive in their writing.

IB: O. Henry felt that if a story was true to the human element, you just had to change the local color so it would fit any town.

ES: That's tending too much toward the formula story to me. I used to know a man who listed all possible stories as formulas. They were fourteen in number, and any story you gave him he could immediately say, "This is the 'Worm-turn' story" or "This is the 'Ain't Love Grand' story" or "This is 'Conflict with Final Success.' " (Laughs.) I don't know, I think that every good story is different. It really never has been written before.

IB: Where'd you meet this fellow?

ES: He was a good friend of mine, actually. He was a mystery story writer who had a seminar in writing in Nashville, Tennessee. And I was having a lean time of it because I had a job at a girls' finishing school in Nashville that I felt I was stifling to death in. It was during the war and I used to go down there to hear him talk—to get out of school, I guess. So I thought he was charming and I thought it was fun to be there, but I didn't believe a whole lot of it.

IB: Did you feel a need to escape the South?

ES: Yes. Part of it was my writing. I felt there were getting to be too many southern writers and that I didn't know if I was different, but I felt because I lived in the same part of the country as Faulkner did, I was seeing the same sights and knowing the same kind of people all my life. I read Faulkner very late, actually, but I realized when I read him—I already wanted some day to be a writer—that my heart sank because he was dealing already with things: people, landscape, the family, history, and everything that I might some day have to be tapping for my own work. In fact, my first novel, *Fire in the Morning,* people said was Faulknerian—I'm not sure it is. It just seemed to me I was drawing on things I'd known around my home town. Anyway I thought if I stayed around the South, it was just going to be multiplying and finding varieties of the same sort of thing that other writers are doing in great quantities now. And then, I just wanted another horizon to bring to bear on that—like learning another language sharpens your own language.

Also, I had done a sort of interesting thing. I had a friend who was working for the State Department in Germany. She went over for the Nuremberg Trials right after the war. She had gotten married over there and wanted me to come. It was the summer of 1949. So I took the proceeds of my first book, got a French freighter out of New Orleans, and went to Europe. I visited them for a while and then I left and went down to Italy. And I thought, "Oh, if I could ever get back." Well, that was part of the dream. But the other part was shaking loose from the *single* environment and trying to bring another to bear upon it. Maybe it was partly instinct, but I thought it would be enriching. However, I always meant to come back.

IB: What was the weirdest thing that happened to you on the freighter? That was a daring thing to do, wasn't it?

ES: I didn't realize how daring it was until we were actually at sea. It was a French lend-lease freighter called the *Wisconsin* (pronounce it in French and it sure sounds funny). The passengers were from Mexico, New Orleans, and the United States generally; some got on in Cuba (this was before Castro) loaded with rum and rumba records. It took eighteen days to cross the Atlantic. We changed the port of entry three times and had to send cables. I should have written *Ship of Fools.*

IB: How'd it feel when you finally got back in the states a few years ago?

ES: Oh, I'd been visiting a lot at home. See, I went to Mississippi

a lot during my parents' last years of life. I always went back to
Mississippi at least once a year all those years except when I was
living in Italy that longer stretch. But getting back to Chapel Hill, that
was a kind of return too, because I'd been Writer-in-Residence here
for a month in 1969, and I'd gotten to know people who didn't go
away, in contrast to other places I'd been, people like Max Steele and
Louis Rubin, and we really kept up the friendships that we made at
that time. Chapel Hill is rather special. My husband says it's
Shangri–la.

IB: You definitely use dreams in your work?

ES: Oh, yes, I think I do. *Knights and Dragons* is full of them.
There's a little dream in the title story of *Jack of Diamonds* that I
thought of cutting out because it certainly goes against my
commandments—you know, don't leave anything that embellishes
what's been discussed. It's where the girl has a dream about the
mother coming from the library.

IB: The librarian promised her a book, which she didn't have . . .

ES: And then she leans down on the pavement and picks up the
very book she was looking for. Now I have no idea what that dream
means. I didn't dream the dream. I had the girl dream the dream, but
somehow I felt like it pertains to the feelings she had for her mother
so I left it in. Do you think that was wrong?

IB: No, I think it works.

ES: But why it works you don't know. It's like dreams themselves.
Why do they work? You don't know.

IB: Are your dreams vivid?

ES: When you concentrate on remembering your dreams, if you
do it the first five minutes after you wake up, you'll remember a
whole host of things. And I tried this—I've got notebooks full of stuff.
Then the second morning you can remember more. I don't know if
you deliver some kind of directive to your subconscious to "start
dreaming now because I'm thinking about what you're going to do."
Then they come thicker and thicker and, if you try consciously to
remember and put them down in the first five minutes, you can
resurrect a whole lot of things out of that.

IB: Any persistent type of dreams?

ES: I used to, when I was a child, be very frightened by a dream I
had about running from a fox. (Laughs.) Isn't that silly? I was never
chased by a fox.

IB: What were the watershed periods in your life?

ES: Oh, Lord.

IB: This follows up on the three—or is it ten—commandments of writing.

ES: Only ten? (Laughs.) I think when I left the Mississippi environment, complete and total Mississippi saturation, and went off to Vanderbilt to graduate school—that was a watershed. Then I tried to go back to Mississippi and teach in a small college and I wasn't content. I got a job in Nashville where I was in graduate school—that new job was confining, too.

The thing that I didn't like about Mississippi, though I love it in a sense, was a sense of confinement because I was brought up by a very strict family, Presbyterian, but the ramifications of my mother's and father's families extended over the entire state. There wasn't anything I could do ever to escape. It was not so much supervision, though there was that in it, but it was people knowing everything I would do. Every part of my life was being scrutinized. It's enough to give you paranoia, but it would be a justified paranoia because it was literally true. When I got up in Nashville, I had a sense of freedom.

I won a prize from the National Institute of Arts and Letters of a thousand dollars, and I went up to New York and got to live off the thousand dollars some way or another because I lucked up on a room that was cheap. The lady went off on vacation and left me with the whole apartment. That was a wonderful summer, and that, again, led me to believe that I could cope with things outside Mississippi and feel freer and happier by doing so. When I left on the Guggenheim and went to Italy, that was another watershed. I suppose getting married was another watershed because it changes your lifestyle. You've got to adjust to another kind of life. And we had to go somewhere where we could make a living. That turned out to be Canada, and I think that watershed almost put me in a backwater because, though Montreal's a big international city, Canada was so much different from the warm country I'd been brought up to care about—the South and Italy. It seemed to me I stayed up there too long. I was always coming back when I left Europe. This latest move to Chapel Hill is definitely a step I was glad to take. Any more? Have I got ten?

IB: You based *Fire in the Morning* on your grandfather. Didn't he die long before the book came out?

ES: Yes, it was an unsullied relationship because I hadn't reached adolescence when he died. I think adolescence is a time for shaking up and disillusion and all that. I think I was writing about a wonderful man, and I hope I caught that wonderful quality in the book. He was a country sheriff for years before I was born, of course, and all those stories about him as sheriff were real. He had prevented a lynching at one time. And there were several men he had to hang. There were a good many stories about his courage. I made up the conflict over the property. But I got in trouble socially because people thought I was talking about them. It was difficult for my parents to survive all that because it was an irritation in the community, and they were heavily embarrassed and had to go and tell everybody that I really didn't mean them. (Laughs.)

IB: Any specific confrontations they had?

ES: Well, I don't know. My mother was very exercised and unhappy, and she begged me to take certain passages out that had bad language in them, and I gave in to her a few times. But the surprise to me—I guess I was very naive—was that I couldn't see people around home really reading a book or caring if I'd written anything. Instead, it went all over the place, and everybody was reading it. A lot of people in Mississippi were writing at that time and there used to be a game that women played around beauty parlors called "Picking Out the People." And they would sit with these books not giving a damn about the message of the book or what its real literary intent was and say, "Oh, isn't that exactly like so-and-so," "Oh, I know that's so-and-so." And then, I guess people being very fond of my mother and caring about how she felt began to say, "Oh, it's really a wonderful book." So she finally got calmed down. But I don't know what confrontations she had to go through because she was torn—she was always torn, always defending me. In the meantime, probably, she really wished the book was in the creek. (Laughs.)

IB: You heard Civil War stories from your grandfather and others didn't you?

ES: My grandfather tried to volunteer and lied about his age, but they wouldn't take him. He was running the whole plantation, a boy of fourteen, because all his family was in the war. I don't know that he had any Civil War stories to tell because he never saw any combat. Aunt Lucy Breckinridge was my older brother's nurse and the family cook for a while. You see Carrollton wasn't in the regular line of action, even when they made forays through northern Mississippi and burned houses—I don't think Carrollton was in that sweep. So they weren't war stories in the sense of being actual troop engagements near there. But there were any number of reminiscences of hard times after the war. Oh, real fury could be awakened out of people of my mother's generation about the Yankees, and about Reconstruction, and if Lincoln had only lived—and how mad they were at everybody. They'd say, "They take every opportunity to put us down," and "We just don't amount to anything." All that hatred of Yankees, I think, made racial segregation more entrenched in the South because the idea was that the Yankees were trying to force us to do these things. And they hated the Yankees so they hated any sort of attempt of the Yankees to do anything, even though it was probably indicated as right.

There was a story my mother used to tell about an aunt of hers who, when Yankee soldiers came by, they thought they were going to burn the house. She was a very pretty woman, so the soldiers said, "Well, play a tune for us," and she played, "I'll Be a Rebel Still" (laughs) which was a popular song in that time. And they just laughed and said, "You're too pretty for us to take any offense at that." So they left.

IB: You wrote in "The Cousins," "Whatever Southerners are, there are ways they don't change." In what ways haven't you changed?

ES: People in Montreal said, "How did you keep your accent?" And I said, "Well, I never tried to lose it, I never tried to keep it—it just stayed." I don't know. I suppose I have good manners because I was made to sit still in those horsehair chairs. (Laughs.) I can't imagine losing a sense of manners because I think manners are very important to kindness in living. The whole thing that I got from my parents that I am really grateful for is a sense of real democracy. And I wouldn't go back on that part of my upbringing because I think it's right. If that means you're a southerner . . . I suppose you could learn that in Nebraska, couldn't you?

IB: Have you received any knee-jerk reactions where you were made, as a southerner, to feel responsible for everything?

ES: I used to get more comments on that than I do now. When I had outlined the book, *The Voice at the Back Door*, people at the American Academy in Rome—it was sort of pre-civil rights era—and a lot of other people out there mocking, made comments. I always felt I had to defend the South, but at the same time I didn't want to seem that I wasn't liberal-minded myself. You can't go to great lengths to explain all that in a social situation where nasty remarks are thrown at you.

IB: Any specific nasty remarks you remember?

ES: I met a black man at a party, and I asked this Jewish musician, "What was his name again?" when the black man left. The black man was sort of drunk and flamboyant and threw his arm around me at one time, and then went on somewhere else, and I hadn't taken offense at that, but I asked his name. The musician told me his name and he looked at me and said, "And he's from a fine old family in Georgia,"—as though this underscored something and took the whole idea of southern family tradition to task. I felt how can I stop all that, so I guess I didn't say anything.

IB: In *The Voice at the Back Door*, Kerney lies about the racial incident and Duncan ruins his career trying to protect the black person.

ES: Oh, I think in politics in the South, in Mississippi, you had to knuckle under. I had a cousin by marriage who was eventually ruined in politics because they smoked him out. He'd been a Congressman under Kennedy, and they sent troops into the University of Mississippi. He had to answer when he was asked point-blank if he agreed with that. He said, "Yes," he did, so he was defeated. Kerney saw the handwriting on the wall if he kept the friendship, so he betrayed the friendship.

IB: What was difficult about writing *The Voice at the Back Door?*

ES: See, for many years, I was a supporter of segregation because I'd never known anything else. I was partially brought up on a plantation where there were descendents of slaves, and there weren't any white people for miles around, except my uncle and aunt. Then I began to place some blame, and, from hearing other ideas, I decided to examine the whole thing in the novel. And the difficult part for me was *I* was maturing in *my* attitudes in writing that novel—it was an evolution and a questioning of my own attitudes from childhood on.

So it was a living, evolving experience for me, and that was the hard part—not to be easy on yourself, and to look at it unflinchingly, so I did. In the preface I wrote to that *Time* edition of that book, I tried to recount some of my feelings.

IB: You seem interested in the southern class structure. You have rednecks, middle class, planters . . .

ES: Well, it's so mixed and so fluid. There were people who have been around in my part of the country for years. My father's family, the Spencers, and my mother's family, the McCains and the Youngs, were there from the earliest times, before the Indians left. But being in the planter class might just mean you had more land than your cousin somewhere who had maybe only two hundred to three hundred acres. So you built a bigger house because you had more money. Then the person with a little land might be married into the family some way. That's what happened to my mother and father. He was an up-and-coming young man who didn't have very much—it was all hard times after the Civil War. My mother's family home burned before she was ever born—it was a big house on a hill overlooking the Delta. They saved very little out of it. Then they built a smaller house on the plantation that eventually got extended and extended until it looked like a planter's house. But they built tack-on rooms for the longest. That's where I spent a lot of time. But the people who made big money after the war were sometimes unscrupulous—it's all in *Fire in the Morning,* how they came up and they gave themselves aristocratic airs—just as in Faulkner, the Snopses ended up buying the biggest house in Jefferson.

IB: It's always seemed to be that the extraordinary people of the South were often even more special because they've frequently had to overcome a lot.

ES: Oh, I know. Everybody's had to fight for their soul in the South, at one time or another. It wasn't that there was just poverty or just losing the war, but also continuing to right things within your own society where people ought to see and appreciate, and people turning against you. You know, that's very hard for people to come out of, I think. It's testing all the time. Maybe it's less now than it used to be because certain things have gotten pretty generally accepted. But in that story in *Jack of Diamonds,* "A Business Venture," that woman is being tested every minute—the one who opened the dry-cleaning establishment—because she's going against the way they thought she should live.

IB: Your stories are reminiscent in some ways of Henry James or Chekhov. Did you read them a lot?

ES: I've read some of James. I enjoyed reading it at the time, but I don't go back to James much. I read some short novels recently that I hadn't read before, and I think the first time you read them, they involve you completely, but then you don't want to work through that again. I think his prose is somewhat labored, but I shouldn't say anything against James. He's really a fine worker. It's really very interesting when he talks about his own work, but I didn't come early to James. I thought *Fire in the Morning* was more like a Thomas Hardy novel than it was like James or Faulkner. I admired Hardy a lot for the way he puts his novel together, but I'm not keen on his philosophy of life. I like Chekhov a lot; I am fond of Turgenev. I don't know, people have been saying that I resemble James. Before, they compared me to Faulkner. I've been compared to everybody. (Laughs.) Sometimes I think it's flattering, in a way. They always pick the very best people to compare me to, but I sort of wish they'd let me be myself. I don't know what's in the way of that—it must be my fault. (Laughs.)

IB: Could you talk about the dramatic elements in your writing?

ES: I've recently written a play! But I think there's been a strong dramatic element in my work all along. I like confrontation and encounter, and I like the sense of nobody being not entirely right about anything—again, situation, desire, event, all colliding and trying to work themselves free. And so I've had a lot of fun with the play, *For Lease or Sale.*

IB: Did it help you to be away from the South?

ES: Well, it does take a lot of pressure off to live abroad for a while. In the South it was a constant daily struggle to maintain your own ideas and beliefs.

A bunch of us from Mississippi were on a trip to Russia last September. The novelist, Ellen Douglas—that's not her real name— and I and several others would all sit around having a drink in our hotel in Moscow, talking about what we went through during different times in our past in Mississippi. And it was just a daily struggle with the people in your own family to keep your sense of humor, not to get your mind poisoned by the things they were saying. I didn't have to live through all that—I was in Canada. But, in many respects before I left, I was feeling that kind of pressure, so I think that that was a strong tide against any creative effort. It was a counter-tide that you were always fighting against. There's an essay that Eudora Welty wrote in *The Eye of the Story* about someone calling her up in the middle of the night. The caller is saying, "What are you going to do about all this, Eudora Welty?" and Eudora asks what a writer owes to current situations. How can you as a writer engage yourself? You don't want to turn out polemic, and yet you want to be on the right side. But, should you devote your fiction to that? I didn't feel that pressure so much when I started writing *The Voice at the Back Door.* *The Voice at the Back Door* came out coincidentally at the time the civil rights issue came to a head on the national level, but I was just responding to pressures I'd felt all my life. But then, I was able to write that because I was in Italy and I wasn't having to contend—I was just remembering and imagining.

IB: When did you feel you were able to write fully in your own voice?

ES: I've always felt that I wrote in my own voice, but I suppose it was weaker as a personal thing at first, and therefore it was easier to find echoes in it of other writers, like Faulkner and different people I had read and admired. But, in point of fact now, I think my style is pretty much my own instrument. I find that I can lend it very easily to the voices of the women that I've written about—in two instances in the stories in *Jack of Diamonds:* the voice of Ella Mason in "The Cousins" and the voice of Eileen Waybridge in "The Business Venture." They seem to me, though two different women, to generally come from the strata in the South that I know best. And it was easy for me to let them talk and tell their stories. And I could feel their personality operating through the voice, and I think that's really exciting for the writer.

IB: Jack London said that civilization has put a pretty thin veneer over this soft-shelled animal we call man. What do you think?

ES: Oh, I think people are pretty primitive—I really do. I think the primitive nature is just underneath the surface. It's close to all of us, but I don't know why that's surprising. (Laughs.) I think people are pretty much like animals. In fact, I often think about people in a favorable sense, really, as being like animals. I knew this guy in Montreal. I thought for ages that he resembled an antelope and I told him that. I don't know whether he liked it or not. (Laughs.) He even wore little black boots, instead of shoes, and they looked like antelope hooves.

IB: All right. What animal are you?

ES: Oh, Lord, I don't know. One of the cat family. You see, I'm tall and have a rather small head. Somebody told me I looked like a cheetah once. (Laughs.) They can run faster than I can.

IB: What would you like an Elizabeth Spencer story to do?

ES: I had several very pleasant reviews of this last book, and one reviewer said of one of the stories that it would change you a little bit. She said that was what she expected a really great story to do. I think I'd like for the story to be something that is part of the reader's life. I can never look back to a time before I read, for instance, *The Golden Apples* by Eudora Welty—it's become part of my life, part of my experience. It wasn't anything I did except reading it! Like Tolstoy, how can you think back before you read *War and Peace?* It's part of you. Not all of my stories can be that to everyone, but maybe some of my stories can be that to each and every reader.

IB: Novelist William Harrison talks about the writer always having to make choices between the secure and the adventuresome.

ES: Faulkner used to say "Don't do what you can do—try what you can't do." Well, that can be overdone, too, because you can do something wild that you aren't equipped to do at all and fall flat. But I do think much in favor of being adventuresome.

IB: Would you do anything differently, knowing what you know now?

ES: Each step seemed the right one at the time, so given the circumstances I suppose I made choices that were best for me. I think when my first books received favorable reviews, I should have stayed home instead of trying to go around giving "interviews," and attending bookstore "signings." I wasn't ready for doing public things, and being at that time excessively shy I used to feel I said wrong and misleading things and I was in general unhappy about the results.

IB: If you had to be personified as one character in one of your books, who would it be?

ES: I think the character that may be a lot like me is in *Jack of Diamonds*. I don't want to make this sound like I am this person because I'm anything but this person, but I think the character Ella Mason has this sense of remembering without judging too harshly the things she remembers or turns over in her mind. She wonders without making too terribly harsh judgments about anything. I'd like to be sort of like that.

Elizabeth Spencer and the Great Big Gong

Max Steele/1988

From the *University Report* [General Alumni Association of the University of North Carolina, Chapel Hill, 36 (January 1989), 14-16. Reprinted by permission.

When I call to arrange a time and place it seems a bit silly to both of us: an interview when we've known each other since she was a Writer-in-Residence here in 1969 and since we talk two or three mornings a week on the telephone.

I have to explain to her that naturally there's a great deal of interest in her since she has a play being produced, a widely reviewed and intelligently-praised book of short stories, and is receiving a $40,000 award. (The play, *For Lease or Sale* will be performed in the Paul Green Theater from Jan. 25 through Feb. 12 by the PlayMakers Repertory Company. The book is, of course, *Jack of Diamonds,* and the award is The National Endowment of the Arts Senior Fellowship in Creative Writing in recognition of the twelve books of elegant, important fiction she has published since 1948.)

She listens as if I am talking about somebody else, then says, "Oh, all that. Well, if you say . . ." I say I do say and she says: "As a matter of fact I got a really funny letter from Eudora Welty yesterday. She said, 'All these things happening to you. It's as if somebody hit a great big gong.'"

I like hearing anything about Welty and envy the fact that Elizabeth Spencer has known her since 1942 when Spencer was a senior at Belhaven. She had asked Welty, newly published, to come over and be a guest-critic at the college writing club. Later Welty brought first Elizabeth Bowen then Katherine Anne Porter down to meet her when Spencer was living at Pass Christian on the Gulf Coast, working on her second novel, *This Crooked Way.*

"Well," I say not to be outdone, "I got a letter from David Hammond about your play." (David Hammond is a professor of dramatic art and artistic director for the PlayMakers Repertory Company.)

170

"Oh, David," she says. She has a girlish quality to her voice and when she says the name of a friend it is especially young and warm. She's told me how much she is impressed by what Hammond knows about the theater and about writing and what complete confidence she had in him while rewriting the play, during one intense month in the early summer of 1987. "I would work with him for four or five hours during the day and then I couldn't go to sleep at night, it was like a tape running through my head."

Hammond's letter is in response to my question: "Why did you select the play?" Not that I doubt or underestimate any type of writing such a talented friend may dare to do. But still it does seem a bit spectacular that she should have her first effort at playwriting accepted for production after having been so successful with fiction. Her first novel was published when she was 27. A Guggenheim Fellowship followed in 1953. *The Voice at the Back Door* won her serious critical acclaim in 1956 and the following year she won awards from both The American Academy and the Kenyon Review.

The Light in the Piazza, first published in the *New Yorker* in 1960, became a bestseller as a book, was made into an MGM movie and received the McGraw-Hill $10,000 Fiction Award.

Then look what she's done with short stories: Five O. Henry Prizes, regular publication in the *New Yorker.* And a year or so after she collected 33 out of 40 or more stories in *The Stories of Elizabeth Spencer* she was recognized again by the American Academy of Arts and Letters, this time with the award of Merit Medal for the Short Story. In 1985 they quit messing around and elected her to a membership in The Academy.

She's waiting for me to read what Hammond has written.

"He says," I say, "among other things, 'I was impressed first of all by her skill in writing stage dialogue. She has been able to make the leap from fiction, which can make points and create atmosphere through narrative, to drama, where everything must be included in the moment of speaking. This is an elusive skill: you can't have stage characters simply expounding their pasts, yet you must convey to an audience all necessary information about the characters and their backgrounds."

"Is that all?" she asks.

I tell her I will show her the letter when we meet for the interview

which will be after the Farmer's Market where we occasionally run
into each other when she is looking for raspberries and date-nut
bread which her British husband John Rusher is very fond of. They
met in Italy and have lived in Canada 28 years but she finally
persuaded him to move South with her two years ago when it was
suggested at the moment of my semi-retirement that we teach
alternate semesters. I will show her the letter in the morning.

The next morning I turn up the suburban street where she lives
and sit for a moment looking at the suburban house. Neat with neat
yard and two gloriously golden maples. It is odd the houses writers
live in. In her first novel, *Fire in the Morning,* the house, "Walston
Cedars," had been of some importance to the plot and to the
understanding of the motivation of the protagonist. And in *This
Crooked Way* the house, "Dellwood," was no less important. The
title of her play is *For Lease or Sale* and the house has great meaning
to the people involved. This house I sit before is a good, practical
house and just right for a couple but there is nothing wildly Southern
or romantic about it. (Later when I tell her this she says, "You don't
like my house?" and when I try to explain that her fictional houses
have been great romantic structures she seems not to understand. "I
love my house," she says.)

When the car door slams, John Rusher opens the door of the
house. He is a handsome man who long ago was prematurely gray
and who now is still prematurely gray which happens if you get gray
young enough. His eyebrows though are still as black as a chow dog.

She comes to the door, too, and then down the walkway. Her
walk, like her voice, is young (she swims and does yoga) and she
looks thin in her deerskin jacket and light wool skirt. I have on a
deerskin jacket too but after comparing them she declares hers better
since the deer was killed by her own father and the skin sent off
somewhere in Missouri to be tanned. I claim my mother killed mine
with her own hands, skinned it with her own teeth and tanned it
Eskimo style in the upstairs bathtub. Like most people with vivid
imagination she never knows what to believe, (its that telling detail
"upstairs bathtub" that almost has her convinced) but she appraises
me shrewdly before laughing enough to show deep dimples.
Dimples, yet, and her a distinguished novelist! But the sophistication
of the white streak she leaves in her sometimes pale-auburn,

sometimes light-brown hair and the steady gaze of her deepset aristocratic eyes remind one that here is a lady to be taken seriously.

At the Farmer's Market the turnip man says as we pass: "I didn't hear nothing about no acorns hitting you on the head." We don't know what to say to him so we smile and say nothing but are both delighted by his remark which is the beginning or end of a fine short story given to us the first thing on a Saturday morning. As we walk about looking for John's bread she is reminded by the absence of tomatoes (pronounced with a broad British "A" for she has lived now half her life out of the South) of Teoc, her grandfather's plantation where she spent so much of her childhood and from which various men kin left for West Point and Annapolis before becoming military heroes.

Pausing before the Chinese garlic she decides she will buy some datenut bread and go home and make a spice cake. "With cayenne pepper in it. That makes it spicier, you know. You can't taste the cayenne pepper but it makes everything else spicier." Nancy Hale once told me that if she cooks a cake she might as well forget writing that day. "Do you like her writing?" she asks but does not wait for an answer.

We walk three times around the market talking about vegetables and the homemade muffins and about the food at the Villa Serbelloni, the ancient luxurious palace where she was invited by the Rockefeller Foundation to work on a book which turned out to be her current book, *Jack of Diamonds*.

"The interview," I reminded her.

"Oh that . . ." she says and glances at her watch.

While I contemplate a pumpkin she disappears and reappears with a small paper bag and is ready to go on for coffee, at Breadman's which we decided will be a good place for an interview. She glances at her watch. She is time-conscious these days because she is reading everything she can about the sixties for her new novel which will be about the Americans who took refuge in Canada during the Vietnam War. Lately, she seems a bit preoccupied as if she's anxious to get back, learn more, do the basic hard work of research after which the imagination will take over and pull seemingly from nowhere people who will start living a story she does not yet know.

On the way to Breadman's she reads from the letter David

Hammond has written: "Elizabeth's dialogue is what I call 'loaded.'
You know everything you need to know about her characters
because their pasts are present in their words and actions. It's
interesting to me that critics have many similar observations about
Elizabeth's stories, although the technique required is very different."

She stops and says that Hammond has showed her how to
shorten, sharpen dialogue for the stage, and how to move a line of
dialogue from one place to another to make it stronger, and that a
long scene has a great deal more impact than two or three short
scenes. She is, as always, generous in her praise of his knowledge of
the theatre. "He knows if a scene will play." She regrets she did not
see his brilliant production of *The Storm* which was performed the
year before she came South. But we both admire his beautifully
staged *Midsummer Night's Dream* and *Marriage of Figaro*.

She reads on: "I think all of her writing is distinguished by the
depth of her perceptions about her characters, and that in this play
she has found a new way to reveal that depth. We are all made from
what we were, and what we were is thus present in what we are, but
few writers can capture moments in which the full natures of our
beings reveal themselves. I think Elizabeth does that, and I think she's
now found a way to do it on a stage."

"Why did he write you this?" she asks.

"Because he didn't want to be misquoted. I've a feeling he's had
the experience all of us have had, of being misquoted in a way that
caused somebody a lot of misery." She leaves the paper bag carefully
on the dashboard.

In Breadman's we order and she minces at her blueberry crumb
cake and sour cream, her face reflecting the pink from her blouse.
Neither of us wants to do an interview and so we talk as always about
other things but not about writing. We talk about teaching, about the
office we use, she one semester, I the following, about the luxury of
cotton clothes, about watermelons that crack just ahead of the knife,
of where we learned to ride horseback, people we both knew or I
knew in Paris, or she knew in Rome in the fifties ending with the
most unlikely: Alice B. Toklas on my list, Krishna Murti on hers.
(There's something about Breadman's, maybe the endless time and
endless coffee or the sympathetic waiters, that makes us talk always
about Europe.)

But we talk this morning, too, about people we knew at Vanderbilt in the forties and the fact that we did not know each other there, about friends from everywhere and books they have or haven't written, restaurants, discount-houses. Neighbor talk. Family talk. I've lost two sisters; she's no longer in close touch with her brother. Cousin talk. Small talk. Southern talk. It doesn't matter what we say, it is the rhythm, the cadence that counts in Breadman's over coffee after the Farmer's Market.

She doesn't know I've seen a recent interview with her that Kim Ruhl has published in *The Phoenix*. In it Elizabeth Spencer says: "I remember Max Steele said to me twice in a row, 'Do you mean you just sat down and wrote a play?' and I said yes and he said, 'Do you mean to tell me you just sat down and wrote a play?' and I said yes."

I want to ask her the same question now and I want to tell her I never say the same thing twice, I mean I don't ever say the same thing twice. But by now I don't need to ask because I know how a theatre group in Montreal talked so much about her writing a play that she began writing one by just thinking of two people talking and then it turned out that it was a niece and an uncle and that they were talking about a house and that it was clear that the house had to go. The play had a successful reading there but something was definitely wrong with the second act and everyone was telling her something different about what was wrong and how to fix it so she just put it aside until she got here. Milly Barranger (professor and chairman of the Department of Dramatic Art) arranged a reading of it at which David Hammond appeared and knew exactly what needed to be done.

She has quit picking at the crumb cake and is sitting as still as only she can sit. One can see her, a young girl on a porch in Carrollton, Mississippi, on a rainy afternoon, fly-swatter in hand, waiting for the right fly to settle. That kind of still. Even her lake-colored eyes are still and there is a still, straight smile on her face, dimple to dimple. I remember that in a *New York Times* review Reynolds Price called her "a smiling sibyl, unafraid of her news." And then I remember that recently Andy Solomon in a penetrating review of *Jack of Diamonds* in the *Tampa Review* quoted Price and went on to say: "Spencer's news is how we move through life grabbing some but not all of its possibilities, unraveling some but not all of its mysteries, feeling much of its joy, much of its pain, as we sense our consciousness dawn with how we are yoked inextricably to others for reasons we feel rather than control." I glance down at my stenographer's pad.

Interviewer: Would you like another cup of coffee?

Elizabeth Spencer: I would, but I really do have reading to do. And I've got to bake John a spice cake.

We pay and leave, and back at her house she takes the paper bag carefully off the dashboard and thanks me for the coffee but not for the crumb cake, which I knew had too many calories. As we walk up the walk, John Rusher opens the door and before he can ask if she remembered his date-nut bread she holds the bag aloft. She walks on up the walk alone in that poised, sure and measured pace with which she has moved through her long distinguished career and with which she will undoubtedly walk onto the stage of the Paul Green Theater in late January when the audience begins demanding "Author!"

I drive back down the curving golden-leafed, suburban road, hearing the twangy voice of the turnip man and above the distant roar of the by-pass traffic, the January applause and the joyous reverberation and melancholy echo of the great big gong.

Mystery in Close Relationships:
An Interview with Elizabeth Spencer
Robert Phillips/1989

Printed with permission of the *New Virginia Review.*

Between 1975 and 1989, Robert Phillips interviewed the fiction writer Elizabeth Spencer several times. Much of that material recently appeared as "The Art of Fiction CX," in *The Paris Review* (#111, Summer 1989). The following unpublished exchanges constitute a totally new interview, and unlike *The Paris Review* piece, focus largely on Spencer's most recent works.

Elizabeth Spencer is the author of eight novels and four story collections. Among her many honors she received the Award of Merit Medal for Short Story from the American Academy and Institute of Arts and Letters in 1983, and a Senior Arts Award Grant in Literature from the National Endowment for the Arts in 1988.

Interviewer: The character Elinor appears in both your first and second novels, *Fire in the Morning* (1948) and *This Crooked Way* (1952.) I feel she represents certain aspects of your own personality. How do you feel about that?

Spencer: I saw her objectively, not as myself. However, several people said the same thing you did. I wanted at first in the second book to give her a new life, a better marriage, etc. But her family's story fascinated me. I felt I knew it already, so I wrote that. Actually, I was intrigued by a story of her own family that she (an outsider) came out with at the Gerrard dinner table. About how her father got his plantation and who her mother had been, and so forth. She told it to "put down" a rather slick Yankee type who was talking of the South in stereotype, *Gone with the Wind,* terms. When casting about for a subject, I thought I would follow that, explore it, see where it led me. My own family had always been in the hills, but close to the Delta, and I knew a lot of stories, a lot of lives.

Interviewer: The town of Tarsus in the one novel and the town of Lacey in the other seem the same.

Spencer: Hmmm . . . The geographical lay-out of both is close to that of Carrollton, Mississippi, my hometown, it's true. I intended just about everybody as fictional. But some maps get engraved on your soul.

Interviewer: I've always felt your novel *The Voice at the Back Door* (1956) would have concluded perfectly with the words, "You just can't tell," in the last chapter before the "Epilogue." That ends on just the right note of hope for improvement in racial relations. Isn't the "Epilogue" anticlimactic?

Spencer: *(Thoughtfully.)* Well, no . . . I still see it as a necessary part of the book. Maybe it goes on a little too long? The book was about all of them, you see: Duncan was no more its main character than Jimmy Tallant or Beck, Tinker no more than Marcia Mae or Lucy. They had all been affected by the events lived through and had to be seen as coping in the future with what was now their past. I also had to have the part about Cissie being fully conscious of what she had done and not giving a damn. Cissie is the Southern Bitch, totally self-confident, entirely self-assured. Someone else, however, also told me the book should have ended just where you said. But to me it is right.

Interviewer: Wasn't William Goyen your editor for *No Place for an Angel* (1967) and *The Snare* (1972)?

Spencer: Yes. It was a wonderful surprise when Bill came to McGraw-Hill as editor. I had been stuck for somebody to work with, as there had been certain departures. Yet they wanted to continue to bring out my work. Bill was a fine writer, as you know—I admire *The House of Breath* enormously—and he helped me get going again after some personal upsets, hangups, whatever. He got enthusiastic about *No Place for an Angel,* and really worked with me on it. Our only trouble was that, both being writers, we would go into spasms of fictional excitement at the same time. Bill's wife, the actress Doris Roberts, is a level-headed girl, and she had a wonderful knack for bringing us both back to earth. Bill also helped get the story collection, *Ship Island* (1968) together. I had a very happy time working with him. He also read one early version of *The Snare* but he left publishing to do his own writing full-time before it was completed. He did, I think, make some valuable suggestions. It's probably my most under-rated book.

Interviewer: Both *The Snare* and *The Salt Line* (1984) seem built upon fascination with the underworld—criminals and countercultures not found elsewhere in your work.

Spencer: Actually, as far back as *The Voice at the Back Door* I had a group of crooks running a gambling syndicate come up to put some capital in a small-town highway operation. I had fun writing about these people who seem, in addition to everything wrong and shady, rather funny. In *The Snare* the sinister gang is much worse. They are perverted, dirty, depraved and altogether despicable. I don't try to point out morals, but I think here that it wasn't necessary. Marnie and Wilma were simply ghastly examples of humanity. They were not even clever or amusing.

In *The Salt Line,* Frank Matteo started out originally to be a little like this, but I saw as he came to life for me that he wasn't all that low. About this time I had access to a lot of material given to me by a friend who is a reporter and had done extensive interviews with certain Mafia types. This gave me ground to move in, as I could see the wide spectrum of types, each was an individual story, the good within the bad which, of all things, strikes me as most touching, as though the good struggles to live and is always being slapped down. Frank had something of this struggle internally, and though the book is not his story, at least that good is not extinguished in the end.

Interviewer: That whole novel seems to be about crossing certain borders and boundaries.

Spencer: The idea occurs and recurs. First, the beginning idea is in the title, but before that it was in my experience. The salt line is a liberating point between the restrictive side of living in small-town Protestant Mississippi and the tolerant attitudes of the coast. In the novel, however, Arnie comes there to cut himself off from the wounding experience of being turned out of his university, to start a new life. And Lex, his nemesis, comes there to score in a materialistic sense, to set himself up in the world. A doom waits for both, but Arnie accepts and converts his doom into a continuance, a life acceptance and Lex—well, it's all in the novel. There is also the crossing to the island, which represents a mystical stepping-up of the Coast experience. There are other ramifications.

Interviewer: This novel marks a departure for you, doesn't it, in that the two protagonists are men? Your recent novels seem to be about women.

Spencer: I found it very difficult to write a story mainly involving men. The central character I saw early on would have to be male, but I had envisaged him as mainly relating to a number of women. Actually he does, if you notice. There are more women than men, or at least as many, in *The Salt Line:* Evelyn, Mavis, Dorothy, Lucinda, Barbra-K. But for some reason the males do dominate the story. One person I didn't particularly welcome in the book was Lex. But once he got into it, I couldn't get rid of him, so I had to make the best of him. My idea is that stories are found, not invented. Having found this story, I had to write it the best I could. Maybe it should have been found by someone else, by a man, rather than a woman. But it wasn't.

Interviewer: Is this novel a glorification of past events, of "the Old South"?

Spencer: One title I thought of for the book was *After the Storm,* or *Wake of the Storm.* Central to my idea was a very American syndrome, the passing of the days of glory. American society does throw people at times into great heroic relief, then events move on and they are dropped, forgotten. They are bound to remember. Memory could become a sort of life in itself, but Arnie knows you have to move on. Evelyn is in counterpoint to this theme, for though she has crossed a boundary—she died—she too is not confined to the past, when she appears it is not to take life back, but to urge it forward. The notion is that the dead continue, not as the past, but continue to live.

I question your phrase, "the Old South." Arnie is not trying to renew the Old South in the meaning it always gives to Confederate ideas. The feeling of life along the Coast was never that. The Coast as I see it related to the Gulf, the Caribbean, Mexico and New Orleans. It does not turn inward, though wars and histories always turn up in its experience. A certain atmosphere, built up through the years, relating to its flora and fauna, traditions and architecture, made it the unique place that it was. This uniqueness is not "Old South" so much as personal. Arnie does not want this entirely obliterated in the storm's wake by new building on the current order. He has, I think, the admirable, correct idea that renewing himself can't be done directly, only indirectly by giving himself to something he can believe in. The novel is about personal renewal, but with the realization central to it.

Interviewer: There seem to be a number of storms in your novels. Do they have any particular symbolic meaning for you?

Spencer: I don't know if my fascination with storms is "symbolic." If you have to live through a brisk hurricane or tornado season, you will probably forget all about symbols before it is over. The house in Carrollton, where I was brought up, was on a hill and we had many violent storms in that place. The effects of cloud and light were fantastic, beautiful and terrifying at once. We never had a direct hit with a tornado, but many people in the Delta nearby had experienced them. I was once in a hurricane in Charleston, South Carolina. The experience I had with Camille was that it destroyed a much-loved place, but only a year after it did I see what its intensity had been when I went to the Coast to do a reading at a college. The effects of what I saw would not leave me.

As for symbols, I think storms often express inner tension which my characters may be feeling. That happened in *The Voice at the Back Door,* when Kerney was suffering guilt after Duncan's death. But not all are like that. In one place I think I relate the hurricane, its shaping and approach and striking, to the cancer which Evelyn had. Both are natural destructive forces. People deal as best they can with such things.

Interviewer: Did you have Shakespeare's *The Tempest* in mind when you wrote *The Salt Line?* There seem to be parallels.

Spencer: Oh yes, *The Tempest!* There are certainly enough feelings about that floating around. The island has a mystical sense to it, and visions there are possible. It is more in feeling than in literal parallels that it gets through. Arnie is in a way a benevolent spirit, like you might think of in connection with Prospero. I think he possibly has some mystical powers. A good deal of that feeling also came from the logs of an artist—a very fine one—called Walter Anderson, who lived on the Coast and constantly went out alone to paint nature on Horn Island. His vision was directed toward the actual natural life he found, yet he was profoundly mystical as his work shows. There are a lot of moon references, too—in relation to the women, but it is not all worked out as some might have done.

Interviewer: Let's talk about your latest book, *Jack of Diamonds*

(1988). It seems to me the themes of the stories are very interrelated. Taken as a whole it is one of your strongest books. Were you consciously writing variations on a theme?

Spencer: The stories were written over a period of about seven years, and I worked on other projects during that time, too. I wasn't conscious of a common theme while I was writing them, they're not inter-related as to character and setting. But when I look back I see there is a related theme. Perhaps it is mystery in close relationships. All the main characters in these five long stories are women, and each has a relationship in which important matters are concealed.

I don't think this is an unusual preoccupation. It only means that in every real—or intense and highly important—relationship, complete openness cannot exist. There is always something mysterious and illusive about "the other." I have dramatized this in various ways in the stories, without consciously trying to do so. Only in the last one, "The Skater," is the search a different thing. I think there, the main character Sarah seems to be searching for a hidden truth first in her lover, then in the young man Goss, but she is really searching for the true nature of herself.

Interviewer: In "Jean-Pierre," on one level, the story seems about what the French went through in Montreal, in the quest for assimilation. But on another, it seems to be about one's inability to understand others. Callie's husband seems especially inscrutable and mysterious. Did your own marriage to a citizen of another country [Englishman John Rusher] in any way help formulate the theme of this story? Or was it all those years you lived in Montreal among the French-Canadians?

Spencer: This story really is about mystery compounded by the deliberate effort of French-Canadians to insist on their separateness. They did not seek, but resisted, assimilation. Callie and Jean-Pierre relate on the level of passion, but he seems from all indication to be in mortal fear of the judgment of the English business community. His side of the story—why he left so strangely—would be very different, I think, from hers. The strain this places upon her is what makes the story work.

As for my husband being English, this does at times present interesting points of contrast in our ways of doing things, our attitudes, and so forth. But the real source of this story was the Québecois.

Interviewer: In "The Business Venture," Nelle seems under the impression she can lead her own life the way she wants to in this day and age. But given the social milieu of her southern town, can she?

Spencer: Nelle had reached the point of seeing her own life as her "crowd" with whom she had been identified for so long. She knew she had to be practical, and following along from one practical point to another, in order to make the business go, she stepped over a lot of lines. But she was superior—of a better family socially than the rest, and perhaps too she had the confidence of the innocent. It's really Eileen's story, not Nelle's—the mystery of Charlie that Nelle is able (all so innocently, just by being there) to make plain. Once the mystery is gone, Eileen sees the plain truth, and her illusion about him goes, too.

Interviewer: In this story, the outsiders are not the French among the Canadians, but rather the blacks, pro-blacks, and non-society figures in the New South. It is the mind of the blacks whom the whites cannot comprehend despite their apparent "loyalty."

Spencer: This is a very old state of affairs. It does figure in this story, because Nelle has evidently been successful in uniting herself to black "loyalty" while the others are uncertain outsiders to it.

Interviewer: Again, in the title story, "Jack of Diamonds," the daughter discovers she hasn't understood the nature of her parents' marriage, or her father; and in "The Cousins," there is an ambiguity of emotions between the cousins, and Ella Mason's inability to decipher the true nature of Eric.

Spencer: I don't doubt the cousins all loved each other, in a family-related sort of way. But thrown into more intimate relationships as they were on their journey abroad, they began to run into mysteries. I look on the triad of Ben-Ella Mason-Eric as being the essential one. She seems to love them equally until she and Eric are thrown together, while Eric is a long suspension of both trying to be like Ben and to be separated from him. When Ben throws the burden of Eric's departure squarely on Ella Mason, she feels she has to go and find him. This was a breakthrough of sorts, but very late, possibly too late, to recover what was there for them both.

Incidentally, everywhere I go people tell me they love "The Cousins." I don't know why—maybe it's because all families have this sort of mystery hanging about them?

As for "Jack of Diamonds," the girl really had all the materials at

hand to know that her mother's state of mind must have contributed
to her fatal accident, but she hid it from herself. It was again her love
that made her not want to face the truth in things. But the discovery
of her father's former relationship with Eva made her inner evasion
no longer possible.

Interviewer: The final story, "The Skater," seems to be about
attachments—to children, mates, lovers, the past. Yet the heroine
seems at a loss without her children, who are grown, and her
husband, who has grown distant. Would you say the young man
Goss is a son-figure more than a potential lover?

Spencer: Sarah seems to be seeking her own nature in her
relationships with Goss and Karl. Many threads tie her to Goss,
among them, their both being Canadian, both having residence in
Westmount. They also both have Ted, her husband, in common, and
have tried together to figure out the old father figure. Goss wants to
be adopted, she wants to adopt. She will skate in wider circles now,
with more confidence.

Interviewer: *The Light in the Piazza* has been the book of yours
which is the public's favorite. Do you have a personal favorite?

Spencer: I often think *This Crooked Way* is my favorite book,
though the writing is not so mature or sustained as in others, like, say,
The Voice at the Back Door. It did have original, deeply-felt ground
to explore. It was something I don't think Faulkner—giving his
awesome genius every due—ever touched on, and when Flannery
O'Connor came along, her strict Roman Catholic point-of-view
prevented her seeing it, to my mind, as it was. But this was before
she started publishing. The religious fervor of the willful, ego-
centered man, his sense of a personal god-mission, the way he took
to express it, the way it took him, the myth of it and the ritualistic
resolution . . . this holds me still as being rendered in an accurate
way, despite stylistic flaws.

Interviewer: And your favorite of your own stories?

Spencer: I don't know. I like "Ship Island" very much. It was
misunderstood by a lot of people, the way *Knights & Dragons* (1956)
and *No Place for an Angel* were misunderstood. But it still stays with
me for some reason, I'm not sure I know why. Perhaps because I
always gravitated toward the Gulf Coast. I also like "The Finder,"
"Indian Summer," "Prelude to a Parking Lot," and "The Girl Who

Loved Horses"—four long stories which I consider to be among my best work.

Interviewer: Who among your contemporaries do you enjoy reading?

Spencer: Well, Eudora Welty, and Katherine Anne Porter—I guess she's still "contemporary"—I love *Pale Horse, Pale Rider.* Then there are John Cheever's stories, Walker Percy's *The Last Gentleman,* and Joyce Carol Oates's stories—I haven't read them all, but want to. And on and on . . .

Interviewer: You recently moved from Montreal to North Carolina. Has that move affected your writing in any tangible way?

Spencer: I moved in June 1986. Nothing so far to report. Currently I'm finishing a novel called *The Night Travellers.* It's partly set in Canada, during the exile of American draft-defectors there, during the Vietnam mess. In the Jamesian sense, I guess it's "an international novel." It's now about finished except for some final revisions, and should be out next year.

The South and Beyond: A Conversation with Elizabeth Spencer

Peggy Whitman Prenshaw/1990

This previously unpublished interview with Elizabeth Spencer took place on 20 and 22 April 1990, at her home in Chapel Hill, North Carolina.

Prenshaw: I'd like to begin by asking about your decision to live again in the South. What effect has your coming back to the South, to Chapel Hill, had on your work?

Spencer: I don't know. I had a good deal of work in progress when I left Montreal. One is the novel I am still working on now. I also had the play script underway with the University of North Carolina PlayMakers. When they decided to produce the play, I put aside the novel. When we first came to Chapel Hill in the middle of 1986, I was busy getting settled. The *Jack of Diamonds* stories were put under contract about that time. I didn't have much more work to do on the stories—rewrites of one or two paragraphs in the final story, "The Skater." There was also the question of my agent's finding the best publisher. We weren't too happy with Doubleday, and we went on to Viking.

I did intensive work on the play with artistic director David Hammond in the summer of 1987 just before you, Jim Seay and I and others went to Russia. I also worked on the novel in the spring and early summer of '87. I did a lot of background reading for it because it's set late in the 1960s, and I had sort of lost contact with my feelings that were connected with the sixties, a time when we were living in Canada. I picked up serious work on the novel the fall of '87 and then later on after I got back from Russia. I had to teach again in the spring of '88. The play, which was put on in 1989, took a lot of time, though it was quite a successful production and I'm glad I did it. So since moving here, my work has jumped from one thing to another. Whether that would have happened elsewhere, I don't know.

Several production companies in Canada had been interested in this play, but it was hard to think of raising money to support the production of a play laid exclusively in Mississippi and dealing with Mississippi society. In the first place, when we gave several reading performances of it with actors, just sitting around the table and reading the script, they decided they wouldn't even attempt the accent. They said, "We'll certainly make a botch of it." When they wanted to hear a Mississippi accent, they asked me to get up and say a few words.

Prenshaw: They asked you to give them a model?

Spencer: I was the authority on Mississippi accents. Earlier a little country theater out from Montreal had presented Beth Henley's *Crimes of the Heart* and had called up out of nowhere and asked me to read a few speeches aloud so they could tape them for the cast.

Prenshaw: Did you compose the play while you were still living in Montreal?

Spencer: Oh yes, but when it was given a reading performance here, David Hammond, PlayMakers' artistic director, said that I had enough material for four and-a-half hours of action. I didn't realize when I wrote it how much time a scene takes on stage—I'm a bad judge of time. But David, who is a real pro—I've never worked with anyone so expert in the theater—liked the language, liked the characters and the situation. So nothing changed in the rewriting except pruning and shaping and dealing with entrances and exits. We did eliminate one character. Certain scenes we must have rewritten a hundred times to get them just right.

Prenshaw: Do you think you will write other plays?

Spencer: I would like to. I had a thrilling time with that one.

Prenshaw: Would you be interested in dramatizing any of the fiction? Would you revisit material that you've already worked with?

Spencer: It doesn't interest me to go back and do in another form something I've already done the best I can. If other people want to dramatize my work, as they did in *The Light in the Piazza*, it's O.K. I would be glad to help them.

Prenshaw: I would like very much to see a movie or play of *The Snare*. I think that would be a terrific drama.

Spencer: It was very attractive at one time to an agent and to the actress Trish Van Devere. But, according to my agent, her husband, George C. Scott, nixed it for some reason. That was soon after it came out. I thought it would make a good movie, too.

Prenshaw: You said you were revisiting the fifties and sixties. I thought *No Place for an Angel* very fully caught the mood and sense of drift of the 1950s and '60s.

Spencer: That was the Eisenhower era, a period of post-war corruption. I think of it as a time of emptiness or vacancy. This period of the new novel is a different thing. It looks at rebellions that set in as a consequence, I think, of those empty, vacant people. There was the rebellion of youth that was heightened and dramatized by the Vietnam War, objections to the Vietnam War. Many of those young people came to Canada and, though we did not know them well, we did know that they were present in Canada with all their objections to what was going on in the States.

I had thought of this novel of a young southern couple, actually from North Carolina, but I had no idea at the time that I would be living in North Carolina. After I moved to Chapel Hill, I went back and expanded the young woman's North Carolina background, adding details that would have been part of her life and have made her make her choices. Since moving here, I've expanded that part of the book. Instead of about twenty pages getting them to Canada, there are now about 150 pages.

Prenshaw: Aside from specific details that would be clearly different from Mississippi, do you find the family traditions, politics, religion and values of North Carolina like that of Mississippi?

Spencer: Well, if I have a choice about things and I'm dealing with the South, I avoid Mississippi. One reason is that, being brought up there, in a way I know too much about it. I want the setting in the new novel to be generally southern without being specifically related to a certain place or tradition. The people could have been from Mississippi. The young man in this case is from south Louisiana, which brings me closer to home. But it's southern in a general way. Of course, most of the people in *No Place for an Angel* weren't Mississippians. I think the artist was from the coast; Catherine was from Texas.

Prenshaw: Jerry Sasser, I remember, was also from Texas. The Blood Union of Messiah's Brotherhood, that whole crazy religion that was a part of Jerry's background, seemed extremely southern. I think of fundamentalism as being typical of Mississippi, but, of course, North Carolina is the more prominent home of the large, media-dominated fundamentalist groups.

Spencer: Yes, North Carolina has always been associated in my mind with religion because I was brought up a strict Presbyterian and we thought of Montreat as the center of the Southern Presbyterian Church. Also, there are meeting centers for the Baptists and Methodists up this way. I think the deep South got so hot that the preachers were glad to get away from the heat—their congregations would send them up here to let them get cool.

Prenshaw: Would you talk about *Jack of Diamonds,* your most recent collection? There are stories set in Canada, but there are also two rich, long stories with southern characters, "The Cousins" and "The Business Venture." What was the central impression that gave you the story, "The Cousins?"

Spencer: I was doing a writing stint at the Villa Serbelloni at Lake Como in Italy. I had thought before I went, "What am I going to write?" *The Salt Line* had just come out, and I had recently sold the story "Jean-Pierre" to the *New Yorker.* I had fragments of "The Business Venture" and parts of "Jack of Diamonds."

Being in Italy started the juices flowing again about Italy. I thought, as I did in writing *The Light in the Piazza,* about how to bring together the two concepts that are the strongest in my life—the South and Italy. I thought, well, let the characters take a trip. And remembering how much my own cousins have meant to me throughout the years, I invented all these cousins, although I set them in Alabama instead of Mississippi. I do have a cousin Jamie, who insists that he might have been part of the model for that guy.

Prenshaw: Was he Jamie in the story?

Spencer: Well, he's tall and skinny and that's about all. All of this was sheer invention. The more I kept thinking about them and hearing them talk and feeling about them and their relationships to each other and people I've known like that, the more it occurred to me that the intellectual southerner has never been done very well. Of course, Quentin Compson, who was mixed up terribly, suicidal because of the family situation, was highly intellectual. But who in literature has written about upper class, well-read southerners? I don't mean upper class in the sense of some fake aristocracy that hangs around, but really upper class, good homes and all. There are—and have been— a great many southerners like that.

Prenshaw: *Lanterns on the Levee,* I suppose.

Spencer: Right, interesting literature springs out of these kinds of people who have an interest in literature. I was thinking along those lines when I invented Ben and Eric.

Prenshaw: Didn't you have such a character in Randall Gibson in *Fire in the Morning?*

Spencer: Oh yes, though he was a heavy drinker.

Prenshaw: He was educated, and he had some of the same qualities of Ben and Eric.

Spencer: Yes, you're right. But thinking of my childhood, of friends and relatives somewhat older than I was, I remember a cousin who was writing poetry in the big house up the street from the time I was an admiring little girl. I guess he would have been a leading American poet, but during World War II he was the kind of person being sent off to intensive language school and he was tapped to go for Japanese language training. They took the very highest IQs for that, and he was sent off to Boulder or Denver, I forget which. He was led from there into a whole preoccupation with Japanese culture. He has spent years of his life in Japan. He became a lecturer on Japan and Oriental studies. There was the loss of a poet but the gaining of a scholar.

Prenshaw: Did the family feel that he was somehow lost to them?

Spencer: Oh no. I think it was expected that he was going to do something important intellectually somewhere, but certainly not in Carrollton, Mississippi. He went to Ole Miss for a time and he might have wound up teaching.

Other people that my brother knew, or knew of, I used to end up meeting and dating. My brother wasn't particularly interested in intellectual things, but he talked books and was interested in literature. The war interrupted a whole lot of those contacts and scattered people. I think all around these little southern towns there were always people who were very well read.

Prenshaw: There is a good deal of scholarship going on now about the intellectual traditions in the South.

Spencer: Can you think of very much fiction that's dealt with southern intellectuals?

Prenshaw: Walker Percy comes to mind. Among the Agrarians, it seemed that it was precisely the combination of a classical education and the love of the land that was so admired.

Spencer: Yes, but did they write about it? I think in *All the King's Men,* for instance, there are some highly educated people. Nevertheless, I had the illusion of tapping into a fairly uncharted social, intellectual area when I started out with Ella and Eric. What better position for the teller to be in than the admiring cousin, you know, one who could never get in first place with either cousin romantically, which is what she wanted? She could only listen. She's really in a kind of halfway comical situation because she's an attractive girl who isn't satisfied with the conversation of the other boys she has been dating but who is thought of by the cousins more as a sister. She had a tough go of it. The other two characters, I thought, were really wonderful. Mayfred and Jamie. There they were—they just kind of came forward and volunteered. They were very real and so I just started writing about them. I thought about setting the trip to Europe in an earlier time because boat trips are binding for the people involved. I drew upon a lot of memories. When I had the Guggenheim in the fifties, that was how you went to Italy. It was kind of refreshing to look back. I don't know much about the Italian scene now, or the French, what you would feel and experience as a young person going there now.

Prenshaw: I was particularly interested in the way you handled the voice, the first person consciousness. At the conclusion of that story, Ella and Eric are sitting on the terrace and she suddenly speaks of the two of them as if she moves outside her own story. In the line, "We are sitting there," you used the word "there," not "here," which is quite jolting. Ella suddenly transforms her entire experience into a self-conscious story.

Spencer: I don't know why I did that; it was just instinct, I guess. I wrote that ending several times. I wrote of her leaving to go and meet her son. That wasn't it either, because, in a way, as she says, she and Eric were always together anyway in a certain kind of resurrection of memory. It's almost like a fantasy that she goes back at all. Somebody said, "Did she really go back, or is she just imagining that trip?" I guess that one word would make you leave that open.

Prenshaw: The word "there" suddenly fictionalized the entire action, as if Ella were indicating her awareness of being the maker of the story.

Spencer: I didn't think of that. But if it works, I'm glad.

Prenshaw: I'd also like to ask about the relationships that seem in a way to be parallel in "The Business Venture" and "The Cousins."

Spencer: Well, they are certainly a different class of people. I think in "The Cousins" there's a certain innocence about them that's kind of refreshing. These guys in "The Business Venture" seemed to me to have gone through all the tricks you could do. There was a certain strain of corruption.

Prenshaw: Yes, but the connectedness that they claim to feel and that they so deliberately cultivate suggests they share something—perhaps an illusion of connection, perhaps desperation. Both groups had to devote such energy to maintaining the group.

"The Business Venture," which takes place in a small town, reminds me in some respects of "First Dark." That earlier story you set in Richton, Mississippi, but you may not have had in mind the actual Richton.

Spencer: I didn't. That was a mistake, pure and simple. I didn't know there was a Richton. I wrote that story in Canada. I thought of Ridgeland, a town a little too near Jackson to be that particular town. I had in mind someone's driving from Jackson on weekends.

Prenshaw: There is a Richton, though, near Hattiesburg.

Spencer: That would have been all right, then. But no sooner did the story appear in the *New Yorker* than here comes a letter that's postmarked "Richton." I thought, "Oh my god, I've had it. Someone is suing me." It was from Daisy Stevens, an old schoolmate, who asked, "How did you happen to choose our town to write your story about?" She was just being very friendly.

Actually, that story could have been set in Carrollton, like so many of my books, because there's a ghost that hangs around Carrollton. There were many, many stories like that, back in the days before paved highways. We lived on dirt roads and gullies and there was a lot of dust at night, as well as daytime. You don't remember.

Prenshaw: I certainly do. The road graders would go out once a month.

Spencer: In approaches to the town coming from Greenwood there was a ghost that would hang around and catch rides with people. In the story the only real person is the ghost, as I always say.

Prenshaw: There are ghosts throughout *Jack of Diamonds.*

Spencer: Oh yes. In the story "Jack of Diamonds," the mother's coming back.

Prenshaw: And in "The Skater" there's a recurring presence, and there's a mystery surrounding Callie and Jean-Pierre. In some ways, it seems you've carried your interest in mysterious women even further in these stories than you had done with some of the earlier characters. Would you talk about Callie and that mirage-like scene in the quarry?

Spencer: That came about in a strange way. I had written half that story and didn't know how to end it, and I just shelved it. A friend asked us down to Burlington, Vermont, one summer, and we drove cross country. One day we went to a picnic in this quarry—it was a startling kind of scene. The pool was bigger than the one I described. Of course, there are quarries all over Vermont. That's where we got all of our Confederate War statues. They're startling, dramatic looking places. I shaped that part of the story after that experience.

Prenshaw: I remember the scene in *No Place for an Angel* in which there was a visit to a quarry. Might there be some link between those images, those characters?

Spencer: I don't think I ever made love in a quarry! As I recall, the Greeks attacked those people, captured them in droves and put them there and starved them to death.

Prenshaw: I don't suppose that's what you want for a love scene.

Spencer: Oh yes, it was. It seems terribly exotic. Don't you remember, they said the vegetation grew out of the bodies?

It was very strange because that is the dry part of Sicily. You go there and the ground slopes down and you enter a pit-like place where there's all this lush growth. . . . It's like the furthest reaching of what you can experience.

Prenshaw: In your fiction one of the most persistent and fully realized attributes of human nature is the mystery of character. In some cases, like Dev in *The Snare* or Gordon Ingram in *Knights and Dragons,* the characters are not only mysterious but vivid and looming. But in the case of the female protagonists, there is just an overriding sense of mystery. In the most recent group of stories, to come back to "Jean Pierre," Callie seems such a character.

Spencer: Well, she's very stubborn. I didn't think Callie was very mysterious. I think the whole key to that story is very plainly sexual. They just had this singular and completely passionate relationship—a strong center to the whole. I don't know whether he stayed or not; I would think maybe he did. The other aspect of the story that operates against their relationship is the very strong social, political background of the French-Canadians and the English. He was afraid of being judged by the business community, but when she turned out to be loyal, as I think she did, it seemed to me that they had a chance.

Prenshaw: She was loyal, but there was something about her that was held in—stubborn and rebellious, but also something insistently withheld. She resembled Mavis in *The Salt Line* in that respect.

Spencer: Well, perhaps. Mavis and Frank Matteo both struck me as having a comical side to them. Some people have said to me that that novel has a happy ending. I don't know whether it does have or not—I just thought those people had a chance at that point.

Prenshaw: All of the stories in the new collection seem to offer some promise of happiness to come, but they are extremely open-ended.

Spencer: A friend of mine wrote me about "The Cousins" that he didn't think the ending was depressing at all because he felt they had a chance to get back together. But the sad part of "The Cousins" to me is that they missed the whole life span. When she says, "Midnight struck long ago, and we know it," I think that is very down beat. But, on the other hand, there they are—still.

Prenshaw: There is a spirit in her and in Eileen Waybridge in "The Business Venture" that's related to Marilee. A real gutsy, take-life-as-it-comes woman.

Spencer: That's right. I like her—those women have a strong spirit and thrive on life, I think.

Prenshaw: If you had written "Jack of Diamonds" from Eva's point of view, we might have another such protagonist. Instead, you give us Rosalind.

Spencer: That story is Eudora's favorite in the book.

Prenshaw: It's a wonderful story, with hints of Welty's *The Robber Bridegroom,* Shakespeare, Cinderella, and a host of other fairy tales.

Spencer: I cut a good deal out of it—the theatrical association and an old buddy of her father's who used to recite Shakespeare.

The whole idea of Rosalind and Shakespeare and everything—I just had to cut it. That story sprang from one day in New York in Central Park—from seeing those apartments overlooking Central Park, which always seem to me rather intriguing.

We used to go down to Lake George a lot, where we knew a woman from New York who visited a friend with a cabin like the one I described in the story. It was beautiful—when you were in the living room you would think you were in a house on the water. And the lake was very clear.

That's a mysterious part of the world. It used to give me very strong artistic feelings. I found out years later that Georgia O'Keefe painted there before she went west. She lived there with Alfred Stieglitz for a long time. John and I used to spend every Easter down there.

Prenshaw: The relationship between the older man and the younger woman, in this instance the father and his daughter, Rosalind, is such a difficult and contradictory one. In other works, such as *Knights and Dragons* and *The Snare,* you depict a relationship that's fatherly but destructive. Is there some inevitable link between an impulse to father and to destroy?

Spencer: I don't know. I never had a very good relationship with my father. There were a lot of comings and goings that sometimes had masked meanings, but he disapproved of me. I think he was very tyrannical in his ways. On the other hand, I had a fine relationship with my Uncle Joe.

Prenshaw: Would you talk a bit of your work as a teacher of writing? In Montreal, I remember, your class at Concordia University included an unusual young man, a very intense young man.

Spencer: He turned out to be one of my best friends. He wrote a weird novel that's based on a kind of satiric version of a guide book, *A Guide to Crocodilium.* It's about a tourist that visits a strange little republic that is run by crocodiles. It is a fantasia of images and word play—really brilliant. I tried my best to have it published, but the publishers didn't think they could make money on it.

Prenshaw: Do you have other students who have published novels?

Spencer: Oh, yes, several of them. There was a young woman in Montreal by the name of Sharon Sparling. She did a brilliant first novel about a runaway girl—*The Glass Mountain*—which was published in England and the States. Then, another student of mine, Scott Lawrence, published a book of short stories. There have been others since.

Prenshaw: How do you conduct your writing seminars?

Spencer: We start out talking about writing and reading. Then I have them do very short things. The more advanced students in the master's program in Montreal started out by bringing in any piece of writing they had, whether it was a completed short story or not. Every time they did a story, they made copies and passed them around to everyone. That way, the whole class could join in and read parts of it and see what went wrong with this—and where. When they were at a loss for something to criticize or talk about on their own in the workshop, we could always fall back on technique—time sequence, structure, character development, good dialogue, such as that.

I always give my students a reading list to let them know what works I admire and why. I have a back-up reading list of texts on writing. *Understanding Fiction* is one I have used extensively. Critical tastes have expanded so much with the newer criticism like structuralism and deconstruction—all of which I don't know much about.

In Montreal I taught another seminar run in conjunction with the fiction writing seminar called "Techniques of Fiction." The first semester would be in the short story and the second semester in the novel. For that I made up very serious reading lists. The students were supposed to analyze stories from the standpoint of how the writer must have written them.

Prenshaw: Who are some of the writers you include on the reading list?

Spencer: The standard ones—Hemingway and Fitzgerald, and all the moderns up to the present time. We used to spend a good deal of time on people like Borges, who was having a vogue at that time because of the recent translations. There was some interesting Canadian short fiction. I tried to stay away from identifying with the southern writers. We would read many of the Russian and French and English writers—I tried to make it eclectic.

Prenshaw: Do you ever find in students' writings a clear indication that the student has come under the spell of one writer?

Spencer: Yes. I told them that was inevitably going to happen—
that they were going to sound like the person they most admired, but
just to go ahead and sound like that. They would feel themselves
becoming more individual through that experience. The boy in
Montreal who fascinated you was hooked on experimental writing.
He had a lot of good material about an immigrant family, such as his
own, who had come to Montreal during the Hungarian crisis in 1956.
There was a great influx of Hungarians during that time. I thought
that experience ought to make a good novel. A lot of people had
written about the French, but few had seen Canada as a real
immigrant experience. But he was hooked on James Joyce and
experimental writing.

Prenshaw: Let me ask you about the community of writers here
at Chapel Hill.

Spencer: Well, there is a huge writing community around here.
Louis Rubin has encouraged a lot of it with his Algonquin Books.
There's Clyde Edgerton. Lee Smith doesn't publish with Algonquin,
but she was a student of Louis's at Hollins. Jim Seay has done
poetry. There are Jill McCorkle and Kaye Gibbons. Also, there is Tim
McLaurin. And, of course, Reynolds Price is nearby.

Prenshaw: These writers have published a great many books in
recent years. Can the young writers just beginning still find
publishers? I am thinking of Louis Rubin's comments and how
difficult it is for fiction writers to find a publisher. The situation seems
to be exacerbated by the large corporation's buying up smaller
publishing businesses.

Spencer: There are very few publishers who are doing well.

Prenshaw: Recently I heard the most startling assertion—that the
largest concentration of publishing houses in the U.S. is in the South.
The speaker was talking of the publishers of religious books. She
claimed that the religious publishing businesses have drawn editors
and designers and other skilled professionals to the South, and that in
the future she expected more and more small, independent
publishing houses to be established in Tennessee or in the Atlanta
area by these professionals.

Spencer: Religious publishing is one form of the business that
keeps up a boom as long as there's a Bible Belt and all of the revival
people.

Prenshaw: Let me ask about the publication of the new novel. Will it be coming out soon?

Spencer: I don't know when it is coming out. I've got the first draft finished and am trying to get the rest of it done by the end of June. If so, it will come out in the spring of 1991. I'm over the deadline specified in the contract, but I understand that is not unusual with novelists.

They have re-issued the stories with a new cover.

Prenshaw: *The Stories of Elizabeth Spencer* is an extraordinary work.

Spencer: I was glad Doubleday brought out the collected stories, though I thought it was too puffy a book. I very much wanted *Knights and Dragons* to be in a collection that finally wound up being issued through Penguin—*The Light in the Piazza* and *Knights and Dragons.* I had wanted all of the stories of relatively common length for the one volume. It turned out that Doubleday wanted to make as puffy a book as they could, so they overruled me. I was glad to have the collection under contract so I let them do what they wanted, but I did think the novella had no place in the book.

Prenshaw: *Knights and Dragons* seems to be a book that has presented problems for you, beginning with the excessive cuts that were initially made. It is such a strange and compelling story, one that never leaves one's head.

Spencer: It presented problems in the publishing. I didn't want to publish it on its own after *The Light in the Piazza* because I thought people were going to be looking for another delicious little romance. As a matter of fact, that's what happened—the critics all jumped on it.

Prenshaw: It came out in *Redbook,* didn't it?

Spencer: Yes, in 1965. *Redbook* bought it and then they slashed it down so awfully that you couldn't tell what you were reading. Later the whole thing was restored as a novel, but it was still difficult for readers. It wasn't easy reading like *The Light in the Piazza.* It has a place, though; it extends what I was trying to do with the Italian scene and Americans abroad.

In the book you wrote about my work, a very good book, you didn't seem to think it fit in with the rest of the things I had done. I've forgotten just what wording you used—that it was outside of me.

Prenshaw: Perhaps in some ways it is more experimental and more lyrical and more subtle than your other work.

Spencer: Yes, it's more internalized than externalized.

Prenshaw: The character of Martha Ingram is connected in many ways with other characters you've created—like Maureen in "I, Maureen" and Julia Garrett in *The Snare*.

Would you talk a bit more of the novel you're working on?

Spencer: It is set in the 1960s and concerns the young people who wander up to Canada and how they got there. The central figure is a young girl who is just finding her way amongst all these forces that seem to be swirling around her. It is not that she is unintelligent, but she is not politically involved in the sense that the boy, who's later her husband, is. So she seems to me like so many people in this crazy world we live in who are heavily influenced by politics and forces they never invented and have no part in having devised, but whose lives are caught up in them. She is one of those.

Prenshaw: There is something about the intense political scene that's contagious. You do get drawn into it.

Spencer: He loses himself in the anti-war movement because of a teacher he had who more or less adopted him, a professor from Johns Hopkins who came back to North Carolina to teach but who had troubles connected with the civil defense agency he was part of for a time in Washington. In that job he learned about certain things that were going on in connection with events that brought on the Vietnam War. Because he knew too much, and didn't like what he knew, he got in bad odor and was let out of the bureaucratic job and so went back to teaching.

The boy, a very brilliant boy, becomes something of a protege. The teacher comes down to take a job at a city in North Carolina, lecturing at this branch of the University of North Carolina—also at another local college. The young man follows him and meets this girl who is not politically involved, though it's a match of great intensity, and other kinds of involvement. They both feel themselves to some extent to be outsiders—she's had problems within her own family. Gradually, notch by notch, they find themselves losing ties in the States and winding up in Montreal. He goes back to complete certain political missions, and she's left up there with a child and a chain of under-ground connections that, supposedly, will supply her with money.

I knew a lot about such arrangements from a friend in Montreal. She was a very free-thinking, left-wing person who used to hide money in her oven. When some representative of the anti-war movement came along and gave certain code words at her door—a proper Westmount, suburban neighborhood—she would go and pull the money out of the oven and give it to them. There was a chain of such people in Canada. I heard a great many stories. One friend told of a barn near a lake that supposedly was devoted to pottery making but was instead the site of a printing press that turned out anti-war fliers. There were a lot of these presses all around. Nobody knew about it, but that's what they were doing back there. They were making some pottery, but the main thing going was the press.

Prenshaw: There was the thought that such activity had to be kept hidden?

Spencer: It had to be kept hidden in the sense that the American authorities had a way of getting in with the RCMP and rooting out the people that they really wanted. You think that doesn't happen, but there are ways in which they encircle and surround and get what they want. Canadians were almost voiceless outsiders during that war, did you know that? They wouldn't even discuss it very much. I know that anti-war people weren't particularly welcome socially.

The Canadians were conservative by nature and, I suppose, thought if a country was at war, boys ought to go to it. Something like that was in their thinking. The anti-war people who were up there found jobs—a lot of them merged with Canadian society. Now, if you didn't know their history, you wouldn't know that they hadn't just come up there for ordinary reasons and gotten a job. There are an awful lot of them in the universities who later became Canadian citizens.

Prenshaw: I remember hearing that the universities put limits on the number of Americans who were allowed to hold university appointments.

Spencer: Yes. They thought their universities were being floated away on American talent. Educated Americans were applying for those jobs and getting them. It was thought that there should be some limits imposed.

Prenshaw: You wrote about the aftermath of the 1960s storm in *The Salt Line.* Does that period continue to intrigue you?

Spencer: Well, it does. As for this novel, it seems to me a natural subject for a person who knew a great deal about Canadian landscape and society but wasn't part of it. I just get subjects wherever I can.

I still think the sixties was a big turning point in American life. I think what I was trying to do in *No Place for an Angel,* maybe half consciously, was to find the emptiness, the vacuum that something had to happen in. With the 1960s, first came civil rights—and then a lot of the civil rights people went into the anti-war movement. That spirit was pervasive.

Prenshaw: I think I found the New England that Catherine Sasser finally ends up in a more satisfying and believable spiritual home than what Arnie Carrington found on the Gulf Coast.

Prenshaw: It seems to me that Arnie almost became like a spirit himself, more than a man with any stake in life for himself. It was as if he were a spiritual restorer, a person who gave himself, hoping other people could be happy. I do think that was the kind of thing he turned into, almost like a person who was inhabiting the coast spiritually. Catherine, too, came to a kind of peace in New England.

Prenshaw: I've never spent any time in New England.

Spencer: We loved it when we were in Montreal. It used to be a big break to go down in the States and some of those villages and towns were just fascinating for their own history and presence and personality. It was such a change. In Canada you find either a classy English style, or many French-Canadian stone villages each with their tin-roofed parish church. New England is very different.

Prenshaw: Earlier you were speaking of the new novel. Have you given it a title?

Spencer: I have a tentative title. It's called *The Night Travellers.* The characters have to spend so much of their time, not at night exactly, but as if they were moving underneath the surfaces of the ordinary life that's expected of them. Not criminals, but almost like outsiders beyond the realm of ordinary life.

I hope I will finish it soon because there are some other things I want to do. I may try to do another play sometimes.

Prenshaw: I'm eager to see *For Lease or Sale.* I'd like to read it, too.

Spencer: The play has four major characters—a mother and her son, his niece, who is her granddaughter, and a boyfriend. They are all in this house that has to be sold because it's too big, too rambling, too rundown for them to keep up any longer. It's "We go, we go, we go," but they never go. The son flirts along with his niece, who's totally devoted to him.

We had an excellent, very pretty actress from Off-Broadway in New York for the mother and this young actor for the son, very brilliant, who was a bit younger for the role than I'd envisioned.

Prenshaw: I understand that one of your stories will be in the new Signet Classic *Southern Short Story* collection that Dorothy Abbot is editing.

Spencer: I didn't really want "First Dark" chosen because I think it's been over-anthologized. I think many of my other stories measure up to that one, don't you?

Prenshaw: Oh yes. You know what I would have liked to see in it? "The Girl Who Loved Horses."

Spencer: Yes, I mentioned that story, but she said it might be appropriate for another collection that will come out later, covering a different time span. "First Dark" was published within her time span.

What story should I read at the Faulkner Festival?

Prenshaw: There is some wonderful dialogue in "The Cousins"— and there's Eileen's voice in "The Business Venture."

Spencer: That makes good reading; it's provocative. You think it is going to turn into a love affair between this black man and this white woman, and you never know, though I don't think they were lovers at all. But the story runs on the edge of whether they were or weren't.

Prenshaw: It's what keeps the whole community tense in the story.

At home last week, as I was walking toward the entrance of the mall, I passed a couple leaving—a white man and a black woman and their two children.

Spencer: In Hattiesburg?

Prenshaw: In Hattiesburg. I saw them walk to their car—there was an expanse of parking lot to walk across, and lots of people coming and going. No one stared at the couple, but you could see eyes registering "black and white." The couple didn't seem to me to be at all self-conscious. Of course, we've had mixed couples on campus for a good many years.

Spencer: I have three black students in my class this year—very bright students. I talk to them about when I was growing up, when southern writing was thus, thus and thus. But I try to keep out of all my conversations any reminiscence of black people I knew when I was a child because they were in the position then of being the servants. It is a road block—and I can't keep walking around subjects that spontaneously occur to me.

Prenshaw: Earlier I asked you about *No Place for an Angel,* which so fully caught the spirit of the fifties and sixties. Would you talk about how you see the world now, in comparison to where we were thirty years ago? You've recently been to the Soviet Union and you've followed the events over the last year in Eastern Europe. Do you sense some change in the world's spirit, or are we all just wishing for that?

Spencer: I don't know. I'm not a remarker on the world. I try to get hold of characters that seem to me to be involved in some way. During the years we were in Rome I began to know more and more people who were Americans abroad and talked about these things continually and lived a rather special experience in regard to politics and policy of the United States and all. In getting hold of the characters, I guess I gave the impression that I understood these things better than I do. I've just let the characters move ahead in their sphere of interests, which did often transect with all the business of the world. In exploring those, I think I discovered that I am also consciously exploring a period in our common experience. It works from the particular outward. I try to make as much fictional use of my sense of the times as I can, but just standing outside, without a character to guide me, I don't know what I could say about the present. It seems to me that the South has become less like the South I knew and grew up with, simply because of all the communication and the good roads and the sense of being a part of a new energy in the United States. At other times you run across things that seem purely southern.

Prenshaw: It feels to me as if there are two strong, contrary motifs at work. There is the globalization that we hear about, which exerts a strong pull against particularity and uniqueness, but at the same time people seem to be demanding more and more local participation and identification and sense of place. Maybe it is the sense of the nation that we are losing—what we'll have is the globe or our own back-yard. Perhaps it's the middle organization that's being eroded.

Spencer: It's so transitional. So many links in everything to other parts of the globe. At University Mall where I do all of my shopping, I've noticed some of the shops are closing or changing names and people are moving out. I was told that the Japanese own it now. It's my shopping place, and I've wondered where my shops are going. It's funny when the Japanese can reach out and control you.

I called my editor one day about a year ago and all of Viking was closed. The reason was that they were scared to death that the Moslems were going to bomb them because they had published Salman Rushdie. The last time I went to New York to go to Viking there were two guards downstairs at the elevator. One of them frisked me, and then they pinned a badge on me to show my name and who I was seeing. They were scared of somebody's coming in and blasting them to kingdom come. What does the Ayatollah, who was alive then, have to do with my life? In fact, nothing, but he was able to keep me from calling my editor one whole day. So many distant things now affect your day-to-day life.

Though I think, as we felt when we were in Russia, too much accumulation of information about people is a kind of safeguard in a way. We used to sit in the hotel in Moscow and talk about anything we wanted to, but mainly we were talking about Mississippi. Do you remember?

Prenshaw: Yes I do. Swapping stories.

Spencer: Every once in a while someone would point upward, as if there were a little microphone hidden in the light fixture. Undoubt-edly there was. But who is ever going to care what my mama said to someone down the street when I was a child? It would be so unimportant—and, anyway, they have too much to listen to.

Prenshaw: Exactly. The sheer volume of it is a protection.

Spencer: It seems to me it is, but people say I am naive. In fact, I've got a statement upstairs that informs me I can get somebody to research my record under the Freedom of Information Act. Somehow it just doesn't interest me.

Prenshaw: Do you think the record was kept because of your life abroad or because you are a writer?

Spencer: I don't know. It may not be anything, though I'm sure my phone was tapped while I was in Montreal. I had a friend who was married to a leading French economist who lectured at the University of Montreal. I had another friend who was highly placed in the international writers' organization, PEN. Every time I talked to either one of those two people, something would happen in the phone line. It would go "clunk," with an irritating effect. It wasn't loud, but it was clearly discernible. We joked, "There they go again. What are they going to hear?" I called the phone company to ask if my line was tapped and why. There was a rumor at that time that the RCMP people were cooperating with the CIA to check on thousands of people.

Prenshaw: One always thinks of Canada as having less of that paranoia.

Spencer: Well, maybe it was the Americans that started it. There were articles written about it later. But finally I got a call from the telephone company, asking me if I had made this complaint. I said, "I just asked the question." They said, "You won't be bothered any more." I said, "Well, why was I bothered in the first place?" They said, "You won't be bothered any more," and hung up. So I feel sure that I was tapped for some reason, but I don't know why.

I expected I might hear more of this when John and I were leaving Canada and collecting all our papers, visas and records through the consulate. Of course, you had to present police records and everything, which I expected to be perfectly clear for both of us, but sometimes things just get garbled. Nothing showed up. With all the records people have everywhere, you're liable to get cross-wired and turn out to be somebody else.

Prenshaw: One hears stories about that sort of thing. Speaking of papers, your manuscripts and literary papers, the early papers, are at the University of Kentucky. And more recently, you've placed your papers in Ottawa at the National Library of Canada?

Spencer: Yes. Some of the things at the University of Kentucky were there on deposit, and so they were placed in the collection in Canada. In addition, the University of Kentucky made copies of all the things they had. So Canada has a complete collection now.

Prenshaw: I'm sorry not to have those papers in the South.

Spencer: Charlotte Capers wrote from the Mississippi Archives. I told them I would dearly like to have my papers in Mississippi. I said, "Kentucky has them and you can purchase what Kentucky has, I'm sure." This was before my decision to place my papers in Canada. She wrote back and said, "We can't give you anything but love." I regret it, but you'd be surprised where people's papers wind up. Elizabeth Bowen's papers are at the University of Texas.

Prenshaw: Yes, I know. Well, we may not have your papers in the South, but luckily we have you now.

Thanks very much for the good conversation—and thanks even more for all the works of great fiction you've given us over the years.

A Whole Personality: Elizabeth Spencer
Terry Roberts/1990

This interview, previously unpublished, was conducted at Elizabeth Spencer's home in Chapel Hill, North Carolina, in three sessions: 16 August, 10 September, and 24 September, 1990.

Terry Roberts: Would you think aloud about the communities, large or small, of which you have been a part? What are the most important groups that you've belonged to in your life, starting perhaps with your family?

Elizabeth Spencer: There was a time when I was growing up when my father and I had a good relationship, but he was a hard man to know, and I gravitated more toward my mother and her relatives for a long time. The people I could relate to and talk to didn't often include the kind of people my father could like. He was always a business man, and business was a kind of undercurrent all the time—what could you do with things? Could you make some money out of things? I got early on to dislike that approach. There were people who didn't have that approach that I gravitated to, and I suppose I still do.

Then there was the closeness I felt with my mother's father, my grandfather, and with her brother, who ran the plantation, and his wife and on and on within the family when I was a child.

In school, I had haphazard relationships with people. There was a bunch of little girls I ran around with, but they never developed into lasting relationships because they had such different interests. I was singular in my little town group for having any interest in literature and the arts. Oh, we were buddies when we were playing tennis or climbing trees, but the whole idea of talking about books was rather boring to them, I guess.

But in the summer, I remember, we had a group of kids around, mainly boys, my cousins. My first cousins used to come there and visit all summer. My uncle and his wife were divorced, and they had two boys who spent the summer with their father, and he sent them to visit my mother and my father's brother. Then I had a cousin up

207

the street who was a very brilliant boy who wrote poetry and read
poetry a lot. There were good times when we were getting along
well, but then, you know, kids fight and so sometimes I was
miserable.

We had a stamp club, swapped and collected stamps. We held
meetings of the stamp club at different people's houses. The Holman
boys up the street were in on that.

There was one girl who moved early on in my life to a neighboring
town. Her father was a funeral director, and she was in the stamp
club and so was I. Sometimes in the winter I used to play with her,
but there again, it was the same thing that ruined my other relationships with girls I knew. Very early on they got interested in nothing
but boys, boys, boys. I was interested in boys too, but I had real
enthusiasms for books as well. I was shoved to one side as one of
these bookish youngsters. I didn't have much companionship.

When I went to college, I tried to be friendly with a lot of girls
there, but Belhaven College was a rather strict school. You had to
sign in and sign out if you had a date, and you couldn't go off
campus with a date until you were a junior, and then you had to have
a chaperone. So I kind of withdrew to myself except for the summers
when I was more free, withdrew into a sort of shell and hardly went
out with anybody. I didn't think that was a very natural way to meet
anybody.

I got to be very studious. I suppose I had a good deal of fun
because early on I was made editor of the school paper. That led to a
lot of activity with people working on the paper, and I got along all
right with them. I went to Belhaven for four years, which seemed like
an incarceration. A lot of people though were more skillful at
managing their lives there than I was. I always felt, again, that the
bookish side of my nature got too much emphasis there.

In the summers I used to have a good time, though I was sent off
in the summer a lot, and that was more of the same. I was sent to a
strict Presbyterian camp, and many of the same people would be
there as at Belhaven.

Oh yes, when I was at Belhaven, my brother was engaged for a
time to a girl from Pickens, which was right up the road from
Jackson. She used to have me up on weekends. She had a large,
talkative, energetic family, lots of brothers and sisters. They were

attractive people, and I had a good time with them. I began to see
when I was with them how I really wanted to live. I wanted to be
around a lot of attractive, talkative people.

TR: And have lots of brothers and sisters?

ES: Well, I was pretty much alone because my brother is seven
years older than I am, and he's often been sort of a bully toward me.
I don't know why. We were never very close.

Then I went off to Vanderbilt. I went during the Second World
War, and most of the guys who should've been there were off in the
service. There were a few very, very bright young men and women
around. That was the first time I really became all the way awake to a
lot of possibilities because these people were not only attractive and
conversant with everything around them but were also interested in
books and ideas. That gave me the idea that I hadn't been wasting
my time as *a whole personality.* That was the first time I didn't have
to suppress my interest in books for fear of being told, "Oh, you're so
smart!" Which is deadly socially.

There people actually liked women who were bright, so I found
myself taken up by first one person and then another as a different
sort of person because I had, if not a sheltered life, a life formed
outside their experience. I had, I guess, a sort of freshness, and I did
make some very good friendships there. I loved Nashville, I loved
studying there, and getting my degree there, though it was uphill
for me.

Then I taught for a year in Mississippi, and that was back to the
same sort of pattern. It was a junior college in Senatobia, Mississippi,
and I was expected to sponsor the paper, the annual, teach a Sunday
School class, and on and on. I was supposed to be an example of
lady-like behavior. Anyway, some of the students were really quite
bright.

There I met the daughter of the president—she was about my age
and in her first teaching job in a high school over in the Delta. She
would come home on weekends, and we became good friends. I
suppose she was the closest friend I ever had. We liked the same
kind of poetry and books, and we exchanged ideas an awful lot—
confidences, too, about men and all that. We began to write each
other, and she turned out for many years to be a very close friend.
We weren't in a group of any kind. We were a twosome. Two young

women with similar ideas and lots of thoughts and feelings about
Mississippi. You see, Mississippi was a big thing with both of us. We
were both from what were called "good" families in Mississippi with a
lot of kin, and certain things were expected of us. We were breaking
out of the mold of those expectations.

TR: Did you resent the burden of being thought "bright"?

ES: There used to be a saying in my mother's family—men are
afraid of women who are too smart. You musn't show that you're
smart. You musn't discuss things. You musn't ever make men or boys
feel that you're superior to them. They gave me all these formulas:
"So and so's attractive. They think she's dumb, but she's not." The
Southern Belle ideal was brought up all the time.

TR: When you were at Vanderbilt, was there any sense of a
community of younger and older scholars who were together
conscious of an intellectual tradition, say the Agrarian tradition? Or
was it rather that the professors, people like Donald Davidson, lived
in their world and the students lived in a different world?

ES: Some of the older grad students, especially the men who
weren't drafted, seemed close to the professors. There was, for
example, a man there from Mississippi named Scott George whom I
admired a lot. He was a married grad student who was just finishing
his Ph.D., and he, with a few other men, was a part of the professors'
circle. But as far as I was concerned, I was not invited to their homes
for anything. I suppose I must have seemed very young, and the girls
who were in that same boarding house where I was were equally not
included in professors' invitations. Everybody talked about these
brilliant professors we had teaching us, and the Agrarian theories
were very much discussed in our group, but for the most part they
were taken with much reservation. We didn't understand the
fanaticism. We understood the brilliant side of Donald Davidson and
regarded it highly, but his fanatical approach to the South we
resented in some ways. We had no desire to quarrel openly with any
of them, but we talked about these men all the time—talked about
their ideas and found them fascinating.

I can't think of anything that wasn't good for me about Vanderbilt.
I worked awfully hard getting my degree, particularly that one
summer that I worked on my thesis. We didn't have to take oral
exams for a master's; I was very, very shy in public at that time. I

could write good papers, but I hardly wanted to speak up in class at all.

After Vanderbilt there was Senatobia, as I said. I got back to Nashville by way of Ward-Belmont, which was also a girl's school and pretty cloistered, but at least it was *in Nashville*. And then I began working for the newspaper. All this time I was either visiting or receiving visits from Carolyn, the girl I met at Senatobia, and we exchanged a lot of letters. That was a continuing relationship.

I was writing all the time and sending stories out and hoping to get a break by publishing the stories and didn't. I had a little money saved up and so finally quit the newspaper and started writing my first novel, which turned out to be *Fire in the Morning*. During that time I continued to have good relationships with grad students at Vanderbilt; some of them who had been there while I was there came back. That bunch really saw me through the writing of the novel—I was either dating one of them or some of us would go out and have a beer together, and we had a continuing interest in each other. And there was one guy up there that I really was attached to for a while. It seemed a shame when it didn't work out because we had such a continuation of Vanderbilt interests. It continued for a long time, but it finally broke up before I went to Italy.

A lot of people did make very successful marriages who were from the same school and shared the same intellectual interests and acquaintances. That was one group that was very important to my life.

I got a job at Ole Miss after the book came out, and Carolyn was my deepest friendship. She got married in Germany. I went to Germany to see her in the summer of '49, and she was going out with this guy that she married soon after that summer. At Ole Miss there was a girl from Brownsville, Tennessee, who was fond of me. She was younger than I, but we used to run around together. She was dating one of of the young professors when I was first there, and that's how I met her. But our friendship didn't last too long.

I don't know; it's funny about friendships. You think they're terribly important—and they are when they're going on—because you need a sounding board for everything you have to confide about or trust somebody with. Trusting people is terribly important I think, though there aren't many people you can trust. Then when time and circumstance break up, when the *place* that holds the friendship together is gone, you find that lasting friendship is rare. But I'm older now. I used not to think in this way. It's just that I've seen it happen too many times.

TR: As you were talking, I was thinking of people who were the closest friends I could imagine having in high school and college, people whose personalities I would associate with the most fundamental things in my life. Now, except for a very few and on very rare occasions, I don't see them.

ES: You know, though, sometimes you think you've lost those things, but if you drift together, you might rediscover the same rhythms.

It is strange, though. Relationships are like plants. They come up and bloom for a while, and then they're gone. But it doesn't make me particularly sad anymore. It used to be heartbreaking. There are very few people who last in one's life. Now, at Ole Miss there was a couple whom we've kept up with over the years. Elizabeth Tillman Hamilton Willis and her husband, William. Her family used to live in Carrollton, and they moved the year before I was born. Their grandparents, the Tillmans, were friends of my grandparents. Her aunt was my mother's *best* friend. The only trip I ever remember my mother taking when I was a child was to Meridian, Mississippi, to see her old friends. When I was at Ole Miss, William Willis was the head of the classics department. One of the first calls I got at Ole Miss was from them asking me to come over. So there are three generations of friendships that have continued down to the present; we saw them last night in Durham. Also, the Blissard family in Jackson, Thomasina and her sister Frances. They date back to college days and have kept up our ties.

TR: Friendships as a still point in the turning world.

ES: Exactly. They have been important to us.

The first year I was in Italy, I was recovering from an operation. I wasn't very well, and I was trying to get back to my work. The social life in Rome at that time was all-consuming. There were a lot of literary people there, and I had very good letters of introduction to the director of the American Academy, and I met Alberto Moravia and went on trips with groups that included him. Rome was in a ferment at that time with these wonderfully placed and creative people. I met scores of writers and artists. But the partying was so intense you almost had to give up your work to meet the fascinating crowd. So I got frantic because I wasn't all that strong, and I couldn't keep up the pace of work, learning Italian, and party going. I know there are women who write novels who have three children screaming at them all the time, but my health at the time just wasn't up to the intensity. So I went up to Florence and took a room with a rather interesting Italian family, a contessa and her relatives, in order to learn the language. Through a friend I met Elizabeth Mann Borgese, who was very hospitable to many creative people who were in Italy then. She showed a great interest in them. She was Thomas Mann's daughter, and she had two little girls. She was the widow of a very prominent Italian critic, Antonio Borgese, an older man who had died. She had a villa outside Florence. There were also an Italian philosopher and his Swiss wife. Invitations and events! But for some reason this didn't bother me as much as it did in Rome because Florence is much more relaxed.

At the pensione where I was staying in Rome we had formed a fascinating group of people. There was a funny old widow from Texas who was very amusing. She had money and was living in Rome to avoid living a provincial life in the South. There was a historian, Garrett Mattingly, who became one of my best friends, and his wife. I used to visit them in New York. Then he was at work on a book entitled *The Armada*. At the time I met them, I was excited to be in this pretty little pensione. It was run by a Danish woman who had come to Rome when she was young and beautiful. She was an old lady by then, but she had come there after the first World War, as a tourist. An Italian man swept her away, and she survived, somehow, the Mussolini period and came to own this pensione. They were all interesting people there, but it was the Mattinglys who made the difference for me.

So there was a California antique dealer and his wife, the Klapperts, the funny widow from Texas, me, and the Mattinglys. We met every evening for drinks, talked about everything under the sun. And when I left to go up to Florence, pretty soon the Klapperts came up and began to ask me out. They apparently had a good deal of money. Then the Mattinglys came up too; he was doing research at that time on *The Armada*. He spent all this time in the great Italian

libraries—the Vatican, I suppose—and in Toledo, Madrid and
Seville. I kept up with him for years until he died. We had a
wonderful, lasting friendship, and even after he died, I tried to keep
up with his widow in New York, where eventually she ended up in a
retirement home.

Another important friendship I made at that time was with
Gertrude Hooker, a woman who worked at the U.S. cultural service.
When she retired, she came back to her home in Connecticut, and
we used to visit her often when we lived in Montreal. We still
exchange a lot of letters.

Then when I came back from Florence, there was John!

We were together an awful lot. He was friendly at the time with a
very attractive Italian-American who had come to Italy for the first
time to meet her relatives. We're still friends as well. She was in
Rome for a whole year when we were there, and she had a car—she
used to take us to the beach. She was fun to know; we still have a
very good friendship. She lives in New York, and we see her
frequently.

You know, I've had some very good long relationships with people
who last after the groups fall away. You can't keep and hold on to
everybody, but it's really remarkable when things do last beautifully.

The girl I knew at Senatobia I don't see anymore because the man
she married has a difficult personality, but still. . . .

TR: Were you aware, early on as a child, of living in an
environment that didn't let you be fully yourself? That there was no
one to share parts of your life with as there has since been?

ES: That *wasn't* true when I was very young. I've recorded over
and over about my mother's reading to me and encouraging me. My
uncle, my mother's brother, and his wife were also special and
receptive. When I was a freshman in college, though, she had
developed cancer and died tragically. It was difficult after that to carry
on with my uncle. We still had a special friendship, but he was way
out on the plantation, and he was running around dating a lot of
women, running down to New Orleans, and just living a very high
life. Then he married again. We were always close. He took a special
interest in my brother and me because he and his first wife didn't
have any children, and they always seemed to feel we were theirs.

The family, especially my mother's family, weren't hostile to books.

It was, rather, with what should have been my peer group that I found myself put off and sometimes even laughed at and persecuted in a strange kind of way, and that made me more of a loner than ever. I kept my thoughts to myself. Also, I was seven years younger than my brother and sort of shoved aside all the time by him. I got this only-child thing. I think only-children constitute one of the unexplored phenomena in literature. In my new book, two only-children fall in love; they understand a lot about each other because of that sense of primal isolation.

I don't know how to describe it. It means you're alone with yourself as if there're two people. It's not a suffering kind of loneliness.

TR: There's a dialogue going on?

ES: Oh yes. Often, as I think, I think of myself as *you*, which is something that crops up in literary technique fairly often. I know that in Robert Penn Warren's *All the King's Men* there are long passages in which the narrator addresses himself as you.

TR: It's a strange kind of second person narrative voice, which is ironic because it's almost as if there's a *second person* there.

ES: If I suffered from the loneliness of feeling unaccepted or unpopular, it was mainly when I was growing up. On the whole, it's not a bad way to be. Certainly now, isolation is not something that I'm afraid of. The only time I really suffered from utter loneliness, I expect, was the one year I spent in New York after I left John. We had gone together and I had gone back to the States and we had said goodbye, and part of it, I guess, was missing his presence. But the whole thing of being on my own in New York! A lot of people record that as one of the worst experiences in life. Everybody in New York that you could be with in a friendly, front-porch sort of way— there just ain't no front porches. Everyone is working. To see anybody is an undertaking; you've got to make plans to have lunch or drinks or dinner. It's not a dropping in or easy, informal telephoning sort of life. There was one woman there who did become a long, important part of my life. She was David Clay's wife, the man who edited *Fire in the Morning*. She didn't work most of the time. She was at home, and we used to chatter on the phone. Otherwise, I just felt at sea in New York, and I think that was one big prod that caused me to respond when John wrote asking me to come back. So when I'd finished the book [*The Voice at the Back Door*] and gotten an advance, I went to England mainly to see him. We decided to get married because . . . well, because it seemed like the thing to do. I kept thinking that if I left him, I'd have to go back to that awful life in New York.

I guess this is more of an account than you bargained for.

TR: Yes, wonderfully so.

ES: Except that I haven't even touched on the most important relationship in my life, except for the couple of times I've been in love that didn't work out, and my marriage. And that was this relationship to David Clay. It was very, very strange.

See, my father and I had a quarrel when I went home from Rome with my novel just about finished. I had to do some revision and I didn't have a contract. He had promised to give me some money to live in New York. He refused the money, and I couldn't go back home after that kind of confrontation. I wouldn't have liked to go through it again. David Clay had been a friend and interested party in my life ever since *Fire in the Morning*. He was the one who found it. He discovered me at Vanderbilt working on a novel. Donald Davidson told him I was there. I met him in Davidson's office and he asked to see the manuscript, and he gave me a contract before it was finished. He edited it and saw it through publication. And then suddenly he left Dodd Mead, the first of his many departures from firms where he was working. His wife explained that the firm hadn't wanted to do certain innovative programs he was working on. But things got more and more curious. They were devout Christian Scientists, and it entered into every phase of their lives. Everything was to be explained by "Science and Health." So I kind of managed to steer a path around that for years because in many ways they were perfectly wonderful, generous people. They didn't have children, not believing in birth, and so they took a special interest in me. Her mother was also a Christian Scientist and so it was all a part of their common talk, which I tried to get used to but never could quite. He had a difficult time relating to people, but even so he made the sale of *The Voice at the Back Door* to MGM, and it meant an income for me at a time when John and I both needed to do as well as we could. He got so many things for me. He brought my work to the attention of all the people he knew. He was a close friend of Robert

Penn Warren; they'd been at Vanderbilt together. *All the King's Men* is dedicated to him and his wife.

I dedicated *The Voice at the Back Door* to them without regret because when I was in New York and on the outs with my father, they were the mainstays of my existence. They helped me get a little apartment to myself. Then when John and I were married and came back, they were very hospitable. They were concerned and interested when we were moving to Canada, and then when I wrote *The Light in the Piazza,* he saw the possibilities of it. After it sold to the *New Yorker,* he generated the interest in it as a separate book. It did awfully well, and he got a movie contract on it with MGM that was a real bonanza.

I thought it was a friendship that could never be broken, but he seemed to get crazier and crazier. Finally, he tried to set up his own agency and get by selling my work and attracting younger artists. It didn't work.

He finally got a job with an advertising firm, so I took that chance to retreat from his agency. I told him I thought it was time, since he had this new job, a different career. Well, he absolutely blew up, and I never saw him again. Just like that! And so this relationship ultimately caused me an awful lot of anguish because I had regarded him as my best friend.

Finally he died in 1984. I found out about it quite by accident. So, this was a relationship that was very, very productive for me, and yet, the cost! I often wonder if I had it to do over again, knowing what I know now, would I undertake it. Because in the end, it was almost paralyzing. For a long time, I couldn't get over the break. At the time it occurred, he was unexpectedly and irrationally furious. A lot of people had explanations. One was that I was his only hope for literary distinction, and that I dashed his long-term dreams by leaving his agency. That's all in the past emotionally now, but for a long time it was a great strain, something that was very hard to get over.

You asked a question without knowing how much I'd say.

TR: True, but it's been helpful because many of the issues you've touched on—trust and alienation within communities and between friends—play an important role in your work. It seems to me that for your characters there's a desperate need to understand self in the context of what is shared with others and what is not shared with others.

ES: Oh yes, and in deciding whom to share with. But you know—there's a hardship involved when you finally learn that the people who understand you least are quite often those who *should* understand you most. It's one of the grave things of life. As the Bible says, your enemies are those of your own household. That's one of the hardest things to accept in life.

TR: On the other hand, do you feel like people in isolation are never quite sure of themselves? I think of characters like Nancy Lewis in "Ship Island," Martha Ingram in *Knights and Dragons,* even Arnie Carrington in *The Salt Line* as going through isolated periods. Is there a sense in which it's necessary for people to be known intimately by others in order for them to know themselves? Must we balance isolation with intimacy?

ES: I think in retrospect of three pieces I've done which have a common element not far from what you're asking—one was "Ship Island," one was *The Snare,* and the third was "I, Maureen," set in Canada. Those three come out of the same impulse. Nancy Lewis in "Ship Island" is thrown into a social milieu that she can't cope with, and in jumping free of it she is suddenly on her own, which is finally *more* satisfying than trying to cope with a community that she's not fit for and is not fit for her.

Julia Garrett, in *The Snare,* leaves the community she was being shaped for because it turns out to be sterile. She finds unlikely sources of energy and belonging in a very, very strange element. She finds a life-giving situation and people on the outside of "decent" human society.

The woman in "I, Maureen" is just psychically unable to bear what most people would think of as a highly fortunate life. She is suddenly thrust by marriage into the circle of a very wealthy Canadian family and can't stand it. So she plunges into a much lower-class environment, which settles her and makes her happy. She was going mad in affluence. These are three women who are out of their element in what seems to be the most attractive circumstances.

TR: What about Arnie Carrington in *The Salt Line?*

ES: He's trying to use the past to revitalize the present. He hates to see the old styles and the old ways vanish from himself and from the coast. In order to reconstruct, he goes back to former times, former lives. But gradually, gradually, he and the characters Mavis and Frank seem to me to all be groping toward a decent, shared community, a new basis.

You know, this idea you've brought up of "community" is a kind of ancient theme as well, a sort of mystical issue of just who your brothers and sisters really are. It occurs over and over again in religious writing. All the central characters in my stories do seem to have that problem—finding out where they belong.

TR: And who they belong with?

ES: Yes, oh yes.

TR: Critics have often remarked how gifted you are at evoking setting. I feel that your settings often reflect the psychological landscapes of your characters. Your landscapes are often figurative as well as literal. It seems to me, for example, that the fluid, even dangerous seascape of *The Salt Line* is a perfect backdrop for Arnie Carrington's struggle.

ES: Arnie has had a longer life than most of my characters. He's on the verge of being an old man. That's one of his pursuing demons, isn't it? He doesn't know if he can reconstruct any sexual present for himself; that's one thing that's haunting him. Life's somewhat diminished for him, his having already lived through so much. Most of the characters I deal with are trying to "discover themselves"; Arnie's discovered himself many times. His attempt to rediscover himself, I feel, is quite poignant because so much of his groping toward other people goes unrewarded.

I do think he's finally at one in a sort of relationship with Mavis at the end because he's become a sort of father figure, a protective figure. And then, he and his son have worked it out in a cycle of encounter and rejection, encounter and rejection and then finally acceptance.

The strange thing about that book was the Buddha; it was actually on the coast. I thought it was washed away, but after the book was published, a woman came up to me at a reading to tell me that the Buddha was safe in the garden next to hers. So it *was* saved from the hurricane somehow. Which is interesting, as it came to mean for me the possible harmony, the harmonious qualities of the East, which didn't exist between these characters until after the irritants, namely

Lex and his wife, are gradually thrown aside, and the harmonies
return between people.

TR: What about religion then? Peggy Prenshaw, in writing about
The Snare, says that the characters are seeking a kind of transcen-
dence. Isn't there a holdover in your work of a literal Calvinist
background?

ES: Oh yeah. I was brought up on such. One of the troubles
between my immediate family and me was that they were so churchy
and I wasn't. I think religion is dangerous. I really do. I think it can
almost poison human relations. I suppose, though, if you get really
strict about it, it's supposed to. You're supposed to have your main
relationships in the church, and that's exactly what seemed to happen
to my family. They were staunch members of the Presbyterian
Church, and my mother's mother (whom I never knew; she died the
year I was born)—her family was from Scotland. Their whole family
down to my day were dyed-in-the-wool Calvinist Presbyterians. I was
made to memorize something called "The Shorter Catechism." It's a
tiny book of 108 pages, full of very involved theological questions,
and at age seven or eight, I had this whole thing by heart. They
called in the Sunday School teacher, who was qualified to hear it
recited. She took the book and asked the questions, and I spun it out
word for word with my mother sitting there, and then I got my
diploma. I had to recite. I also had to go to Sunday School, church,
Young People's, and church at night. All day Sunday was a disaster of
straight-laced behavior, usually long visits from your relatives in the
afternoon after a long Sunday dinner. It was infinitely constricting in
a strange sort of way, and I'm sure that quality has gotten into my
stories.

My grandfather was the only one who never went to church.
Somehow he was exempt. People revered him for his goodness. It's
hard to think about anybody rejecting his behavior. We—he and I—
had such a good relationship.

But I think finally I did get caught up in the whole idea of belief as
something I didn't reject. I don't reject it yet. I don't think anybody in
the modern world can say with absolute certainty that these things
are true, but on the other hand, nobody can say with absolute
certainty that they're not. There's something there, I think.

I joined the Anglican Church for John and his family. But I don't think I could ever accept the kind of dictums and regulations that Catholics take on, for instance. That takes a kind of systemization of your faith that seems to me an intrusion. The church shifts its theological positions from time to time, and you have to think of the generations of people who were made to toe the line while the church officials were debating. That to me is out. You should have as little dogma in your life as possible. Faith and love matter so much more.

TR: Do you think your characters seek a harmony, let's say, in personal relations that is spiritual even when it is not dogmatic?

ES: My own feeling is that there's a pattern in things, mysterious though it may be, that is asserting itself in the lives of humans. And if that pattern is there, at times it finds us. I suppose I'm more mystical than anything else. Many Scottish, Celtic people are mystical in their orientation.

TR: Fey?

ES: Sure. A lot of my stories are about supernatural things. There are a lot of quite intentionally mysterious elements.

TR: Forster says that in the best novels, even in those that are most realistic, the sense of the supernatural is never very far away.

ES: I think that accounts for the feeling you have from my novels that a setting or place has a spirit. That has always seemed to me to be at the edge, though unsaid, of Eudora Welty's thinking about place. To me, the pagan and the Christian are never very far apart. And I think there's a pagan belief that's common in southern writers. Place is sacred. There's a spirit there to be worshipped or violated. I think this feeling, though she never goes so far as to say so, is at the heart of Eudora's work. She keeps it on the level of the permeation of observation and the like, but I do think that in stories like those in *The Golden Apples* she almost gets palpable with the spirit of certain places. I think it's very strong.

TR: And it's there equally in yours, this spirituality of place?

ES: It's strong in both our works because it's really there.

TR: It seems that mysticism permeates your work, particularly material set on the Gulf Coast. Somehow when you cross the "salt line," you're entering the territory where visions occur.

ES: Yes, the coast is my personal affinity.

TR: You've talked a lot about *The Voice at the Back Door* as a book of exploration, that you wrote it to examine your own beliefs. Has that been true of other books as well?

ES: Well, the segregation that *The Voice at the Back Door* explores was really a tenet of faith in the white South before World War II. To challenge it was to challenge the rightness and righteousness of your forefathers. So, reexamining that whole system was really different from examining a dramatic or human situation such as I had done in other novels.

TR: Do you normally find yourself starting with a central image?

ES: Oh, I often start stories with an image that I want to explore. Novels are different for me though. I always begin them with a firm idea of what the central characters are, what their relationships are and will become, and where their lives together are likely to go. It may change as I write, but it's not going to change a lot.

With a story I find I can begin with an image, say, a character in a room, and ask why is this so kinetic for me. The exploration leads out much like a straight line, though it may double back to catch threads from the past.

TR: Has any story ever taken you any place that was totally unexpected?

ES: I've always thought that the experience you describe is one of the most exciting things in writing. The best example I can think of is *This Crooked Way.* I foresaw it up to the end of the next to last section, a crucial point where there's just been a murder. Then in the last section, there's a rather sudden shift of voice. I didn't foresee what would happen after the murder, but when I got there in the writing, I felt that the energy was coming from the central character. He at this point had either reached a dead end in his life or he had to take off in a new way. Well, suddenly the writing itself took off in the way *he* wanted it to go. It wasn't foreseen at all. I remember I wrote half the night. Oh, it was thirty or forty pages that just went rolling, rolling. It carried on its own force.

Another example of a book that seemed to take its own, unexpected way was *The Salt Line.* I had whole blocks of *The Salt Line* that I had to throw away because they didn't pertain to the central images in the book. Those images I think are what controls that novel. If I tried while writing that book to follow the narrative line and left the images, it just wouldn't work. But when I stuck to the central vision, things just flowed.

10 September 1990

TR: Since we talked a few weeks ago about the groups in your life, you mentioned that there was a group of people in Montreal who had been very important to you.

ES: Yes. I suppose that the experience is so recent that I still think of them as part of my group, even though we've been here now for four years. This group evolved kind of naturally in that a friend introduced us to an extraordinary couple of people. First there was a man who's a lecturer in classics at McGill University in Montreal named Paolo Vivante, a Siennese gentleman who's been in Canada since World War II. He and I had this Italian background to talk about, and he and his brother, the poet and short story writer Arturo Vivante, became our friends. This started a new phase in our lives in Montreal because, though we had had friends there, we'd never had friends of such closeness. His wife Vera is English, and she and my husband get on quite well. They took to both of us quickly.

The Vivantes used to give a lot of interesting evening gatherings. At one of these, an Italian woman came up to me. She and her husband, who is English, had travelled through much of Europe and the Middle East. There again the fortunate English-Italian connection. She came up to me and immediately began talking about books of mine she'd read. She apparently had been reading them for years. She'd checked them out of US Cultural Service libraries everywhere they went; apparently some of my books are in the Cultural Services Library in Vienna where they were stationed for a time. So this made a nice opening, and John and I both liked her husband, William Brind, a movie producer with the National Film Board.

So we immediately fell on our feet with those two, and I already had a friend there named Joan Blake from Pinehurst, North Carolina. She and I used to think of ourselves as the only two southern women in Montreal. We became close friends because of our mutual southernness. She was a widow but had a friend we liked too. And so the eight of us were a very close unit. We were always passing around invitations. It just went without saying that we would all see each other every week or so. We still see Joan when she comes down to visit her mother, and we talk to the others on the phone often. It's an important and continuing thing. I had many other close individual relationships in Montreal, and many students I became close to.

TR: When you returned to the South four years ago, did you feel a certain sense of coming home? Or had you been in Montreal long enough that you felt you were leaving there more than coming here?

ES: I relate to the South on a very down-home, personal level, and I relate to southerners in a very immediate, clued-in way. It's been a great dimension of my life to find that I can relate to people elsewhere, but I still feel most at home, most relaxed with southerners.

TR: To change subjects abruptly now, I'd like to talk more about certain aspects of the books. The more I've read your work, the more certain I've become that you're a master at creating a structure and a style that matches the theme of a book. For example, if *No Place for an Angel* is about the rootlessness and alienation prevalent in post-World War II America, then the constant shifts in time and place give the reader a real sense of a kind of dislocation, of disjunction, a sense that none of these characters are at home, that there is no place in which the angelic nature of any character can grow.

ES: I think that, without realizing it, reviewers of *No Place For an Angel* criticized me harshly for doing exactly what I was trying to do—convey the shifting, uncertain nature of experience, how these people's lives never find a root.

I intended the shifting nature of human experience to be reproduced for the reader in the book's structure. I rather enjoyed trying to put it together without confusing the reader as to time and place. It wasn't successful critically, I think, because they felt it lacked a focus. If I'd had a focus, I would have destroyed my idea.

TR: There would have been an angel.

ES: Just so. Some people thought I meant that Catherine, the solitary woman at the end of the novel, was the angel. I didn't mean that at all. All of them had dimensions of their natures that might have been angelic, given the right atmosphere, the right environment.

TR: In *This Crooked Way*, did the structure play an important role in conveying your message?

ES: In *This Crooked Way* I meant the narratives to be as crooked as Amos Dudley's life. I began with an omniscient third-person piece, and then I developed it through a series of accusations that this man had to answer because he was living so within the closed circle of his own beliefs, his own drive. I brought the three people in who had the most to make him answer for. I hoped with each to advance the story even though not along a *straight* line.

Then the last part was his coming around, his recovery, part of which is our discovery of his voice—his finally speaking for himself.

Somebody said I had a choice at the end of the third indictment to make it either a tragedy or to relate it back to the strong, life-giving elements in the story. I obviously chose the later, although I don't know if it's fair to call it a comedy.

In order to return to his wife and plantation at all, he had to give up his self-obsession. Up to that point, he thought the life force in him was the only thing there was. He had to get outside himself in order to belong.

TR: At the end of the novel, Amos Dudley brings all his flooded-out family back to live with him and his wife, and there is the comic sense of synthesis, of the union of extremely disparate elements.

ES: Yes, she had to give up some of her pride to descend the steps and welcome this comic crew of a family. Just as he had had to give up some of his pride in order to return with them. So they both had to surrender some part of themselves in order for this reunion to occur.

TR: The uprooting of Amos Dudley's family by the building of an artificial lake raises the issue of uprootedness in general. The sense of having lost one's treasured home is everywhere in *No Place For an Angel*. Are we of the twentieth century a rootless generation?

ES: Oh, I don't think most southerners of even the recent generations have lost their deep-seated sense of home, especially if they were brought up in or had much contact with the countryside. The Jesuits say, "Give us a child until he's six years old and. . . ." It strikes me that the same could be true of the southern language, whether you're white or black. If you live in a place 'til you're six, you belong to it.

We used to say our sense of ourselves as southern stemmed from our history—Civil War and Reconstruction—but that's not remembered so much any more. I think the southern landscape has an enormous influence on people whose senses and memories it permeates.

And you know, it might be the heat. I have a theory that when you're outside in the South during the summer, the heat enforces a slower, more sensitive, more meditative pace. You can't constantly be in a hurry to get anywhere.

TR: *Fire in the Morning* is written in third-person omniscience, but Randall Gibson, the laconic, well-read country lawyer, narrates a long section in the middle of the book. It struck me, as I read, that he serves as a sort of community chorus. Isn't Randall Gibson in a sense an incredibly sensitive mouthpiece for the town of Tarsus? A sort of community voice?

ES: Yes, I think so. That type of character seems to reappear in my work. In the play, *For Lease or Sale,* the mother becomes a kind of human voice for the house and what the house means and in a figurative sense is.

Randall Gibson is the acute observer and voice. When he leaves Tarsus, another lawyer comes on the scene, and in our few glimpses of him he is beginning to take on Gibson's role. I like the structure of that book, but I think the style is rather immature.

TR: You mentioned earlier that the development of *The Salt Line* was controlled by the imagery of the novel rather than by a plot in the traditional sense.

ES: Yes, the water tower, the light house, the Buddha, Arnie Carrington's island, the coast itself. The whole book was very strong visually to me as I wrote it.

TR: I think of Arnie's climbing the water tower on a whim, and by chance his nemesis Lex, standing below with a rifle, tempted almost beyond endurance to kill him. It seems that image delivers a tremendous amount of information about both men and their relationship. I think that most critics read past the images searching for more traditional plot lines and so misunderstand it. Often, I think, what's misunderstood in your better novels is the structural medium through which the story is being told.

ES: That's interesting because, to be honest, I feel as though I've almost always been misread even when I've been praised.

TR: What about *Knights and Dragons* in this respect? In that story, don't you communicate your message partly through the imagery of Martha Ingram's rooms in Rome, the depth and complex darkness?

ES: Yes, in fact that story went so deeply internal that some who can take that sort of exploration really responded to it. A lot of poets liked that story. Dana Gioia and James Merrill, for example, have written me in admiration of it. And yet it got kicked around no end by critics who liked *The Light in the Piazza.*

TR: Well, *The Light in the Piazza* is a much more accessible story with a much more traditional plot. There's a sense in which *Knights and Dragons* would seem static almost if you read for plot. Whereas if you read it as psychological exploration, it's much more sophisticated. Perhaps it's fair to say that critics have refused to read some of your novels on their own terms.

ES: I have thought so. Perhaps one of the things good teachers and scholars do is show us how to best read, how to be conscious of what, perhaps, even the author was unconscious.

TR: Is there another book which comes to mind that you felt was not read on its own terms?

ES: I think *The Snare* has been very underrated. It had bad publishing luck to start with, and then when it finally did get reviewed in the *New York Times,* Madison Jones, whom I like personally, failed to praise it. He said that the narrative shifts slowed the reader up and didn't work. He admitted there were minor redeeming features, but on the whole he didn't seem to get at all what I was writing about.

I think the overlay and interplay of past and present, of memory and current life, is true to anyone's experience. For Julia Garrett in *The Snare*, the past is quite important and must be understood in relation to the present.

TR: You once said that *The Snare* is the most intensely thought out book you've written. How does that exhibit itself in the book's structure?

ES: There were layers of discovery that she went through—all of which is constantly playing in a sort of symphonic way with the city of New Orleans, where the book is set.

New Orleans is a very sexy place, and I needed a very sexy heroine to make that connection plain. Most of the men who are attracted to her are attracted sexually. Her early experience with her guardian mentor, Dev, a French Cajun man who may or may not have seduced her, had a profound effect on her.

This shady part of her life was happiest and yet at the same time was not subject to approval by the proper side of New Orleans, of which her family was a part. She kept trying to make these two parts of her life come together. In search of a synthesis, she went deeper and deeper into seedy, cruel, even criminal life. Finally she hit rock bottom, and it's a wonder she even survived.

I don't know if her character and the book work together. Someone told me that you had to be fascinated with Julia Garrett to enjoy the book. What I hoped would happen is that the reader would catch the connection between Julia and the city and so read it as an exploration, in depth, of both simultaneously. She's a human compendium of the city. New Orleans reveals the woman and the woman reveals New Orleans.

24 September 1990

This session centered on Spencer's only play, *For Lease or Sale,* written between 1986 and the spring of 1989. It was first performed on stage by PlayMakers Repertory in Chapel Hill, North Carolina, on 25 January 1989.

For Lease or Sale is set in a large, antebellum house on the edge of a small but growing Mississippi town. As a result of urbanization in general and rezoning laws in particular, the owners of the house, the Glenn family, will apparently be forced to sell out to "progress." Edward Glenn, a lawyer in his late thirties or early forties, has been called home from a mysterious exile in Mexico to help his elderly mother and eighteen-year-old niece, Patsy, cope with the dilemma. Matters are only complicated by the appearance in the second act of Edward's ex-wife, Aline, just as he is attracted to a new woman, Claire.

As the story unfolds, we discover that in addition to the family crisis each of these characters is undergoing an emotional crisis as well. Each is suspended between a deeply disturbing past event—for Edward and Aline, their divorce; for Patsy, the loss of her parents; for Mrs. Glenn, the loss of her husband—and an unsure future.

Mrs. Glenn dies suddenly, partly from the shock of Edward and Aline's renewed conflict. In the aftermath of her death, Patsy decides to leave with a young suitor, and Aline goes as well, leaving Claire alone with Edward. The ending is ambiguous in tone; it is not quite clear whether or not Claire can help Edward regain a stable life in the old home.

TR: You've said before that when you first imagined the story that would become *For Lease or Sale,* you "heard" it as two characters talking on a stage. Would you say a little about that?

ES: I think I made it sound a little more mystical than what actually happened; I didn't just suddenly have a vision.

Playwriting was on my mind at the time; there was an English theater group in Montreal formed to combat the prevailing French influence. I don't know what the laws were at the time, but the English got to feeling that their theater and their way of doing things were being stamped out. The new civic center that was built—*Place des Arts*— was built to French specifications, not architecturally but in terms of performances allowed there. So the English theater community in Montreal began to feel in danger of being stamped out.

Several people I didn't know very well got together to establish a group dedicated to bringing English-speaking theater to the city. They asked me to be a part of it; "maybe you could write a play for us," they said.

I refused on the grounds I'd never written a play, but the idea got in my head. I admitted to a few of them that I'd always wanted to write a play. The group sort of fizzled out, leading to another group with more backing and eventually to the revitalization of English theater in Montreal. I wasn't involved in all this except that I began working on *For Lease or Sale.*

There was also a woman there who was directing an English speaking group called the Playwrights' Workshop, and she was very interested in my play. She arranged a reading performance for it, and

I invited some friends and she invited some friends, and actors just sat around the table and read it and that's when I—for the first time—got turned on by it. The response was terrific. People laughed at the right times and even though the actors didn't attempt southern accents, they read the lines awfully well. The woman who played the mother was just marvelous. So it met with a wonderful response, and the group and I were to go on editing and shaping.

But things happen to theater groups. This bunch came under new management just as we began to plan our move to North Carolina, so it seemed pointless to push things there. It never got produced in Montreal but it did get on its feet there. When I got to Chapel Hill, some members of PlayMakers Repertory also gave a reading performance, and I got turned on again, and that's when David Hammond, the artistic director at PlayMakers, first heard the play.

From there, one thing led to another.

TR: By the second or third page of the script, there begins to be an organic connection between at least two of the characters, the mother and son, and the house where the play is set. To me one of the strongest things about the play is the way in which the setting itself is such a deeply-rooted part of what is going on, almost as if it's another character. Edward tells Patsy that "this is where our knowing is."

ES: That and some other core lines were in the script from the first draft on. There were some very significant pieces of the script that weren't changed at all, not during all the time that I and others worked at the play both in Montreal and in Chapel Hill.

What did get edited, particularly by David Hammond, were those spots that were repetitious. David would say, "Look, Elizabeth, you don't have to tell the audience something but once." And I'd say, "Well, seeing it on the stage they might forget, so I like to repeat it." "Forget it," he'd say. We had a lot of fun really. We never really argued, you know. Once, I got so exasperated that I told him to write it himself. He said, "I can't write." And there was laughter again.

TR: You mentioned the strong, underlying relationship between Edward and the house.

ES: The basic relationship in the play is between Edward and Patsy, his niece. But the root system that feeds it all is made up of mother, son, and house.

TR: After the mother's death, does Edward take on the same relationship with the house that she had before?

ES: I wondered that, too, about the end of the play. I put a lot of hope in Edward's relationship with Claire, and perhaps through it, he will continue a stable life in the context of that old home place. I got differing opinions from spectators who saw the play here in Chapel Hill, so the ending seems to have been ambiguous in effect, which is what I wanted.

I don't know enough about the kind of reaction a play is supposed to produce in its audience to know just whether that ambiguity is desirable or not.

At any rate, Claire has enough sense to take Edward in hand and bring out his strong points. She's from the same class, is well-educated.

TR: She has intelligent manners, as Edward says.

ES: Exactly, and by the end of the play she understands Edward as well as anyone. She may be willing to stay there with him or she may even get him out of the old house. But either way, she has inspired in him the beginning of a new cycle. New life. One person who saw the play told me that Claire shouldn't be there at the end. It should be Edward alone, a tragic figure entombed in the huge, old house. But I just don't see life that way. It shouldn't give the sense that their lives are over when the play is over.

TR: It seems to me that this sort of extension backwards and forwards in time is very much a part of the sensibility of the play. The house, which contains the entire action, is a sort of symbol for all of the family that has lived there, previous generations, the dead father, Edward's brothers and sisters, and Aline. And the mother is as sensitive to their presence as she is to that of Edward and Patsy. If the house is the embodiment of this family and its collective spirit, it can only continue to be so if a new "family" springs up out of the ashes at the end of the play. Edward alone could well be tragic, but Edward with Claire . . .

ES: Could renew the life of the house.

TR: Tell us about the chandelier. I know it was one part of the original script that got cut.

ES: At the end of the next to last scene, Edward, while quarreling

with Aline, snatches up his umbrella to threaten her. It's done half in
self-mockery, as is much of what Edward does. He swings it over his
head and accidentally hooks the chandelier, which begins to swing
back and forth. I had thought to incorporate the tingling glass and
the wildly swinging lights as elements of the on-stage tension. And
then it falls, barely missing the mother. It's such a shock, though, that
she goes to her knees in an effort to pick up the tiny pieces of broken
glass. And then she has the fatal heart attack.

David said the whole business had to go. First of all, it would be
too difficult to stage. And second, the chandelier idea had been used
in Beth Henley's *Crimes of the Heart.* I didn't remember that at all,
though I'd seen the play. So we tried to substitute a vase. I don't
know if that damn vase broke the nights you were there or not. Half
the time it didn't break. They ordered that vase specifically—broken
and rewired—from a theatrical house. It was supposed to break at a
touch. And night after night, I had to sit there in the theatre and
watch the damn thing *not* break. It lost all effect.

TR: If drama is the genre of crisis, the play covers a crucial
moment in the history of the house—after all, it may be destroyed—
and of Edward. His mother dies, Patsy finally breaks free of him and
the house, and there also seems to be a final, true break between
Aline and Edward. There is a sense at the end that all who don't
belong and don't understand are gone. Claire is the last one, and she
alone stays with Edward. I had the sense in the theatre that we were
witnessing a birth—not of a child, though that may come, but of a
relationship.

ES: Yes, the trauma that precedes the birth of a new relationship is
very strong.

TR: They are dancing at the end, almost in a ritual.

ES: To the tune "Dancing in the Dark." Dancing takes on a heavy
note of romanticism and insecurity during the play. When you dance
with someone in the dark, falling in love with someone you don't
know, you cannot tell just what will happen.

TR: There's the sense, suggested by Claire's inability to get the
screen door open at the end, her flattening herself against the screen
like "a large white moth," that she is bound by the house, captured
almost.

ES: There *is* the sense that she half wants out. She has enough sense to know how dangerous Edward is. And yet, subconsciously at least, she wants to stay. She wants to belong.

TR: The strength of the "ties that bind," a line you use in *The Snare.*

ES: The strongest ties always bind somehow.

TR: Earlier in the play, the mother tells Claire that what has happened there in the house never stops happening. It's a fascinating comment in the context of this large "haunted" house. It suggests the cyclical quality of human life. That things ebb and flow, turn and return. But also, it adds a mythic quality to the events which occur there.

ES: She was a very mystical person, the mother. She had the strong sense that she communicated regularly with people who had died. She tells Patsy and Edward that it's fairly common, and I agree. Communication goes on even though a person's gone. She talks things over with her dead husband in a very matter-of-fact way. I don't think she, or I, meant it cyclically so much as just the feeling that he wasn't really gone.

She found Edward's argument with Aline so dreadful because she'd had to be the audience when they'd fought so much there before. It was as if this awful part of the past was all coming back on her. That accounts for her extreme action.

TR: There's a sense also that the mother is striving to hold them all together—Aline as well as Claire. She would take them all in and make them family, bind them together.

ES: She wanted to love people and have them love each other, no matter what the obstacles, and so the argument strikes forcefully. She's very healing. Her age and experience give her a quality of acceptance.

TR: Isn't Edward Glenn, the restless, articulate lawyer, a figure that appears more than once in your work?

ES: There's Randall Gibson in *Fire in the Morning.* The southern lawyer is a character in everybody's work on the South. The lawyer is most always the university trained individual on the scene and so became the traditional spokesman of a community. The law was the profession for the gentry to go into. Both Randall and Edward are well-read, conscious of themselves and of the larger community. I touched on this type of educated southern man in "The Cousins" also. I'm not sure that this character has ever been fully treated in southern literature. There's Faulkner's Gavin Stevens, whom I find overdone. He's so garrulous and so much concerned with other people's business without any life of his own. He doesn't act; he only talks. Let's see, there's Scout's father in *To Kill a Mockingbird*.

That type of intellectual southerner really existed and has seldom been fully realized.

TR: Percy's *Lanterns on the Levee* treats it fully, but in non-fiction of course.

ES: That's a fascinating book even if it contains some misguided thinking on certain topics. The Percys were very important in trying to keep alive a tradition that seems at first glance like snobbery. But I don't think the Percys, at least, were snobs; rather, they struggled to keep alive a sort of Jeffersonian ideal of virtue and talent.

TR: You know I've always thought that Edward in *For Lease or Sale* uses his training and intellect to manipulate language in remarkable ways. His power of speech, his poet's sense of language, he uses to control the distance between himself and others. He can be charming and attractive as well as cutting and sarcastic, drawing others to him but always keeping them at a safe distance.

ES: It's certainly in his nature to use language to manipulate, to mock himself as well as others—to attract, to defend, to attack. He's a good lawyer, or would be if Claire puts him to practicing it seriously.

TR: One more question. Now that you've left the play and gone on to another novel, is there anything that you'd say you learned from playwriting about writing fiction?

ES: I have a new tendency to forget that I have to fill in the background behind the conversations in this novel. There are also a couple of dramatized chapters in the new novel that exist almost in a vacuum. I've thrown several passages into a sort of disembodied dramatic form as a way of suggesting the natures of the characters and situations. It's exciting. We'll see if it works.

Index

235